CONTENTS

Strategic Business Finance

USING FINANCE FOR STRATEGIC ADVANTAGE

Edited by
Tony Grundy
and Keith Ward

YOURS TO HAVE AND TO HOLD
BUT NOT TO COPY

First published in 1996

Kogan Page Limited
120 Pentonville Road
London N1 9JN

©Tony Grundy and Keith Ward, 1996

British Library Cataloguing in Publication Data

A CIP record for this book is available from the British Library.

ISBN 0 7494 1937 7

Typeset by Saxon Graphics Ltd, Derby
Printed and bound in Great Britain by Clays Ltd, St Ives plc

Contents

LIST OF FIGURES

LIST OF TABLES

THE CRANFIELD MANAGEMENT SERIES

The Cranfield Management Series represents an exciting joint initiative between the Cranfield School of Management and Kogan Page.

As one of Europe's leading post-graduate business schools, Cranfield is renowned for its applied research activities, which cover a wide range of issues relating to the practice of management.

Each title in the Series is based on current research and authored by Cranfield faculty or their associates. Many of the research projects have been undertaken with the sponsorship and active assistance of organizations from the industrial, commercial or public sectors. The aim of the Series is to make the findings of direct relevance to managers through texts which are academically sound, accessible and practical.

For managers and academics alike, the Cranfield Management Series will provide access to up-to-date management thinking from some of the world's leading academics and practitioners. The series represents both Cranfield's and Kogan Page's commitment to furthering the improvement of management practice in all types of organisations.

THE SERIES EDITORS

Frank Fishwick

Reader in Managerial Economics
Director of Admissions at Cranfield School of Management
Dr Fishwick joined Cranfield from Aston University in 1966, having previously worked in textiles, electronics and local government (town and country planning). Recent research and consultancy interests have been focused on business concentration, competition policy and the book publishing industry. He has been directing a series of research studies for the Commission of the European Communities, working in collaboration with business economists in France and Germany. He is permanent economic adviser to the Publishers Association in the UK and is a regular

14

consultant to other public and private sector organisations in the UK, continental Europe and the US.

Gerry Johnson
Professor of Strategic Management
Director of the Centre for Strategic Management and Organisational Change
Director of Research at Cranfield School of Management

After graduating from University College London, Professor Johnson worked for several years in management positions in Unilever and Reed International before becoming a management consultant. Since 1976, he has taught at Aston University Management Centre, Manchester Business School, and from 1988 at Cranfield School of Management. His research work is primarily concerned with processes of strategic decision making and strategic change in organisations. He also works as a consultant on issues of strategy formulation and strategic change at a senior level with a number of UK and international firms.

Shaun Tyson
Professor of Human Resource Management
Director of Human Resource Research Centre
Dean of the Faculty of Management and Administration at Cranfield School of Management

Professor Tyson studied at London University and spent eleven years in senior positions in industry within engineering and electronic companies. For four years he was lecturer in personnel management at the Civil Service College, and joined Cranfield in 1979. He has acted as a consultant and researched widely into human resource strategies, policies and the evaluation of the function. He has published 14 books.

THE CONTRIBUTORS

Ruth Bender MBA BA FCA DipM, is a chartered accountant who specialises in corporate finance. She joined Grant Thornton, one of the UK's larger accounting firms, after completing her degree in accountancy, qualified with the firm and remained with them for some 15 years, the last 5 as a Partner.

During her time in the profession she has worked in audit and accounting, investigations and corporate finance, dealing with a wide variety of businesses. She also spent a period working as a training associate in fhte firm's national training centre. In 1989/90 she undertook as a secondment to a City venture capital firm, as an Investment Manager. She has also been a member of a District Health Authority and a non-executive director of Bedford Hospital NHS Trust.

Ruth took the Cranfield MBA in 1993/94 and joined the faculty in October 1994.

Adrian Buckley PhD MSc BA FCA FCT, is Professor of International Finance at Cranfield University and past Director of its MBA programme. He qualified as a chartered accountant and is a business graduate. Before entering academic life, his business experience embraced five years of management consultancy, two years in merchant banking, and six years' work in financial planning and corporate treasury. He was the first group treasurer at Redland plc. He has written extensively in his field and has contributed over 100 articles to professional journals and is author of the widely adopted texts *Multinational Finance*, *The Essence of International Money* and *International Capital Budgeting*, all published by Prentice Hall. He is also a chief examiner for the Association of Corporate Treasurers.

John Fielding is Lecturer in Accounting and Finance at Cranfield University. Following articles with Ernst and Young, he worked for 6 years with RTZ. Since 1974 he has taught at Cranfield School of Management and has also carried out a number of teaching and consulting assignments for multinational companies. His current research interest is in the field of efficient capital markets.

Tony Grundy MA MBA MSc FCA PhD, is a Senior Lecturer in Strategic Management at Cranfield University. He is also Director of Cambridge Corporate Development. After qualifying as a chartered accountant with Ernst and Young, he worked in senior line management at BP and ICI, and as a senior consultant at KPMG and PA. He has a PhD in strategic and financial decision making from Cranfield and is the author of four books on strategy, finance and organisational change.

D R Myddelton MBA FCA ACIS. After qualifying as a chartered accountant and graduating from the Harvard Business School, he worked in manufacturing companies as a management accountant. He taught part-time at Cranfield from 1965, then lectured in accounting for three years at the London Business School before becoming Professor of Finance and Accounting at Cranfield in 1972. He was Head of the Finance and Accounting Group from 1972–81, and Acting Director of the School in 1985–86. In addition to many articles he has written books on Tax Reform, Inflation Accounting and Accounting Standards and text books on Financial Accounting, Management Accounting, Financial Management and Economics. He is a managing trustee of the Institute of Economic Affairs, and Chairman of the Academic Advisory Council of the University of Buckingham.

Keith Ward MA FCA FCMA, studied economics at Cambridge and then qualified as both a chartered accountant and a cost and management accountant. He has worked both in the City and abroad as a consultant, and held senior financial positions in manufacturing and trading companies (the last being as group financial director of Sterling International). Keith then joined Cranfield School of Management and progressed to Head of the Finance and Accounting Group and Director of the Research Centre in Competitive Performance.

His research interests are primarily in the fields of financial strategy, strategic management accounting, and accounting for marketing activities. He is the author of *Corporate Financial Strategy*, *Strategic Management Accounting*, *Financial Management for Service Companies* and *Financial Aspects of Marketing* as well as co-authoring *Management Accounting for Financial Decisions*. He has also published numerous articles and contributed to several other books, including as an editor.

PREFACE

Strategic business finance seeks to unify the borderland between corporate strategy and finance. This task is an ambitious one, particularly in view of our past legacy.

Formerly, finance was regarded as being primarily a technical discipline, focusing either on measuring historic performance or following on from strategy's march into the future. At best, it was assumed to play an *enabling* role. At worst it was thought to play a *constraining* role, both in terms of rationing funding and in risk assessment.

Strategy was seen (by contrast) as being visionary and future looking and as focusing on the external environment. Strategy was viewed as going ahead of finance, and of necessity therefore was concerned with the qualitative and judgemental – and of course the uncertain. Strategy also seemed to have more focus on *management process* than finance, whose concerns were intensely analytical and focused on the 'content' of business decisions.

In military terms, strategy was viewed in equivalent terms to the front-line tank divisions, finance as being comparable with support functions, logistics and ultimately with 'counting the dead' after the battle.

But in practice (and now in theory too) we see finance playing a much greater front-line role. Finance provides front-line intelligence (particularly in valuing business strategies, options and decisions). It also plays a major role in the assessment of strategic fit between resources and the external environment in terms of both opportunities and threats.

It can also make a particular contribution to assessing 'whether battles are likely to be worth fighting at all'. It can help our judgement as to whether the battle environment is liable to shift over time towards or against economic advantage. In reality both strategy and finance have common roots – in economic theory.

Forever crucial is the interface between the army and its ultimate commanders – in strategic business finance these are the capital markets. And finally finance can play a major role in assessing uncertainties (as well as specific risks).

We hope that our breakthroughs at Cranfield enthuse managers and management academics alike to explore these borders with more enthusiasm and confidence than in the past. Otherwise we are destined to view the business market with a strategic and financial double-vision.

We would like to thank our colleagues for their contributions to this book and our secretaries, Sheila Hart, Marjorie Dawe and Pat Edwards for preparing the manuscript with their normal skill and patience.

Tony Grundy and Keith Ward
Cranfield School of Management
Cranfield University
October 1995

Part One

INTRODUCTION

1

STRATEGIC BUSINESS FINANCE – AN OVERVIEW

Keith Ward and Tony Grundy

A DEFINITION

Strategic business finance integrates financial and strategic management tools and techniques in order to manage both internal and external resources for the enhancement of long-term shareholder value. These tools and techniques cover strategic decision evaluation, decision making and implementation, as well as performance evaluation and control measures.

INTRODUCTION

A strange syndrome in modern management theory is the apparent polarity between strategic management and finance. While strategic management continues to develop and embrace an ever-increasing range of perspectives on management, conventional financial theory seems to be stuck in one, perhaps mechanistic, dimension. Our book makes the case for making closer links between strategic management and a number of strategic elements from finance which we call 'strategic business finance'. This chapter provides an introduction to the book by putting forward a new framework for seeing how finance can be managed for strategic advantage.

We begin by re-examining the role finance can play in managing corporate value and managing that value strategically.

CORPORATE VALUE AND ITS ROLE IN PRACTICE

By 'corporate value' we mean the economic value of cash streams generated by a group. Thus, these future cash flows are adjusted to their equivalent net present values. This incorporates not merely the operating subsidiaries but group headquarters and the internal interfaces among business units.

Corporate value is not necessarily exactly the same as shareholder value. An over-emphasis on shareholder value suggests that taking a shareholder perspective gives an absolutely superior way of measuring economic value. Management may have superior information on the economic value of the group's future cash flows. The truly rational answer does not therefore lie in adopting a purely shareholder perspective – hence our preferred use of the term corporate value.

To get a better handle on the two terms of shareholder value and corporate value we differentiate between:

- The creation of shareholder value as being the drive by management towards satisfying, if not out-performing, the required returns of the capital market. This is mirrored in the financial value currently placed on the company by the capital markets, which is based on the imperfect information available to existing and potential investors.
- Corporate value is the present value of the expected returns from the combination of current business strategies and future investment programmes, based on the information available to management. (One important role for management should be to ensure that corporate value is properly represented in the company's market value.)

(This difference is illustrated in the Philip Morris case study below.)

A number of major companies including BP, ICI and National Power have begun the attempt to manage corporate value strategically. In some areas therefore, we find that theory needs to catch up with practice, and in other cases vice versa. Theory and practice are thus out of step, providing an opportunity to generate fruitful debate.

We now explore and illustrate how the disciplines of strategic management and finance can be welded more closely together. We therefore begin with a quick review of the literature to highlight areas of fit between strategic management and finance. Next, we develop an overall framework which helps us to explore and explain many of the issues encountered in both theory and in practice. This is illustrated with empirical examples from BP and Marlboro (Philip Morris).

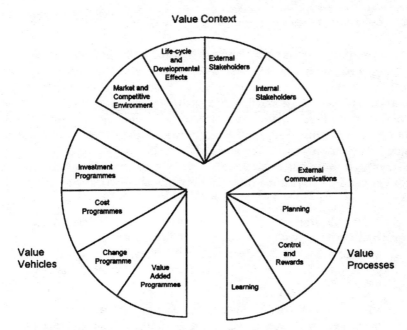

Figure 1.1 The three domains of corporate value

The overall framework also suggests a number of key implications for management practice, and for the process of management learning on this topic. Figure 1.1 demonstrates the range of components which are involved in creating corporate value (and in translating this corporate value into shareholder value). This framework is used throughout the chapter to indicate how the elements comprising strategic business finance can contribute to enhancing corporate value.

OVERVIEW OF THE EXISTING LITERATURE

In approaching this topic one might easily take the view that:

> If something exists, then it must have been written about somewhere. In fact, it has probably been done to death. If managers have a problem, then there is probably an awful lot of theory around it.

While agreeing that there is invariably some piece of literature which is of some relevance, in this particular problem even the literature is fragmentary. This literature is also very prescriptive (with relatively few exceptions, for instance Barwise, Marsh et al, 1988, Grundy, 1992) and does little to explore how managers cope in practice with integrating strategic management and finance. On top of this, we find a conspicuous absence of high-level maps of how the different parts of both areas of theory link with one another.

Strategic Planning

The literature on strategic planning is, with a few exceptions, relatively unhelpful in guiding us towards an explanatory model of how corporate value might be managed strategically. Early models of corporate strategy, such as positioning grids like the growth/share matrix (see Davidson, 1985) provide little enlightenment on how to link strategy and financial (or corporate) value. These grids are very limited in helping us make linkages as they are primarily qualitative in nature.

Although there has been a strong critique of rational models of strategy development (most recently from Mintzberg, 1994), we are of the view that:

- Managers do both seek and benefit from some planning frameworks, providing these avoid becoming over-bureaucratic.
- Corporate value, in practice rather than in theory, is complex and requires some form of analytical process to unravel this complexity.

It is best therefore to look at three key areas which, to differing extents, have sought to interrelate strategic management and corporate value. The three areas are: corporate financial strategy, strategic management accounting and strategic value management. Each of these three areas has been developed to date largely independently and one of the key principles of strategic business finance is to draw them together into an integrated whole.

Corporate Financial Strategy

Dealing first with corporate financial strategy, this discipline should not simply be equated with corporate finance as it addresses a range of issues which interrelate financial markets and also competitive markets. Corporate financial strategy is the process which matches external sources of finance to strategies for corporate development. Corporate financial strategy (as discussed in Chapter 2 and in more detail in Ward, 1993) highlights:

- The need to reflect the expectations and aspirations of shareholders, particularly in strategic decision making and in the ongoing management of financial performance. This suggests that organisations should pursue activities and behaviours which are directly targeted at adding to corporate value. This requires that the specific risks associated with different strategic options are properly taken into account.
- The requirement for financial plans to reflect both short- and long-term goals – and accordingly reflect the full resource requirements of achieving those goals.
- The need to take into account life-cycle effects. For instance, the maturity of the organisation may have a bearing on its most appropriate cap-

ital structure, as will the level of financial sophistication which is acceptable to the financial markets from which financing is being raised.

Corporate financial strategy is therefore a framework for matching group strategy and investment plans with financing requirements. It therefore deals with a number of key interfaces between strategic management and finance which are represented in Figure 1.2. These deal primarily (but not exclusively) with the capital market interface. This interface doesn't figure particularly strongly in the strategic management literature yet it is of considerable importance for the external assessment of the likely returns from particular industries and companies.

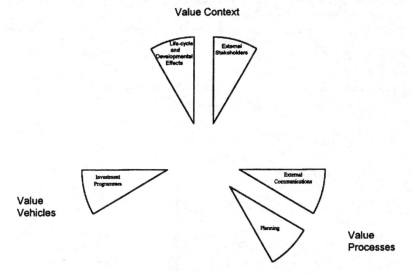

Figure 1.2 Corporate financial strategy

Corporate financial strategy is more than just financial planning and treasury management because it involves a continual dialogue between strategy and financial requirements which is not merely a constraining dialogue but actually an enabling one.

Strategic Management Accounting

Strategic management accounting (SMA) deals with the collection, analysis and dissemination of financial and competitive information about business performance. Unlike traditional management accounting which focuses principally on the internal measurement of (mainly financial) performance, SMA relates financial data to its competitive context (Simmonds, 1980; Ward, 1992).

SMA is not just conventional management accounting with frills attached to it (see Chapter 5). It provides the central focus for measuring strategic and financial performance. SMA helps gain competitive advantage by linking financial and strategic business information as a single whole. For instance, SMA can help management to:

- Identify the source of sustainable competitive advantage
- Value that competitive advantage
- Explore the cost base not merely internally but by comparative information relative to competitors
- Evaluate the relative financial attractiveness of different kinds of customers, or distribution channels
- Analyse key variances to compare what actually happened with what was planned to have occurred under a particular scenario. It is not just about comparing actuals against forecasts – the latter may have become irrelevant due to changes in the actual business environment.

SMA helps the company actually to deliver the additional value (ie super profit) which is needed to satisfy and exceed shareholder expectations, enabling strategic and financial planning to be more effectively integrated. Its key constituents are depicted in Figure 1.3.

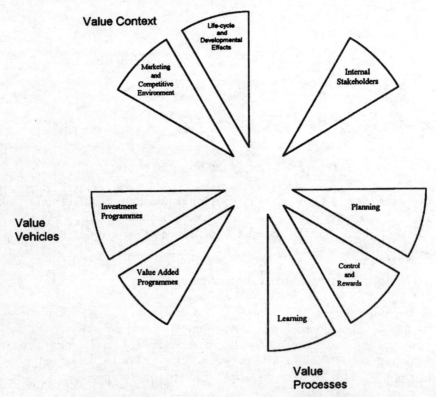

Figure 1.3 Strategic management accounting

Strategic Value Management

Strategic value management (Grundy, 1990–93) focuses on the key vehicles which deliver value in a company (see Chapters 7 and 8). These include:

- Organic investment decisions and acquisitions
- Cost programmes
- Change programmes
- Programmes for adding value.

A short example of strategic value management in practice is that of value-based management at BP begun by Bob Horton (then chairman) in the late 1980s. At that time BP's top managers and planners sought to revolutionise thinking about their businesses. At BP, strategic questioning and analysis now goes hand in hand with financial questioning and analysis. This played a major role in refocusing the businesses BP were in. Value-based-management has provided a framework to manage through the recession of the early 1990s (Grundy, 1992).

The market and competitive environment had become more harsh during the 1980s and early 1990s with problems of overcapacity in the oil-refining and chemicals businesses. Markets were mature in life-cycle terms. Other life-cycle effects were that of the highly volatile oil price and economic cycles. In parallel, to satisfy external and internal stakeholder expectations, BP Group had sought to diversify into newer, less volatile industries (for instance, BP ventures, BP nutrition). BP's style of planning was characterised by Goold and Campbell (1987) as then being 'strategic planning' – ie centralised, and top down.

BP's value process had historically been primarily orientated towards seeking businesses with high levels of return on capital employed (ROCE). Although investment appraisals were based on discounted cash flow (DCF) evaluations, the basic planks of value (the business strategies) were until the mid 1980s not so evaluated. Financial control was based on a mix of ROCE and (to a lesser degree) economic (cash-based) evaluations. Rewards processes were firmly linked to ROCE. Major investment decisions were appraised using DCF but other cost, change and value programmes were evaluated principally using accounting-based measures, with varying time horizons (often short term). This gave rise to some degree of difficulty internally.

Following on from the BP case, let us now turn to the key vehicles of value generation, and more specifically of investment appraisal (organic and acquisitive), cost management and change management.

First, although financial theory characterises investment appraisal as being largely concerned with applying discounted cash flow techniques, in practice issues such as uncertainty, intangibles and interdependencies fog the decision process (Grundy, 1993). These problems can be reduced if sufficient strategic thinking is brought to bear. Strategic thinking is particularly helpful in the stage before the very detailed financial quantification of value.

Second, acquisition appraisal offers potential for much closer integration of strategic and financial appraisal (Haspeslagh and Jemison, 1991). Companies managing acquisitions may need to reflect on how they add value for each and every acquisition, before the deal, during the deal and also after the deal during integration (see recent work, too, by McTaggart et al, 1994).

Third, it has also been argued (Shank and Govindarajan, 1993) that a radically different approach should be taken to costs from conventional, financial budgeting – that is strategic cost management. In strategic cost management (SCM) costs are managed explicitly for both financial and competitive advantage (see Chapter 8). This overcomes the false dichotomy of many traditional practices where cost management is equated with cost reductions which erode business strategy.

Shank and Govindarajan's framework makes extensive use of value-chain analysis and also highlights the need for competitive targeting of costs. It also makes explicit reference to Porter's generic strategies of cost leadership and differentiation. We also argue that many cost programmes can be usefully viewed as quasi-investment decisions. These decisions can then be appraised using economic valuation methods or at least subjected to a business case approach which spells out short- and longer-term benefits and costs, internally and externally.

Fourth, change programmes are also value vehicles. Yet it is not common to find them evaluated as if they were investment decisions (Grundy, 1992). Often the programmes are not very well targeted either financially or non-financially (Schaffer and Thomson, 1992). For instance, a particular popular change theme since the early 1990s has been business process reengineering (BPR) (Hammer and Champy, 1993), yet there is very little mention of financial targeting in the BPR literature.

Change programmes like BPR and other programmes aimed at adding value (for instance, total quality management, customer focus) represent a major financial commitment which is being implicitly justified by improving competitive position. Yet there is an absence of specific guidance on how these can be simultaneously strategically and financially targeted.

The key constituents of strategic value management (SVM) are therefore shown in Figure 1.4. Besides the diversity of vehicles which drive value, Figure 1.4 brings in planning, control and learning processes. It is worthwhile now to introduce shareholder value theory which is the antecedent of SVM.

Shareholder value has origins in corporate finance theory and also competitive strategy. There are different flavours of emphasis in shareholder value, for instance those which are primarily financially driven

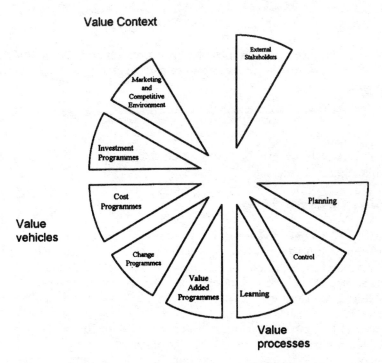

Figure 1.4 Strategic value management

(Copeland et al, 1990) through to the more even balance between finance and competitive strategy as seen in Rappaport (1986) and Reimann (1990). One of the key reasons for calling this framework strategic value management is to highlight the equal role in these two strands of thinking.

Rappaport emphasises the need for a deep understanding of key value drivers which form the linkages between competitive and financial analysis. (Value drivers can be defined as 'those key external or internal underlying determinants of value'. These can include, for instance, direct drivers such as the level of margin through to often more important (indirect) drivers, such as competitive rivalry or impact of new competitor entry.) Yet the mainstream literature in strategic management seems to have neglected this useful notion of value drivers. This may be partially to do with a discernible shift towards more process-orientated, and 'softer' views of how strategy can be managed more effectively as we enter the mid-1990s. We argue, however, that an increased emphasis on strategic management as a learning process does not preclude targeting and quantification, even in financial terms (see Grundy, 1994).

Beside value drivers as an adjacent notion is that of value destroyers. These can be a more important area to manage than value drivers per se in many businesses (as discussed in Chapter 7).

INTERIM CONCLUSION

From this literature review, despite apparent fragmentation, there are many clues as to how to frame a model for the strategic management of corporate value.

KEY IMPLICATIONS OF THE MODEL

Our argument has a number of key implications, particularly for theory and management research.

Implications for Theory

Our discussions have a range of implications for theory, particularly at the interfaces of strategic management and finance. First, although the banner of 'shareholder value' helps draw attention to the perspective of external, financial markets it does so at the expense of over-emphasising the external 'constraint'. In order to lessen the perception that shareholder value is some kind of (harmful) imposition, it is suggested that 'corporate value' is a far more workable concept – both for development of explanatory frameworks (theory) and for practice.

Second, there does seem to be benefit in integrating strategic value management and management accounting more closely. Along with corporate financial strategy we would probably benefit through simplification by calling the trio 'strategic business finance'. This also links into a fourth and particularly underdeveloped area of knowledge – the combined strategic and financial analysis of a company's annual report and accounts. This fourth ingredient we should call 'strategic financial accounting' as this deals with managing publicly available financial data (see Figure 1.5 and Chapter 10).

Both SVM and SMA thus have a critical role in helping finance interface with competitive strategy. These both deal with the financial interpretation of the external and competitive marketplace.

An Illustration

Below we take a closer look at an actual, recent, globally significant case, known as Marlboro Friday, which highlights how important these issues are in terms of corporate financial strategy, strategic management accounting and strategic value management. This case shows how a strategic business finance perspective can shed different light on a strategic move.

Marlboro Friday – Case Study

On 2 April 1993, Philip Morris staggered the business world by announcing 'across the USA' a significant price discounting programme of what

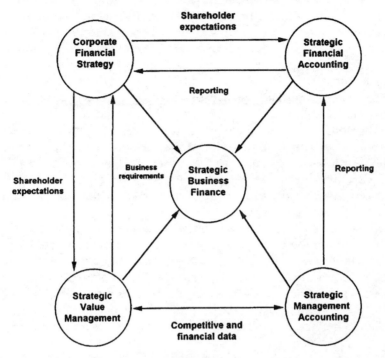

Figure 1.5 Strategic business finance

was perceived then as the world's most valuable brand, Marlboro cigarettes. On 20 July 1993, this 'promotion' was turned into a permanent
price reduction, which was also extended across all Philip Morris' full revenue tobacco brands in the USA. This dramatic change in competitive
strategy, now known generally as 'Marlboro Friday', resulted in a dramatic
fall in the share price of Philip Morris and, not surprisingly, of all its competitors. This was due to the predictable drop in the future profits generation from the USA cigarette market (which had historically been, and still
remains today, the world's most profitable cigarette market). Brand valuation pundits have also argued that this move reduced Marlboro's brand
value so significantly that it has now been replaced as the world's most
valuable brand name.

It is our contention that this dramatic event can be used as a good
example of the problems of current financial and strategic management
processes, which can be improved by the adoption of a strategic business
finance mindset. Using a strategic business finance approach, the Philip
Morris change in strategy can be argued to have increased the real (as
opposed to the 'perceived') value of the brand. It also put significant
financial pressure on key competitors in other markets at a time of high
strategic investment opportunities; thus potentially constraining their
ability to instigate a broad round of strategic initiatives.

The background to the brand's repositioning is clearly important. The USA cigarette market had been declining in volume terms at an average rate of 3 per cent per year. However the major companies in the market had been improving profitability on their USA operations by implementing real price and margin increases during this period; Philip Morris had a publicly stated financial objective of achieving 20 per cent per annum compound growth in earnings per share. Marlboro had, for many years, been the dominant full revenue brand in the market, but these increasing real prices had opened up new pricing segmentation opportunities. Consequently two new product categories had developed (value for money and extra low price categories) in recent years and these products had taken increasing shares of the total market volume, albeit at much lower profit margins to their manufacturers.

All these issues were public knowledge and hence should have been fully reflected in the Philip Morris share price and the associated estimation of Marlboro's brand value. However less publicly available in the short term was the disturbingly rapid decline in the market share of Marlboro during the last few months of 1992 and early 1993. Such information is obviously available to the senior management of the company and should be used as the basis for strategic moves designed ultimately to enhance shareholder value.

From a strategic business finance perspective, the rationale for the substantial and sudden reduction in selling price is based on a resulting significant increase in market share, combined with forcing the two other product categories to be consolidated into a single, even less financially attractive segment. This logic is based on the premise, which could be (and was) thoroughly tested before implementing the strategy, that consumers still preferred the Marlboro product but were unprepared to pay the excessive price premium now being charged by the company.

Clearly a substantial price reduction, with its automatic impact on net profitability, requires an even greater proportional increase in sales volume if overall profits are to be unaffected. Such a level of increase in share could not have been anticipated by Philip Morris (not least because they had carried out a test market in Portland, Oregon, on the price reduction and therefore would have good information on the likely consumer and competitive responses). If the net result was likely to be a decrease in profits and cash flow generation, how could such a competitive strategy be 'designed to enhance shareholder value'?

The key issue is, what levels of future profit and cash flows are assumed in the absence of the new competitive initiative? The share price of Philip Morris, prior to the move, appeared to be based on the historic, growing level of profits being extrapolated into the future. In other words, the company could continue to extract more value from a declining market through real price increases. In addition, Philip Morris was using Marlboro as its key brand in its global strategy, where many cigarette markets were either growing or opening up to the major Western producers, or both. As the international brand positioning was based on the USA heritage of the product, the continued domination by Marlboro of the USA cigarette market was vitally important to the success of this global strategy.

Given these strategic issues, the rapid decline in market share in the USA would have been of critical concern to Philip Morris. If this decline was not rapidly reversed, the future profit generation from both the domestic market and the rest of the world could be significantly reduced. Hence the comparison against which the new competitive strategy should be financially assessed must be adjusted (against) future cash inflows expected from the 'do nothing' alternative. In this 'do nothing' scenario, it is clearly likely that the company would assume a continuation in the decline in market share, and the rate of decline may indeed accelerate over time. (This would certainly be the case if the brand started to lose distribution as its rate of sale fell below required levels.)

The lack of movement in the share price, prior to the price reduction announcement, merely indicates that shareholders had not yet assimilated this very recent adverse change in the future prospects of the company. It is an important role for managers to see that this adverse change is minimised by implementing any potential strategic moves. A strategic business finance perspective will make this assessment possible even before the external financial markets have responded to the new situation.

To summarise, the Marlboro case highlights the impact of interdependencies between strategic moves, competitor responses and different strategic and financial scenarios. Corporate value creation can be regarded not merely through offensive strategy but also through protective strategies which avoid marked, financial decline (through strategic value management).

The case also highlights the need to weigh business information by linking both competitive and financial advantage (via strategic management accounting).

Finally, it also highlights the imperative to evaluate financial results not merely on a historic trend basis but also against their competitive context (strategic financial accounting).

CONCLUSION

Strategic business finance is not intended as a prescriptive programme to follow other management and theoretical fashions. It does not extol a single mechanistic process applied across industries and organisations, plain vanilla style. It does, however, have a common philosophy based on integrating strategic and financial thinking. This philosophy needs then to be operationalised through identifying a workable set of possible processes (or menus) to support actual practice.

For instance, it suggests that major strategic change programmes can be subjected to strategic value analysis. For example, business process reengineering or culture change programmes can be competitively and financially appraised, targeted and controlled. Also cost programmes can be managed strategically through strategic cost management (see Chapter 8). Again, the precise form which implementation actually takes would vary among companies (closely tailored to their value context) but this would again contain some common elements.

Finally, the philosophy of strategic business finance will take a lot of time and effort to diffuse through the learning process to the vast population of practising managers. Managers often struggle with the more basic elements of finance and it may seem counterintuitive to seek their involvement in the more advanced, and sometimes conceptual, field of strategic business finance. However, our experience to date has indicated that it is possible to make advances in insights, particularly using case studies (gathered from research and also in-company experience).

And what now of strategic management; how can it benefit from this emerging field? Strategic management (particularly strategic planning) may not hold the place it justly deserves in management thinking precisely because of its association with the long term and with very high-level, non-financial thinking. Strategic business finance can help give the commercial bite, that sense of immediacy, that strategic management often lacks in practice.

Strategic management and finance have thus traditionally been uncomfortable bedfellows. By and large they have developed separately – resulting in a widespread schizophrenia both in theory and in practice. We would dearly like to see the beginning of the end to this schizophrenia, which is harmful and counterproductive.

To summarise, therefore, in this introductory chapter, we have mapped the common elements of these programmes and interrelated them. We were also able to show how corporate financial strategy, strategic value management, strategic management accounting and strategic financial accounting can come together as one in 'strategic business finance' (SBF). Strategic business finance may provide a more coherent framework for managers and academics alike to explore the interesting borders between finance and strategy more effectively in the future.

The core chapters in this book focus on how finance links to both business and corporate strategy generically. In particular Chapter 2 (Ward) deals with the interaction between financial markets and product/service markets. This theme is followed up in Chapters 5 and 6 (Ward) by a more detailed analysis of how management accounting information (financial and non-financial) can be used to steer external competitive strategy.

Chapter 7 (Grundy) explores the various ways in which companies destroy (and alternatively, create) shareholder value. One theme is pursued in greater depth (Grundy) in examining how cost can be managed strategically (Chapter 8).

More specifically still Ward, Bender and Quinlan examine in Chapter 9 the strategic financial analysis of outsourcing in the NHS.

A further important contribution is how financial statements can be used for strategic advantage (Chapter 10). The more specific, financial issues are pursued in depth in relative to financial measurement over time and the distorting effects of inflation by Myddelton (Chapter 11).

In addition to core themes, the calculation and derivation of the cost of capital warrants a more in-depth, technical treatment (Fielding, Buckley) in Chapters 3 and 4. Also the specific but nevertheless behaviourally very important issue of executive incentives is discussed in the final chapter by Ward.

Collectively strategic business finance brings together recent research by the Finance and Accounting Group at Cranfield School of Management, Cranfield University. We are currently pursuing these and other directions including valuing business change, acquisitions and linking strategy with finance.

References

Barwise, P, Marsh P, Thomas K, Wensley R (1988) *Managing Strategic Investment Decisions in Large Diversified Companies,* London Business School.

Copeland, T, Koller T and Murrin J (1990) *Valuation-Measuring and Managing the Value of Companies,* John Wiley.

Davidson K (summer 1985) 'Strategic Investment Theories', *The Journal of Business Strategy,* Vol 6, No 1, pp 16–28.

Goold, M and Campbell, A (1987) *Strategies and Styles,* Basil Blackwell.

Grundy, A N (June 1995) 'Destroying Shareholder Value – in 10 Easy Ways', *Long Range Planning,* Vol 28, No 3, pp 76–83.

Grundy, A N (1994) *Strategic Learning in Action,* McGraw Hill.

Grundy, A N (1993) 'Putting Value on a Strategy', *Long Range Planning,* Vol 26, No 3, pp 87–94.

Grundy, A N (September 1990, October 1990, February 1991, October 1993) 'Strategic Value Management' (pp 1–4) *Management Accounting.*

Grundy, A N (1992) *Corporate Strategy and Financial Decisions,* Kogan Page.

Hammer, M and Champy, J (1993) *Re-engineering the Corporation,* Nicholas Brealey Publishing, London.

Haspeslagh, P C and Jemison, D B (1991) *Managing Acquisitions,* Free Press.

McTaggart, M, Kontes, P W and Mankins, M C (1994) *The Value Imperative,* The Free Press, Macmillan, New York.

Mintzberg, H (1994) *The Rise and Fall of Strategic Planning*, Prentice Hall.

Rappaport, A (1986) *Creating Shareholder Value*, The Free Press, New York.

Reimann, B (1990) *Managing for Value: A Guide to Value-Based Strategic Management*, Basil Blackwell.

Schaffer, R H and Thomson, H A (1992) 'Successful Change Programs Begin with Results', *Harvard Business Review*, January–February.

Shank, J K and Govindarajan, V (1993) *Strategic Cost Management*, The Free Press, Macmillan, New York

Simmonds, K (1980) 'Strategic Management Accounting', London Business School Paper.

Ward, K (1992) *Strategic Management Accounting*, Butterworth Heinemann.

Ward, K (1993) *Corporate Financial Strategy*, Butterworth Heinemann.

Part Two

CORPORATE FINANCIAL STRATEGY

2

DEVELOPING FINANCIAL STRATEGIES – A COMPREHENSIVE MODEL

Keith Ward

INTRODUCTION

Most of the research, and consequently the majority of the ensuing academic literature, in the strategy field concentrates on the development and implementation of specific competitive strategies at the divisional or strategic business unit level. Even where the overall concept of corporate strategy is considered, the focus of attention is normally on the implications of different types of organisation structure or managerial style (a good example of such research is Campbell, Goold and Alexander, 1994).

This chapter argues that another important area of potential added value is through the development of an appropriately tailored financial strategy. Indeed, such an appropriate financial strategy is essential if any of the competitive advantages which are developed by the business are to be successfully translated into added value for the shareholders in the company. It is also argued that the continuing creation of shareholder value requires that the financial strategy needs to change over time, with changes in the competitive environment and with changes in the specific competitive strategy being used by the business. Thus there is no such concept as the 'right' financial strategy for all businesses, or even for a single industry; each company should develop its own, unique financial strategy which takes account of the requirements of all its specific stakeholders.

This need for a tailored financial strategy may appear, at first sight, to run contrary to modern financial theory which argues that capital structure and dividend policy are irrelevant in valuing a company. However, as explained in detail in this chapter, these theories rely on very restrictive assumptions which make them inapplicable to today's companies in today's capital markets. Hence the model developed in this chapter is considered to be wholly consistent with modern financial theory, as by simply removing the unrealistically restrictive assumptions of theory, the implications for a developing, tailored financial strategy are highlighted.

RISK AND RETURN –
THE ESSENTIAL FINANCIAL RELATIONSHIP

Probably the most fundamental underlying concept in business finance is the requirement by all the stakeholders in a business for a positive correlation between risk and return. As their perceived level of risk increases, they require an increased rate of return to compensate for their bearing of this greater risk; this is diagrammatically illustrated in Figure 2.1.

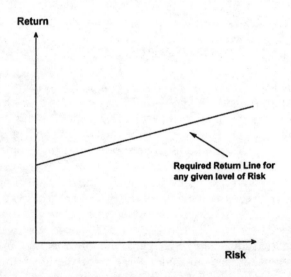

Figure 2.1 Positive correlation between risk and return

This very rational model raises two immediate questions: what do we mean by 'risk' and what is meant by 'required return'. Different groups of stakeholders can receive their returns in very different ways and many of these returns are not directly financial (eg job satisfaction for employees). This chapter, not surprisingly, concentrates on the financial returns from investments and these take two basic forms: an income stream (ie dividends for shareholders and interest for lenders) and/or a capital gain (ie share price movements for shareholders). The ways in which these returns are interrelated is a key part of the later discussion.

Although there is still some discussion regarding the definition of risk, it is widely accepted that, in financial terms, risk relates to *volatility in future expected returns*; in other words the risk free investment shown in Figure 2.1 should produce guaranteed, certain future returns. If future expected returns are likely to be highly variable, investors will logically require a greater return to compensate for their higher risk perception. (This means a *higher* expected value of these more variable returns.)

This idea is very useful, particularly if we break this overall risk down into two components, business risk and financial risk. Business risk relates to the volatility associated with the industry in which the company operates and the particular competitive strategy which it is implementing. Thus new, start-up, high-technology companies (such as those in biogenetic engineering, artificial intelligence, or virtual reality technology) have very high business risks; if they are successful, the future returns will be very good but there may be no future returns at all. As the industry matures, the business risk normally reduces (ie the volatility in the returns achieved reduces); this can easily be explained by reference to the product life-cycle. As diagrammatically shown in Figure 2.2, all the risk elements associated with any product or industry exist at the start of its life-cycle. As the business moves through the stages of its life-cycle, some of the total risks are removed (obviously if the risks are not removed, the business will not progress to the next stage).

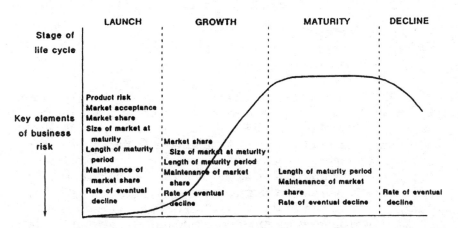

Figure 2.2 Changing business risk profile over the product life-cycle

There is therefore a normal trend over time for the level of business risk to reduce; this should lead to a similar proportionate reduction in the required rate of return. However the company can influence its total risk profile by deciding on the level of financial risk which it undertakes.

Business risk is determined by the industry and competitive environment in which the company operates, while financial risk depends upon the capital structure and financial policies adopted by the company. As risk levels are determined by the volatility in future expected returns, a high level of debt financing will result in a high perception of financial risk (interest has to be paid as a fixed expense irrespective of the relative profitability of the company). Conversely a company which uses exclusively equity funding will have a much lower level of financial risk. The important risk measure is the combined level of risk perceived by the investors (both shareholders and lenders) as this overall risk will determine the rate of return which they require.

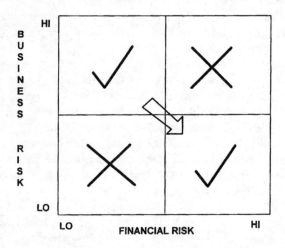

Figure 2.3 Business and financial risks

This enables an appropriate combination of business and financial risks to be established for any company, as is shown diagrammatically in Figure 2.3. (For ease of pictorial representation, the axes on the matrix in Figure 2.3 are of equal dimension, but it should be made clear that business risk is normally the dominant determinant of total, combined risk.) If a high business risk company uses largely debt finance, its combined risk profile will be excessively high and its probability of total collapse will increase dramatically. Interestingly the shareholders in this company may find this risk profile quite acceptable, despite the prospect of losing all their investment if the company fails. The potential upside on their investment if the company succeeds is likely to be very attractive, due to the fixed return payable on the high proportion of debt funding used by the company. It is, in fact, the lenders to such a company who should find the high business risk and high financial risk combination unacceptable. The only volatility which affects a normal lender to a company is the downside potential if and when the company gets into trouble, as lenders do not participate in the excess successful financial performance of the business. Consequently, lenders should only focus on safeguarding their loans against the potential bad news of underperformance.

The resulting financial strategy is that high business risk companies should adopt a low risk financing policy, which involves utilising equity funding. This is now fairly well understood but the subsequent development in the financial strategy still causes problems. Over time, as illustrated in Figure 2.2, the business risk should reduce but the company is also likely to become profitable and cash generating as it successfully matures. This means that it will move down the vertical axis of Figure 2.3 and can very easily find itself in the bottom left-hand box of the matrix. This combination of low business risk and low financial risk is also considered inappropriate for the creation of shareholder value.

Such a low business risk company which has strong consistent profits and cash flows could easily raise debt financing at a cost which is significantly lower than the rate of return which is required on its equity base. This is particularly true for a tax-paying company when the tax deductibility of interest expense is included in the analysis. However many such companies would argue that, since they are now highly profitable and cash positive, they do not need to raise debt financing for their business. This, for a publicly quoted company, is a dangerously 'fat and happy' attitude which has led to many companies being taken over by aggressively 'lean and mean' corporate raiders. The corporate raider is looking for exactly this type of target company, ie one with a sound competitive strategy but with an inappropriate financial strategy. By introducing a significant proportion of debt financing as part of the take-over financial structure, the raider hopes to increase dramatically the value of the equity which they inject into the company. Very often, the new owner will make no significant changes to the competitive strategy of the underlying business; their added value has been the repositioning of the financial strategy into line with the business risk profile of the company.

COMPANY LIFE-CYCLE

This inverse correlation of business risk and financial risk and their changing relationship over time is now used to develop an overall financial strategy for a single product company over its life-cycle. The restrictive assumption is that the company is not allowed to reinvest the profits and cash flow generated as the product matures in new products and marketing. This type of reinvestment strategy ultimately creates the type of diversified conglomerates created in the 1970s and early 1980s and which are subsequently being dismantled. The reasons behind this are explained as the model is developed.

Hence our company is started by launching a new product and the financial strategy model is considered in the four main stages of the life-cycle: launch, growth, maturity and decline as shown in Figure 2.4.

When a company launches a new product into an existing market, it will,

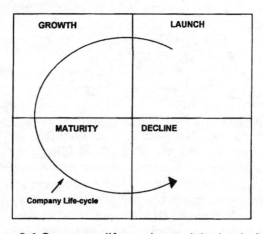

Figure 2.4 Company life-cycle model – basic format

by definition, have an initial low share of the market but will normally select a high growth market. (If a new product is launched into an already declining market, the company will start in the bottom right-hand box and stay there; what we often describe as an example of a 'Wally' strategy.) Its position will, therefore, be in the top right-hand box of the market. The key strategic thrust of the business at this launch stage should clearly be to focus on both research and development and market research for the new product, as the potential success of any new product can be severely curtailed if its entry into the market is so delayed that competitors have become solidly established. Given this strategic focus, the most appropriate management style is entrepreneurial and innovative, in order to stimulate the drive and enthusiasm to create and launch the new product which, quite frequently, requires very substantial obstacles to be overcome.

BUSINESS RISK

It is now possible, as is shown in Figure 2.5, to add in the business risk profile of the company at each stage of development. During the development and launch stage, this business risk is very high because the product may not work properly or, even if it does work, the market research indications may prove to be wrong with the eventual demand being too small to justify financially the total required investment.

GROWTH	LAUNCH
HIGH	VERY HIGH
MATURITY	DECLINE
MEDIUM	LOW

Figure 2.5 Business risk

Should the product launch prove successful and the sales volumes start to grow, the strategic thrust changes to market development, but particularly to market share development. It has been consistently demonstrated that it is much easier for a company to increase its market share while the market is growing rapidly. Again this result is not surprising because even if the particular company grows its sales at 50 per cent per year while the market is expanding at 40 per cent per year, its main competitors would still be expanding their own sales volumes quite rapidly on a year-on-year basis. It is possible that they may not even notice that their market shares are declining or, if they do, they may be capacity or capital constrained from increasing their output sufficiently rapidly to maintain their previous shares. If a similar market-share growth objective was set for a mature, very low-growth product, the competitive response is likely to be much more severe; as the increased sales volumes would almost all have to be achieved at the expense of *lower* sales volumes on the part of competitors. Consequently it is a sound business strategy to try to achieve the maximum desired market share before the market itself reaches its maximum size. This requires a clear focus on market share development, but a *leading* company in a high-growth industry should also invest in ensuring that the market matures at as large a size as is financially justifiable. Financial expenditure on market development (ie increasing the size of the overall market, rather than increasing the company's own share of this market) is very difficult to justify if the company has only a small share of the market. If only a 10 per cent share is held by the company, 90 per cent of any general market development expenditure can be argued as being to the benefit of competitors.

Such a concentrated strategic focus on market development and sales growth requires a shift in management style to 'marketing-led' management, where the emphasis is not necessarily on continually changing the product unless that is required to achieve a competitive advantage in the marketplace. Some management teams seem to be capable of operating successfully in both entrepreneurial and marketing-led modes whereas relatively few have been able to make the required transitions to incorporate the later styles of management. The business risk profile during this rapid growth phase has declined somewhat from the very high level of the launch stage but is still high. The main business risks now relate to the ultimate market share achieved by the company and the length of this period of sustained growth which together dictate the sales volumes which will be achieved during the maturity stage of the life-cycle.

As already stated, the sales growth will eventually slow and the product will enter its mature phase. If the company was successful in implementing its marketing strategy during the period of rapid growth, it should enter the maturity stage with a very high relative market share of a large total market. This is important because it is during this stage that the company recoups the investments made during the earlier stages. As shown in Figure 2.6, the net cash flows in the launch phase are heavily negative and they are normally reasonably balanced or slightly negative during the high growth stage, depending on the rate of growth and need for additional investment in fixed assets or working capital. Once the rate of growth slows this cash outflow reduces, while the cash produced from sales revenues increases (high sales volumes at a good profit per unit) resulting in a strong positive net cash flow. During the final decline stage of the life-cycle, both cash inflows and outflows are severely reduced, but the net cash flow must be at least neutral as otherwise the product should be culled instantly. (No company should be a net investor on a long-term basis in a dying product.)

Clearly this move into the maturity stage of the life-cycle represents a

CASH INFLOW - from sales HIGH	CASH INFLOW - from sales LOW
CASH OUTFLOW - Marketing, fixed assets working capital HIGH	CASH OUTFLOW - R & D launch marketing HIGH
NET CASH FLOW NEUTRAL	NET CASH FLOW NEGATIVE
CASH INFLOW - from sales HIGH	CASH INFLOW - from sales LOW
CASH OUTFLOW LOW	CASH OUTFLOW LOW
NET CASH FLOW POSITIVE	NET CASH FLOW NEUTRAL

Figure 2.6 Net cash flows at different stages of development

very significant change in the strategic thrust of the business. As previously mentioned, any attempt now to increase significantly market share is likely to be fiercely resisted by competitors, particularly where the cost structure of the industry is substantially fixed and committed on a long-term basis. (In other words, if significant exit barriers from the industry have been erected, there may well be intense competition to maintain market share.) The most appropriate management style during this phase can be described as 'controller' mode, because the business should be maximising the return which can be generated over this mature stage of the life-cycle. It is important that the business does not switch suddenly from its marketing-led growth strategy to a 'cost-cutting', short-term profit maximisation mindset. This type of change could lead to a rapid decline in market share and a dramatic shortening of the period over which high profits and strong positive cash flows can be generated. The key objective is to maintain market share as long as the total market demand justifies the required level of marketing support, but at the same time to look for efficiency gains which can improve the overall return on investment. This fundamental change away from a growth management focus to a profit improvement emphasis is very difficult for many management teams to accept and implement, with the result that many businesses try to grow when market conditions and competitive pressures make this financially very unattractive. If such growth is impossible in their original business, they may turn to a diversification strategy by investing in new product areas. For the purposes of this financial strategy model, such a diversification strategy is not open to the company.

Once again this move along the product life-cycle reduces the level of business risk as, in the maturity stage, the main risk relates to the length of this period of stable sales volumes and high total profit levels. From the economic viewpoint of the shareholder, this cash positive phase is the justification for the initial investment in the development and launch of the product. Indeed financially rational investors would like the company to move as rapidly as possible around the product life-cycle until the maturity stage is reached, and then the company should stay in this cash generating phase for as long as possible. Unfortunately the earlier styles of innovation and growth tend to be more attractive to many managers, who can find the appropriate controller style of the maturity phase very boring. Many shareholders find it far from boring to see increasing profits and cash flows generated year after year!

In fact for some groups of managers the declining stage of the product life-cycle may be more exciting as the dominant style now becomes 'cost-cutter', in order to ensure that the cash flows do remain at least neutral. The product is now dying, although the process may take many years and some spin-off ideas may be relaunched as new products in their own right. However, even in the move from the maturity stage to the declining phase, the business risk can still be argued as reducing. The only remaining business risk associated with the product is how long it will take to die. No dramatic positive cash inflows are expected from this phase and, if no further cost savings can be made to keep the cash flow slightly positive or neutral, the product may be closed down by the company before the market demand completely disappears. One major practical problem, caused by the failure to change managers during the progression of a product through its life-cycle, is that it is very difficult for the managers who have developed, launched, grown and then maintained a product to accept that it is now time to kill what has become part of their lives (one of the family!). Far too often, products are kept going too long in the vain hope that the market will pick up or that a new way will be found of reducing the associated costs still further.

FINANCIAL RISK

It is now possible to develop the appropriate financial strategy for each stage of the product life-cycle by using the required inverse correlation between business risk and financial risk, which was considered earlier. Since the associated business risk decreases as the product moves through its life-cycle, it is logical that the financial risk should be correspondingly increased without creating a completely unacceptable combined risk for the shareholders and other stakeholders in the company. This is illustrated in Figure 2.7 and leads to the obvious question of what impact this potentially increasing risk profile has on the financial structure of the business. A key element in financial strategy is the change from 'will' to 'should': the business risk *will* decline and the financial risk *should* be increased. The financial risk will not automatically change; it requires positive action on the part of the company.

As is clearly illustrated in Figure 2.7, the financial risk profile should be very low during the very high risk stage of product development and launch. The relatively low risk nature of equity funding has already been discussed, when considered from the company's point of view. For start-up businesses, it is desirable to use low risk equity sources of funding and this can be achieved by raising capital from specialist investors who understand the high business risk associated with the company. This funding is properly described as venture capital (unfortunately many investment funds nowadays describe themselves as providing 'venture capital' when, in reality, they invest in existing, successful businesses rather than green field, start-up companies; they should be more appropriately described as 'development capital' investors or even 'leveraged capital' investors.) A sensible venture capital investor will have a portfolio of similarly high risk, start-up investments and will require a very high potential return from each investment made. This type of investment strategy, which is still focused on high risk projects but diversifies the risk

GROWTH *Business risk high* **LOW**	**LAUNCH** *Business risk v. high* **VERY LOW**
MATURITY *Business risk medium* **MEDIUM**	**DECLINE** *Business risk low* **HIGH**

Figure 2.7 Financial risk

of any single project, allows for the quite possible total failure of a start-up business during the very early stages of the product life-cycle. As long as a reasonable proportion of the total venture capital investments made actually deliver their expected high financial returns, the overall return on the portfolio should be satisfactory. In other words the very high return *required* by the venture capitalist investor is simply caused by the very high business risk associated with this type of investment.

A primary interest of such venture capital investors is how do they get to realise or receive these high returns on their successful investments (ie what is their exit route?). As previously explained, the product will eventually become cash positive when it matures but this may be many years away, whereas venture capitalists tend to have a relatively short investment time horizon (the normal period is between 3 and 5 years, with a 7-year investment period being the maximum acceptable). This short term focus is exacerbated by their high requirements for financial return, which force them to invest in high risk projects. As businesses successfully develop and mature, their associated business risk tends to reduce and, consequently, so does the level of return which can be expected from these less risky, more mature businesses. Thus staying as an investor until the product is significantly cash positive is a very unattractive proposition for such a venture capitalist. It is also unattractive for the company as the required rates of return of venture capitalists make their funding seem very expensive once the business has a successful track record.

Hence identifying a relatively early exit route, once the product has been successfully launched on to the market, is an important prerequisite of designing a good venture capital investment. The funds to buy out these venture capital investors will not be available from within the company, as its cash flow during its rapid growth phase will be neutral at best. Therefore new appropriate external sources of funding must be identified to replace the initial launch financing and to provide for the growth of the business during this next stage of the product's development. The business risk associated with the growth stage is still high, so that the ideal financial risk should still be low. This means that the source of this new replacement and growth funding should still be equity. However these equity investors will have a slightly lower risk appetite than the original venture capitalists, and will accordingly demand a lower return on their investment.

The best way of achieving this type of exit route for venture capital initial funding is through the flotation of the company on to a public stock market, where a much broader range of equity investors can be attracted to buy shares in the company. Such an initial public offering (IPO) is not normally possible for a start-up company as, by definition, the business has no track record which can be used to indicate its existing success or its realistic prospects for the future. In essence, an investment at this stage is made on the strength of a product concept, with possibly some prototypes and some market research, and a business plan indicating the future prospects for the successful, eventual product. Such investments are normally only attractive to a small number of specialised, professional investors whereas, once the product is launched and initial sales growth can be demonstrated together with substantial future growth prospects, a much larger body of potential investors becomes available to the company.

The changing source of funding is illustrated in Figure 2.8 and this indicates the fundamental change which can occur when the product matures. This maturity stage reduces the associated business risk so that a medium level of financial risk can now be taken on by the company. The cash flow from the product has also turned significantly positive at this time and this combination allows the company to borrow funds rather than only using the equity sources of funding which have been accessed so far in its development. It is also important to consider the business from the perspective of the rational investor, who quite rightly regards this cash positive, mature stage as the most attractive phase of the lifecycle. So far equity funding has been injected into the business to develop and launch the product and then to increase both the total market size and the company's share of that market. If more equity funding is required during the maturity stage, this investment starts to look a lot like a financial black hole; money keeps going in, but nothing ever comes out.

Therefore the only logical source of additional equity funding during this maturity stage is for some of the profits being made by the company to be reinvested into the business. It must be remembered not only that these profits should be substantial in order to justify the investments made earlier in the cycle but also that additional financing can be raised through borrowing money. This is now practical because the positive cash flow of the business provides the source of servicing the debt (ie paying

GROWTH	LAUNCH
Business risk high *Financial risk low*	*Business risk v. high* *Financial risk v. low*
EQUITY (GROWTH INVESTORS)	EQUITY (VENTURE CAPITAL)
MATURITY	DECLINE
Business risk medium *Financial risk medium*	*Business risk low* *Financial risk high*
DEBT AND EQUITY (RETAINED EARNINGS)	DEBT

Figure 2.8 Source of funding

the interest) and of repaying the principal. If debt financing is used at the earlier stages of the life-cycle, the absence of such positive cash flow means that the repayments can only be made by rolling over the original loans or by raising equity to repay the debt funding.

This highlights a key issue regarding the use of debt and equity funding; the risk associated with debt funding from the viewpoint of the lender is lower than the equity investors' risk, due to the security taken and legally granted priority on full repayment. (Remember that the risk ranking is reversed when viewed from the perspective of the company, ie the user of the funding.) Risk and return are positively correlated, so that the return required on debt funding should always be less than that required on equity financing for the same company; ie debt is cheaper for the company. This is completely logical from the company's perspective because, as debt is higher risk funding for the company, the company should demand a cost saving to justify incurring the extra risk.

Therefore so long as increasing the financial risk through borrowing (increasing the 'leverage' of the company) does not lead to an unacceptable total combined risk, the cheaper debt funding will increase the residual profits achieved by the company. Thus the profits generated by the mature company, which uses some debt financing, will be enhanced and the return on equity will look even better, as less equity is required to fund the business.

This is even more important when the product moves into the decline phase of the life-cycle, and it becomes clear that the product is dying. If debt is cheaper than equity, it is financially beneficial to the shareholders to extract their equity investment from the dying business as early as possible by replacing it with debt. Clearly it should not be acceptable to a lender to take on an unacceptable, equity type risk, but it is often quite practical to borrow against the residual value of those assets which are, of necessity, tied up in the business until it is finally liquidated. These funds can then be distributed, effectively representing a repayment of capital, to shareholders so that their present value is increased, without adversely affecting the position of the lender who is suitably secured on the residual value of the asset (such as land and buildings, some non-specialised plant, cars, debtors and certain other working capital items) and receives a risk-related rate of interest. Consequently the principal source of funding for the declining business is debt finance with its associated high financial risk, partially offsetting the low business risk associated with this final stage of development.

COMPARISON WITH FINANCIAL THEORY

This model argues quite clearly for a changing capital structure over time and as the risk profile of the company changes. Modern financial theory states categorically that capital structure is irrelevant from the perspective of the shareholder (see Modigliani and Miller, 1958) and this apparent contradiction requires some explanation. Modigliani and Miller's theoretical model was based on the world of perfect markets and perfect competition. Thus as the debt ratio increases, the required rate of return increases in proportion to the change in risk perception. However the financial justification for increasing the debt ratio is that the company can invest the funds raised at a rate of return which exceeds the cost incurred in borrowing these funds. As a consequence the expected return on the equity invested in the company will also rise as the debt ratio increases. Under the assumptions of perfect capital markets, these increases (in the required and expected rates of return) exactly offset each other. This creates the result that the value of equity is unaffected by the debt: equity ratio of the company; this can be most easily shown graphically in the form of Figure 2.9.

The theoretical result follows from the fundamental assumptions required for perfect competition and the ensuing perfect capital markets; namely that expected rates of return always equal required rates of return, and there are no transaction costs and no taxes. Even Modigliani and Miller, in 1963, acknowledged that taxation did have an impact on capital structure. Taxpaying companies could increase the value of the company's equity by raising tax-deductible debt finance but after a while the tax benefit was offset by the increasing perception of risk. This is shown in Figure 2.10 where the company can add shareholder value by moving from point A to point B.

However Figure 2.10 also shows that, if the financial risk is increased too far, the value of the company's equity can be reduced, ie point D to point C. This recognises the fact that the costs of financial distress (eg administration, receivership and ultimately liquidation) are not borne evenly by the equity and debt holders. All the costs are borne by the equity holders until they have lost all their investment and only then do the

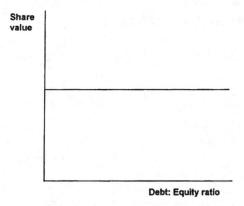

(Note: the same horizontal line would be drawn if total company value
was on the vertical axis)

Figure 2.9 Modigliani and Miller: Impact of debt: equity on share

debt holders have to suffer financially. Thus, as the risk of financial distress increases with rising debt levels, the value of the equity investment
may fall.

The theoretical argument is still that the market is efficient enough to
adjust so that the required and expected rates of return offset each other
in the middle ground, ie between points B and D. This debate has gone
on (see Myers, 1984) for many years and still rages among some academics.

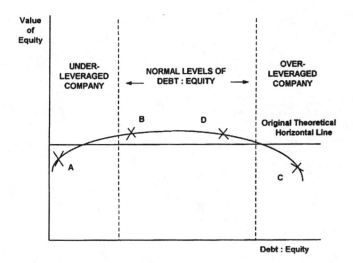

Figure 2.10 Modigliani and Miller, including taxes and financial risk

A LOGICAL DIVIDEND POLICY

Throughout this discussion on increasing levels of financial risk, the issue of how investors receive their required financial return has been critical. Ordinary shareholders can only receive this return in two ways; either the company pays a dividend or the value of their shares increases so that they can sell and achieve a capital gain. Obviously the total return can take the form of a combination of dividend yield (the actual dividend received divided by the value of the investment) and capital appreciation but, theoretically, the shareholder should be indifferent as to whether the company pays a dividend or not. This is because, if the company does not pay a dividend, the value of the shares should increase to reflect the present value of the future cash flows which should be generated by the reinvestment of these profits which were available to be paid out as dividends.

Once again the relevance of dividend policy has been the subject of fierce academic debate. The perfect competition argument of Miller and Modigliani, 1961, not surprisingly again concludes that dividend policy is irrelevant to the value of the company. This is based on an assumption of an infinite stream of potential reinvestment projects which are available to the company and which all generate a rate of return which is equal to the shareholders' required rate of return. Reinvesting at the shareholders' required rate of return neither creates nor destroys shareholder value and, therefore, in the additionally assumed absence of transaction costs and taxes, the indifference of the shareholder to the company's dividend policy is not surprising.

The theory is not wrong, merely irrelevant to the real world due to its restrictive assumptions. Attempts have been made to incorporate dividends and capital growth into a valuation model and this was first done in 1938 by Williams. This work was updated in 1956 by Gordon and Shapiro and again by Gordon in 1959. They developed a very simple dividend growth model which was based on two main assumptions: a constant proportionate rate of reinvestment and a constant rate of return on this reinvestment. These assumptions result in a constant compound rate of growth in earnings per share. The constant rate of reinvestment assumption automatically leads to a constant dividend payout ratio and thus dividends grow at the same constant compound rate as earnings. This leads to a very simplified valuation model which is intuitively attractive because it shows, as in Figure 2.11, that the return to shareholders is composed of the current expected dividend yield and the future growth in the earnings and dividend streams. This Gordon dividend growth model (as it is now normally known) is totally dependent on its own restrictive assumptions, of which the growing supply of investment projects with a constant rate of return is about as realistic as the Miller and Modigliani assumptions.

The Gordon/Shapiro model shows that:

$$P_0 = \frac{D_1}{(K_E - g)}$$

$$K_E = \frac{D_1}{P_0} + g$$

so that the return to shareholders is composed of dividend yield and earnings growth

Figure 2.11 Gordon/Shapiro dividend growth model

The debate about the relevance of dividend policy to shareholder value has continued since these early publications (some of the better articles on the subject include Porterfield, 1959, Brennan, 1971, and Myers, 1984).

Many other dividend growth models have been developed with slightly less restrictive assumptions about either the rate of growth (eg a linear growth model rather than compound growth) or the time period over which the growth continues (eg a finite time period rather than an infinite period). These theoretical developments are discussed in much more detail in Ward (1993) and the theoretical arguments considered here are gathered together and reviewed in Ward (1994).

Clearly this argument is based on the various assumptions regarding the availability of attractive reinvestment opportunities, but such assumptions of an infinite number of attractive reinvestment projects is not relevant if the company is restricted to one product, which progresses through its life-cycle.

Hence for the current structured analysis, it is possible to indicate a logical dividend policy for a company at each stage of development, and this is diagrammatically shown in Figure 2.12. During the cash negative launch phase it is completely illogical for shareholders to expect a dividend from the company. They are supplying all the funding and therefore, if the company was to be able to pay a dividend, they would have to increase their investment in order to pay part of it back to themselves! Consequently a nil dividend pay-out ratio is appropriate for these start-up, venture-capital-funded businesses; all the high required return being in the form of capital growth. There is also a very simple practical restraint on many such companies paying dividends. In order to pay dividends, companies require both cash and distributable profits, eg profits after tax generated either in the current year or retained from past years. During the launch phase, the business may be generating accounting losses and therefore may have no distributable profits from which it can declare a dividend.

Even when the company has moved into the high growth stage of the life-cycle, the cash flow is still, at best, only neutral and the source of funding should still be equity. Thus a high dividend pay-out policy is still illogical and this is made even more clear when the key strategic thrust at this stage is considered. The business is trying to increase its market share while the market is still growing strongly; a logical investor would want the company to take advantage of these attractive growth opportunities while they exist and this could be constrained if current profits are paid out as dividends. As new investors are being attracted into the company during this stage in order to replace the existing venture capitalists and to finance the rapid growth, it may be logical to pay a nominal dividend out of the increasing profit stream. However most of the required investor return would still come from capital growth in the value of the shares in the company.

Once the maturity stage of the life-cycle is reached, the dividend policy should change for a number of reasons. The cash flow from the business is now strongly positive and debt financing is now a practical and sensible alternative source of funding. Accounting profits should now be high and relatively stable so that a high dividend pay-out can be properly supported. More fundamentally, it is important that the dividend pay-out ratio is increased as there will be restricted opportunities for reinvesting the whole of the current profit stream in the existing business. There is a strong possibility of the law of diminishing returns setting in on incremental levels of reinvestment. As already stated, if a company cannot reinvest funds at the rate of return demanded by its shareholders, it destroys shareholder value by retaining these funds. Consequently, as profitable reinvestment opportunities reduce due to the lack of growth in the now mature business, shareholder value can be maximised by paying out these surplus funds as dividends.

This required change in dividend policy represents a potential conflict in agency theory because senior managers will normally prefer to retain these surplus funds within the company. These funds provide them with operational flexibility should an attractive opportunity be identified in the future and they also act as a buffer in case there is an unforeseen economic downturn or adverse change in the competitive environment. Neither of these arguments is based on the concept of maximising shareholder wealth, but is more closely focused on a concept of reducing either managerial risk or accountability.

Inevitably the strong cash flows and high profits will die away as the product starts to decline; yet Figure 2.12 then advocates a total dividend

GROWTH	LAUNCH
Business risk high *Financial risk low* *Funding equity*	*Business risk v. high* *Financial risk v. low* *Funding equity*
NOMINAL	**NIL**
MATURITY	DECLINE
Business risk medium *Financial risk medium* *Funding debt*	*Business risk low* *Financial risk high* *Funding debt*
HIGH	**TOTAL**

Figure 2.12 Dividend policy–pay-out ratio

pay-out ratio. In this context, 'total' means all the free cash flow generated by the business which, during this declining stage, is likely to be in excess of the profit levels reported by the company. During the maturity phase, the company produces high profits and high net cash flows, out of which it should pay a high proportion as dividend. This dividend yield will represent a substantial proportion of the total return expected by the shareholders, because future prospects for capital growth are now relatively low (profits may increase in future years due to improvements in efficiency levels etc). However once the product starts to decline, this future growth becomes negative with the result that the company may not want to reinvest to maintain the existing scale of the business. This means that the depreciation expense (which is, of course, a non-cash operating expense charged in arriving at the post-tax profits out of which dividends are paid) may not necessarily be reinvested in replacing the assets which are being used up. This would increase the level of free cash flow generated by the business which could be paid out as dividends to shareholders. The dividends could be further increased if the residual value of essential assets was raised by borrowing and the cash distributed to shareholders, as mentioned earlier, clearly highlighting that part of the high dividends paid by declining companies really represents a repayment of shareholders' capital.

This changing picture of the dividend pay-out ratio and its offsetting relationship with expected capital growth in the share value must always be considered in the context of a decreasing overall risk profile for the company as it matures. The reducing risk profile means that investors demand a lower total rate of return; the sort of relationships which can apply between dividend yields and capital growth are illustrated in Table 2.1

Table 2.1 *Illustrative example of changes in total shareholder return and its component elements*

Stage of maturity	Total annual required return (ie K_E)		Generated by: Dividend + Capital yield growth		
Launch	40%	=	0	+	40%
Growth	25%	=	2%	+	23%
Maturity	15%	=	12%	+	3%
Decline	12%	=	18%	–	6%

(These total returns are illustrative only. Tax is ignored, but does not affect the logic of the analsyis. However the different tax positions of various groups of shareholders may make companies in particular states of maturity more or less attractive to them.)

UNDERSTANDING THE PRICE/EARNINGS MULTIPLE

It is clear from Table 2.1 that the capital growth component of the total expected shareholder return reduces as the product passes through its life-cycle. This is very logical because the future growth prospects for the product start off very high and reduce as these prospects are actually achieved; obviously if the product is unsuccessful, these future growth prospects may be destroyed very quickly, rather than being delivered over time. The development of future growth prospects over the life-cycle is illustrated in Figure 2.13 which highlights that the future growth of a mature product is relatively low and that a declining product will experience negative growth in the future.

What is unfortunately seemingly not very well understood is the very

GROWTH	LAUNCH
Business risk high *Financial risk low* *Funding equity* *Dividend pay-out nominal*	*Business risk v. high* *Financial risk v. low* *Funding equity* *Dividend pay-out nil*
HIGH	**VERY HIGH**
MATURITY	DECLINE
Business risk medium *Financial risk medium* *Funding debt* *Dividend pay-out high*	*Business risk low* *Financial risk high* *Funding debt* *Dividend pay-out total*
MEDIUM/LOW	**NEGATIVE**

Figure 2.13 Future growth prospects

tight relationship between these future growth expectations and the appropriate price/earnings (P/E) multiple for any particular company (Figure 2.14). The P/E multiple for a company reflects the expected future growth in earnings per share which is already incorporated in the share price. Hence the share price will only move due to changes in this expected growth or if the actual performance shows greater or lower growth than has *already been paid for* by current investors in the existing share price. Merely achieving some growth in earnings per share (EPS) is therefore no guarantee of a rising share price; particularly for a high P/E company.

This can be mathematically explained very clearly by considering how the P/E multiple for a steady state, no growth company should be derived. Such a type of company, which may be impractical but provides a very useful conceptual model, would need two main assumptions in order to maintain over time the constant *real* levels of profit which are essential to the only rational financial definition of 'steady state'. First, depreciation would need to be based on true replacement cost accounting and the annual depreciation expense would have to be reinvested in the business; if this was done the business would be capable of producing the same physical level of output over time. Second, all of the constant real profits achieved after charging this replacement cost depreciation must be paid out as dividends. If any of the profits are reinvested the business should grow, whereas if dividends paid out are greater than the profits earned the business will get smaller over time; therefore, a 100 per cent dividend pay-out ratio is essential. (Obviously there are some other more general assumptions required such as either the absence of inflation, or the maintenance of real net profit margins and a neutral influence on net working capital.)

The result of these assumptions is that the company can be valued on both the P/E multiple basis and the present value of the future dividend stream, as is done in Figure 2.15, shown on p 62. As can be seen from

GROWTH	LAUNCH
Business risk high *Financial risk low* *Funding equity* *Dividend pay-out nominal* *Growth high*	*Business risk v. high* *Financial risk v. low* *Funding equity* *Dividend pay-out nil* *Growth v. high*
HIGH	**VERY HIGH**
MATURITY	**DECLINE**
Business risk medium *Financial risk medium* *Funding debt* *Dividend pay-out high* *Growth medium/low*	*Business risk low* *Financial risk high* *Funding debt* *Dividend pay-out total* *Growth negative*
MEDIUM	**LOW**

Figure 2.14 Price/earnings multiple

(1) P_o = $\dfrac{PAT}{No\ of\ shares}$ x P/E multiple

(Price)

= EPS x P/E

(2) P_o = Present value of the future dividend

(Price) stream

= $\displaystyle\sum_{1}^{\infty} \dfrac{D_t}{(1+K_E)^t}$

But the dividend stream will be constant over time (steady-state company), ie

$D_1 = D_2 = D_t = D_\infty$

and dividends will equal earnings per share (100% pay-out ratio).

Therefore (2) can be restated as

$P_o = \dfrac{EPS}{K_E}$

representing the present value of a constant perpetual annuity

But from (1)

$P_o = EPS \times P/E$

Thus

$P/E = \dfrac{1}{K_E}$ (for a steady state company)

Figure 2.15 Valuation of a steady-state company

these equivalent values, this shows that for a steady state company the appropriate P/E multiple equals the inverse of the company's cost of equity capital (K_E). It cannot be emphasised too greatly that this relationship only holds for a steady state company. This argument and critical relationship is also dealt with by other researchers (see Clarke et al, 1990).

For a growth company, the P/E multiple will be greater than this inverse of the cost of equity capital whereas, for a declining company, the P/E multiple will be lower reflecting the expected decline in the future potential stream of earnings and dividends. Hence this very simple relationship provides a very powerful reference base for assessing both the risk profile and the future expectations signalled by any P/E multiple *given to* a company by the financial markets. It must be remembered that, in reality, the P/E multiple is mathematically calculated by dividing the share price by the current or expected EPS, rather than the computation being the other way round; hence it is more correct to say that the share price drives the P/E multiple.

The risk profile of the company is indicated because the steady state P/E multiple is given by the inverse of the company's cost of equity capital at the time when it becomes steady state, and this cost is driven by the risk free rate of return (K_F) together with the risk related premium needed for the particular company. Using the risk profile of the company, the base steady state P/E multiple can be assessed and then it is perfectly possible to calculate the amount of future growth included in any specific P/E multiple given to a company.

It is therefore useful to think of the P/E multiple as being a signalling device by current and prospective shareholders (ie the capital market) to the company, giving a clear indication of their future expectations regarding growth in EPS. These signals can be compared to the signals sent out by the company's managers to the financial markets regarding their own views on future growth prospects, which are included in the dividend pay-out ratio. Thus a low dividend pay-out ratio, with the consequent high reinvestment strategy, signals an expectation of high future growth; if the stock market agrees with this high growth expectation, it should give the company an appropriately high P/E multiple. Alternatively an increasing dividend pay-out ratio can be used by managers to signal to the market that the future growth prospects are decreasing; the stock market should respond to such a signal by reducing the P/E multiple applied to the shares in that company.

One of the main problems encountered in the financial strategies of major publicly quoted companies is that senior managers, and especially chief executives and chairpeople, do not seem to accept the inevitability of a declining P/E multiple as their company matures. This overwhelming desire to maintain over time, if not to increase, an already high P/E multiple can become the dominant driver of the corporate and competitive strategy of the business, often leading the company to diversify into new areas of potential growth even though the organisation has absolutely no competitive advantage in this new sector. It is quite likely that this obsession with the level of the P/E multiple is increased by the types of short-term financial incentives given to these senior managers.

The type of progression of P/E multiple which can be experienced as a business matures is shown in Table 2.2. This highlights the very high real growth in EPS which is already included in the share price when a very high P/E multiple is applied to the company. The delivery of this expected growth will not make the share price increase because it has already been discounted (ie taken account of) in the current share price. The share price will only rise if the company can actually exceed this expected and paid-for rate of growth, or continue to grow at this rate for longer than expected. However in the first three stages of the life-cycle it is quite possible for the company to deliver strongly growing EPS, as is shown in Figure 2.16.

Table 2.2 *The inevitability of a reducing P/E multiple*

Stage of maturity	Appropriate P/E multiple	×	Current earnings per share	=	Market price of share
Launch	40	×	2.5p	=	100p[1]
Growth	20	×	5p[2]	=	100p (base price)
Maturity	10	×	10p[2]	=	100p (base price)
Steady state	7	×	14.3p[2]	=	100p (base price)
Decline	4	×	12.5p	=	50p[3]

1. The current price of 100p includes a very high expectation of future growth. In order to support this existing price, the company must deliver over its life-cycle the growth in EPS indicated as item 2.
3. As indicated in Figure 2.18 the share price starts to fall when the product moves into the decline phase, as both the P/E multiple and EPS fall.

THE RESULTING SHARE PRICE MOVEMENTS

This continued period of rapidly increasing EPS is very important from the shareholders' point of view because, as was made clear in Table 2.1, during the launch and growth stages almost all their financial return is generated from capital growth in the value of their shares, the company having a very low dividend pay-out policy at this time. Consequently generating only that rate of growth in EPS which merely maintains the existing share price would be considered a very poor performance by the company. The EPS growth during the launch and growth periods should drive up the share price so that an acceptable overall annual rate of return is achieved by the shareholders. This needs to take account of both the declining P/E multiple which will be applied to these earnings as they grow and the changing dividend pay-out ratio which should reduce expectations of future growth as the company matures.

GROWTH	LAUNCH
Business risk high *Financial risk low* *Funding equity* *Dividend pay-out nominal* *Growth high* *P/E high*	*Business risk v. high* *Financial risk v. low* *Funding equity* *Dividend pay-out nil* *Growth v. high* *P/E v. high*
LOW	NOMINAL
MATURITY	DECLINE
Business risk medium *Financial risk medium* *Funding debt* *Dividend pay-out high* *Growth medium/low* *P/E medium*	*Business risk low* *Financial risk high* *Funding debt* *Dividend pay-out total* *Growth negative* *P/E low*
LOW	DECLINING

Figure 2.16 Earnings per share

Table 2.3 *Earnings per share growth required to deliver total required shareholder returns (ie capital gain element in addition to the growth already included in the share price)*

Stage of maturity	1 Length of stage (in yrs)	2 Appropriate annual capital gain required through share price (from Table 2.1)	3 Compound factor ie (2)[1]		4 Required share price at time of change to next stage	5 Future growth related P/E multiple		6 Desired EPS by end of stage
Initial value at time of first external investment 100p								
Launch	2	40%	1.96	x	100p ➤	40	x	2.5p
Growth	5	23%	2.82	x	1.96p ➤	20	x	9.8p
Maturity	10	3%	1.34	x	552p ➤	10	x	55.2p
Steady State	N/A	Nil			742p	7	x	106p

Thus the growth in EPS over the 17 years, which this company takes to get to its steady state position, is from 2.5p to 106p, not to 14.3p as indicated in Table 2.2. Growth to 14.3p will not increase the share price as required by the investors during the initial periods when nil, and then very low , dividend yields are received and the associated risks are quite high, as shown in Table 2.1.

NB The final EPS of 106p at the steady state stage will all be paid out as dividends (required 100% pay out ratio for steady state to occur). This will generate the required dividend yield of 14.3%, which is the demanded return by shareholders at this stage of development (ie P/E multiple of 7 is the inverse of the company's cost of equity capital).

The dramatic impact which this additional requirement for share value growth has on the need to generate EPS growth is mathematically illustrated in Table 2.3. This shows that for a particular, relatively short life-cycle the growth in share price which is required to give shareholders their expected total annual return, including the capital gain element, is itself quite dramatic (eg from 100p to 742p over the 17-year life-cycle period to the steady state stage as shown in column 4). However, due to the declining P/E multiple which is also correctly applied as the company matures, the required increase in EPS needed to generate this final share price is even greater (an incredible growth from 2.5p to 106p, as shown in column 6).

The underlying assumptions for these illustrations have been deliberately kept consistent so that the scale of the changes can be seen quite clearly as the analysis is made more comprehensive. This enables the overall analysis to be completed by adding in the share price of the company over the company life-cycle, as is done in Figure 2.17.

This figure shows both the movement in the actual share price over the life-cycle (ie on the left of the diagonal dividing line) and the associated volatility (ie on the right). The share price is obviously the result of multiplying the P/E multiple and the EPS level, and its required trend over time depends on the proportion of the total shareholders' return which must be delivered through capital growth. As highlighted in Table 2.3 the share price should be increasing during the launch and growth stages, and then stabilising during maturity, before declining during the product's final phase of its life-cycle.

During the very early period of the launch stage, any financial valuation exercise is very speculative as nominal (or even negative) earnings are being multiplied by the very high P/E multiple which reflects the expecta-

GROWTH	LAUNCH
Business risk high	*Business risk v. high*
Financial risk low	*Financial risk v. low*
Funding equity	*Funding equity*
Dividend pay-out nominal	*Dividend pay-out nil*
Growth high	*Growth v. high*
P/E high	*P/E v. high*
EPS low	*EPS nominal*
GROWING/VOLATILE	**?/HIGHLY VOLATILE**
MATURITY	**DECLINE**
Business risk medium	*Business risk low*
Financial risk medium	*Financial risk high*
Funding debt	*Funding debt*
Dividend pay-out high	*Dividend pay-out total*
Growth medium/low	*Growth negative*
P/E med	*P/E low*
EPS high	*EPS declining*
STABLE/STABLE	**DECLINING/VOLATILE**

Figure 2.17 Share price/volatility

tions of strong future growth. As already discussed, this stage of invest-ment is really an area for sophisticated professionals who appreciate the high associated risks and, potentially, commensurately high financial returns. The considerable potential for complete business failure or out-standing success results in very high volatility in share prices during this stage of the life-cycle.

Once the product moves into the growth phase, this volatility will decline somewhat but will still be high due to the continued expectations of significant future growth in share values, EPS, market share, and the total size of the market. Failure of any of these factors (which are of course interlinked) can lead to a rapid decline in share values, while unpredicted favourable developments can create quite spectacular growth in share prices. However during the maturity stage, when the major element of shareholders' return comes from dividend yield, the share price should become much less volatile. This is because the strong positive cash flow and ability to use debt financing should enable the company to maintain the expected dividend payments even through nor-mal economic cycles, so that the share price is consistently supported by this stable dividend stream. It is also much easier to value this type of income-generating share by reference to equivalent risk-adjusted interest-earning alternative investments; thus high-dividend-paying shares tend to move very directly as a result of any changes in interest rates which affect the yields on corporate bonds and other such investments.

This period of relatively low volatility comes to an end as the single product company moves into the final phase of its life-cycle because the volatility of the now declining share price increases again. In spite of the reducing business risk, the share price is now controlled by a total divi-dend pay-out policy and the investors' view on the length of time for which such payments can be maintained. Consequently small external influences on the rate of decline of the product and its consequent cash generation capability can have very significant impacts on the share value, thus increasing the volatility.

IMPACT OF A DIVERSIFICATION STRATEGY

So far in this chapter consideration has been concentrated on single product companies as they, and their products progress through the life-cycle. The analysis in this chapter does highlight that the inevitable liqui-dation of the single product company is not necessarily of great concern to the shareholders in the company; although these shareholders are likely to change over time as the relative balance in the form of their financial return between capital gain and dividend yield changes. A major reason for such changes in shareholder structures is the different taxation treatments applied both to different shareholder groupings and to the different types of return available to each of these classifications of investors. As usual, these taxation differences create inefficiencies in the way capital markets operate which is why most theories of finance are based on assumptions of no taxes at all. Major improvements from this point of view have been achieved in several economies around the world during the 1980s and 1990s by the reduction in corporate taxation rates and the simplification of the related tax systems to reduce some of the main distorting factors.

Clearly rational shareholders may be unconcerned about the forthcoming decline and death of any one investment from which they are currently receiving very high dividends – which partially represent a repayment of their invested capital. If *they* wish to preserve the value of their total investments, they could reinvest this capital repayment in other companies. Indeed it is fairly obvious that rational investors can generate any desired mix of capital gain and dividend yield by investing in a suitable portfolio of companies. Similarly they can create a portfolio with any desired overall risk profile by suitably weighting the different types of available investments. Thus no sensible investor is forced to accept the reducing risk profile and increasing dividend yield which should be offered by a maturing company. A readjustment to the overall portfolio can be made either by reinvesting this increasing income stream in higher risk, higher growth companies or, more rapidly, by actually selling some shares in the now mature business.

The costs of these changes to the investors' portfolios are normally very small and, more importantly, such changes should be easily planned well in advance if the company and the capital markets are using the appropriate signalling procedures discussed earlier in the chapter. Therefore there is no obvious need from a shareholder's perspective for a company to implement a diversification strategy, when the growth prospects from the original core business reduce due to the product's maturity. However such corporate strategies of utilising the strong positive cash flow from the successful, but now mature core businesses to invest in new higher growth potential products lie at the very heart of diversification strategies. As clearly demonstrated in Figure 2.6 the growth and decline stages of the life-cycle are both broadly neutral in terms of net cash flow. The strong positive net cash flows of the maturity stage, which are not required for reinvestment in the core business, are therefore often used to fund the launch of other new products, which are at the beginning of their life-cycles. Inevitably, over time, such a cross-subsidisation reinvestment strategy will create a diversified conglomerate style group which, due to its continued high level of reinvestment, should be considerably bigger than an originally similar, but still focused business which had followed a financial strategy of increasing its dividend pay-out ratio over the same period. The major question is whether shareholder value has been increased or destroyed by the diversification alternative strategy.

Shareholder value is increased by developing and maintaining a sustainable competitive advantage. It is therefore critical whether the business can develop such a competitive advantage in these new areas of commercial endeavour. Obviously it may be that the new products utilise some technological breakthrough which was developed in the core business, and thus the company is not truly diversifying. Similarly the new areas of investment may build on an existing strength of the business so as to increase the overall competitive advantage held by the company. If a key competitive strength of the existing business is built on the current product attributes or strong branding which have created very loyal customers, a strategic thrust for continued growth could be based on umbrella branding of new products with comparable attributes. This would utilise the major intangible assets of the company which are these loyal customers. Such a customer based competitive strategy has been implemented by many retailers, highlighted by the development of 'retailer' brands. Alternatively the existing product may have reached maturity in its current markets but other markets may be less fully developed, and so may represent additional growth opportunities. Once again this growth strategy is based on an existing competitive advantage of the business; it successfully managed the launch and growth stages of the product in its original market, but its managers need to be very careful to ensure that any required modifications to their previous strategy are made to reflect the new competitive environment.

These growth strategies can be successfully developed from an existing competitive advantage but, as with the case of the growth strategy focused on the original core business, the external business environment must be consistent with the strategy selected. Thus for growth of the core business to be financially successful the product must be at the right stage of development; similarly, for the customer led strategy the new products must have similar attributes so that they appeal to existing loyal customers and any umbrella branding is appropriate. For the market development strategy, the dynamics of the new markets must be sufficiently similar to enable the company to make use of its existing competitive advantage developed in its more mature home market; there are many examples of very expensive failures from this type of product globalisation strategy and far fewer examples of success. This area is discussed in more detail in Chapter 5.

APPLICATION INTERNALLY TO THE DIVISIONS OF A GROUP

It is quite difficult for a large diversified group to communicate a clear overall financial strategy and thus ensure that it is properly valued by the financial markets. Consequently the threat of takeover and break-up is potentially on the horizon for many large diversified groups, so that it is important that this analysis of appropriate financial strategies is applied internally by them to their individual operating divisions. In other words, the target financial return set for each division should be based on an assessment of the associated risk; thus a start-up division would be treated as having venture capital funding, with a consequently high requirement for financial return. Also the form of that financial return would be dictated by the stage of development of the particular business so that cash (ie dividends paid by the division to head office as the only shareholder) would only be extracted from mature divisions, where the opportunities for reinvestment were less attractive.

The establishment of very clear, specific, tailored financial targets for each division of a large group can greatly help to focus the attention of divisional managers on those objectives which can create the maximum impact on the value of the total group. This would not be achieved if all the divisions tried to maximise short term profits or cash flow, or even used some form of return on investment as the principal measure of divisional performance. Unfortunately, in many large groups, this level of financial sophistication is still not being applied today; in many the hurdle rate for financial investments throughout the group is taken to be the weighted average cost of capital for the group and almost all divisions are expected to contribute towards the overall dividends paid out by the group to its shareholders. The almost inevitable result of this type of control system is that the divisions themselves start to develop a portfolio of businesses which are in different stages of development, so that they can then manage their financial resources across their own portfolio.

An alternative and interesting response to this apparent complexity of managing a large, diversified, multi-stage group has been to focus on only one stage of development. This focus means that, although the group may have a wide range of products selling to many different customer groupings, the financial strategy signals externally and the required internal financial control systems need not become confusingly complicated. A very successful example of this kind of strategy is Hanson plc, which has a number of relatively independent businesses around the world. However each of these major businesses is at the mature stage of a relatively low technology, and hence long, product life-cycle. This enables this vast group to be controlled by very few people at the centre because similar financial controls can be applied to all the divisions. Even more importantly it enables the expectations of the financial markets to be managed through clear signals on dividend policy and sources of funding. Given the mature nature of these businesses, it is not surprising that most of the growth by the group has been by dynamic acquisitions of mature, similar businesses. Indeed the ideal acquisition target for a group like Hanson is another diversified group which is still being managed for rapid growth even though its major businesses have now matured. Once purchased, some rapid changes in its financial strategy can create significant increases in shareholder value, albeit for its new shareholders.

CONCLUSION

The relevant financial strategy must be selected in the context of both the current business strategy and its associated risk profile. It is also helpful to understand how the financial strategy should be modified as the company develops over time and the expectations of rational investors change.

Shareholders can receive their risk adjusted return in the form of either capital gains (as the share price increases) or dividend income, or a combination of both. Theoretically there is no difference in value to the investor between a zero dividend pay-out policy and a 100% dividend payment but this relies on the company being always able to reinvest its current profits at the investors' required rate of return. In reality, as a company's core business matures, the profitable reinvestment opportunities decline so that it becomes financially sensible to increase the dividend pay-out ratio, rather than continuing to retain the high proportion of profits which can be justified during the launch and rapid growth stages of the life-cycle.

Obviously an increasing proportionate dividend pay-out ratio leaves the company with less cash retained in the business for reinvestment. However the business risk associated with this maturing company should be reducing and therefore the financial risk can be increased at this stage of development. This enables more debt financing to be raised than would have been appropriate earlier in the life-cycle. This additional source of funding can be important as a way of balancing the desirability of increased payments to shareholders with the reinvestment requirements of the business.

The different stages of company development should also condition the expectations of future growth on the part of shareholders. This is reflected through the price/earnings (P/E) multiple applied to the current earnings per share in order to arrive at a current share price; thus, as expected future growth in earnings reduces, so should the P/E multiple. There is no conflict between using either this P/E multiple based method of share valuation or the present value of the future expected dividend stream method, as the link is provided by the shareholders' cost of equity (K_E). This demanded (or required) return by shareholders is not only used as the discount rate which is applied to the future dividend stream, but it also acts as the basis for assessing the P/E multiple for a steady state, no growth company (this steady state P/E multiple is actually the inverse of the shareholders' cost of equity). The actual P/E multiple applied to any particular company is calculated by adjusting the steady state P/E multiple in accordance with the expected future growth or decline in the earnings per share.

References

Brennan, M (1971) 'A note on dividend irrelevance and the Gordon Valuation Model', *The Journal of Finance*, 26 December.

Campbell, A Goold, M and Alexander, M (1994) *Corporate Level Strategy: Creating Value in the Multibusiness Company*, Wiley & Sons.

Clarke, R G Wilson, B D Daines, R H and Nadauld, S D (1990) *Strategic Financial Management*, Irwin, Homewood, Illinois.

Gordon, M J and Shapiro, E (1956) 'Capital equipment analysis: the required rate of profit', *Management Science*, 3 October, pp 102–110.

Gordon, M J (1959) 'Dividends, earnings and stock prices', *Review of Economics and Statistics*, May.

Higgins, R C (1977) 'How much growth can a firm afford?', *Financial Management*, Vol 6, No 3, pp 7–16.

Miller, M H and Modigliani, F (1961) 'Dividend Policy, Growth and the Valuation of Shares', *Journal of Business*, Vol 34, No 4, October, pp 411–433.

Modigliani, F and Miller, M H (1958) 'The cost of capital, corporation finance and the theory of investment', *The American Economic Review*, Vol XLVII, No 3, pp 261–297.

Modigliani, F and Miller, M H (1963) 'Corporate income taxes and the cost of capital: a correction', *The American Economic Review*, June.

Myers, S C (1984) 'The capital structure puzzle', *The Journal of Finance*, Vol XXXIX No 3, pp 575–592.

Porterfield, J T S (1959) 'Dividends, dilution and delusion', *Harvard Business Review*, November.

Ward, K R (1993) *Corporate Financial Strategy*, Butterworth Heinemann, Oxford.

Ward, K R (1994) *Strategic Issues in Finance*, Butterworth Heinemann, Oxford.

Williams, J B (1938) *The Theory of Investment Value*, Harvard University Press, Cambridge, Massachusetts.

3

UNDERSTANDING THE CHANGING FACE OF CAPITAL MARKETS

John Fielding

INTRODUCTION

Few subjects have caused more controversy between academics and practitioners than the efficient market hypothesis (EMH). In 1978, at a conference called to discuss a number of anomalies, Michael Jensen, a leading
proponent of market efficiency claimed, 'I believe there is no subject in
economics that is more firmly established than the efficient markets
hypothesis'. However since that date much of the evidence has tended
not to support the EMH.

The purpose of this chapter is to summarise briefly the findings of
research carried out in the last 50 years into the operation of the stock
market and to relate these findings to decisions faced by practising managers. The work can be neatly divided into three sections. The first considers models of how the market prices securities, the second how
efficiently these securities are priced and the last section considers a topic
of considerable topical interest, the volatility of the stock market.

Before moving on, it is essential that we clarify the meaning of the
term efficiency. When we refer to the efficiency of the stock market we
mean its ability to price securities correctly with respect to all available

information. We are not referring to the level of transaction costs or to how effectively the market allocates funds to companies to secure an optimum allocation of resources. Of course, low transaction costs make it more likely that prices will reflect information which is available to investors, and a market which correctly prices securities may be helpful in allocating funds in an optimum manner. However in this chapter we are solely concerned with the ability of the market to price securities correctly given the information which is available.

Fama (1970) has usefully provided three categories of market efficiency.

Firstly there is the weak form in which no excess returns, i.e. returns giving investor's compensation for risk they have borne, can be earned by studying the historic sequence of prices. In a weak form efficient market, charts are useless for predicting future prices.

Secondly there is the semi-strong form in which prices reflect all publicly available information. Excess returns cannot be earned by analysing this information. Stock market prices are set as a result of trading by highly paid professionals, who carefully analyse company reports, industry statistics and other public information. Competition between these professionals ensures that prices include all this information.

Finally there is the strong form, which asserts that even private or insider information is fully reflected in security prices. Proponents of this form argue that private information leaks into the market. Thus, even insiders cannot consistently earn excess returns from their privileged knowledge.

To measure excess returns, a soundly based model is needed and it is to the development of such a model that we must now turn our attention.

HOW THE MARKET PRICES SECURITIES

It is well known that the value of a security is represented by:

$$V_0 = \sum_{1}^{n} \frac{D_1}{(1+r)} + \frac{D_2}{(1+r)^2} + \dots \frac{D_n}{(1+r)^3}$$

where V_0 is the share price, D_1 is the dividend per share at the end of period 1 and r is the interest rate per period. In other words, the share price represents the present value of all future dividends discounted at an appropriate interest rate. Since dividends represent a risky stream of cash flows they should be discounted at an interest rate which adequately compensates investors for the risk of their investment. A major concern of corporate finance has been to develop a model which provides an equilibrium rate of return that adequately compensates investors for the risk they bear.

To help us understand this model we need trace very quickly from the foundations of portfolio theory, Markowitz (1952), the two fund separation theorem of Tobin (1958), the capital asset pricing model attributed to Sharpe (1964) and, finally, to the market model. Both Markowitz and Sharpe were awarded Nobel prizes for their contribution to the theory.

Markowitz – Risk and Diversification

For many years it had been well understood that investors should hold diversified portfolios. The return on a portfolio is simply the weighted average of the return on the individual securities (the weights being given by the proportional value of each of the holdings in the portfolio). The risk of holding a single share is given by the standard deviation (a measure of the dispersion) of its expected return. Shares considered risky have large standard deviations while less risky shares have low standard deviations. Portfolio theory therefore depends on returns from shares being normally distributed with measurable standard deviations.

The risk of a portfolio depends not only on the proportion invested in each security and the expected standard deviations of the securities in the portfolio but also on the forecast correlations between the expected returns. For example, an investor holding a portfolio consisting of shares in an umbrella maker and in an ice cream manufacturer would receive a return based on the weighted average of the returns of the two companies. However the riskiness (standard deviation of expected returns) of the portfolio of two shares would be reduced since one would expect the shares in the umbrella company to perform well in a wet summer while the ice cream manufacturer's shares would perform well in a dry summer.

Markowitz argued that investors should try to form portfolios lying along what he called 'the efficient frontier' by selecting shares which would give the best return for a given level of risk. This was to be achieved by selecting securities, whose expected returns were forecast to be lowly correlated with the securities already in the portfolio. In this way investors could select portfolios which matched their risk return preferences. This is shown in figure 3.1.

Markowitz's ideas required, for their practical implementation, estimates of the expected return for the securities being considered, the expected standard deviations of their returns and also an estimate of the expected correlation between the return of each security in the portfolio. A formidable drawback to the practical application of Markowitz's ideas was that the number of correlations between securities increases rapidly as the number of securities increases. For example, if it is decided to study

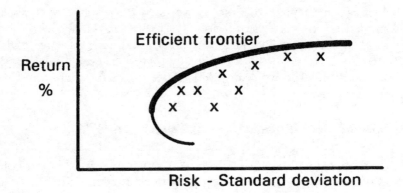

Figure 3.1 Efficient portfolios

100 securities for possible inclusion in a portfolio then there are 4950 correlations between the securities to calculate. Given the primitive computing facilities available in the early 1950s calculation of the necessary statistics was a formidable undertaking far beyond the capabilities of most practitioners. By the 1990s the task has become both trivial and routine.

Tobin – Two Fund Separation

Nobel prizewinner James Tobin extended Markowitz's work by introducing the possibility that an investor could hold a risk free asset (normally assumed to be treasury bills). It can be easily seen from Figure 3.2 that if the investor holds a proportion of their portfolio in a risk free asset and a proportion in the portfolio marked M, then they can achieve a better risk return trade-off compared with the efficient frontier. The straight line R_f M dominates the efficient frontier and gives a higher level of return for any set level of risk. Thus the best strategy for any investor is to hold part of their portfolio in a suitable risk free asset and part in portfolio M, ie in two funds. The proportions which they hold will depend upon their risk return trade-off. They can further improve their return by borrowing to buy investments. In this way the straight line R_f M is extended to the right of portfolio M to a point which we will call X. However, as well as increasing their return, their risk is increased. This of course is just the same as the gearing effect that is well known to accountants and financiers. The reader will have noticed that the line R_f M X is straight. This assumes that investments can be made at the risk free rate, which may be true, but also that the investor can borrow unlimited funds at the risk free rate, which clearly is not true. In the real world borrowing rates are higher than lending rates and the line R_f M X is kinked downwards from point M when the investor starts to borrow to fund further purchases.

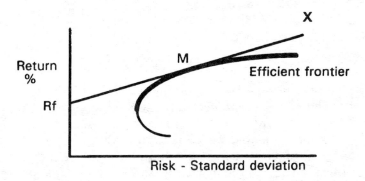

Rf is the risk free rate of interest

Figure 3.2 Efficient portfolios with lending and borrowing

Sharpe and the Capital Asset Pricing Model

We saw earlier in this chapter that the standard deviation was a measure of risk for the returns from a single security and that for a portfolio, risk could be reduced through diversification. The portion of a security's risk that can be eliminated through diversification is known as specific risk. What remains is non-specific risk. In the literature a number of alternative terms are used and these are summarised in Table 3.1.

Table 3.1 Terms describing risk

Risk related to holding one security	Risk related to holding a fully diversified portfolio
Specific	Non-specific
Non-market	Market
Diversifiable	Non-diversifiable
Unique	Non-unique

Since investors can easily eliminate specific risk by diversification they will not be concerned with this risk. They will only be concerned with the risk that cannot be eliminated by diversification. This is known as market or non-specific risk. Figure 3.3 below shows that if 30 securities are held then just over 60 per cent of total risk is eliminated, leaving market risk at a little under 40 per cent.

Sharpe (1964) and others developed the ideas of Markowitz and Tobin further into what has now become the capital asset pricing model (CAPM). This states that the expected return on a share is made up of two parts. First there is the risk free rate and secondly a premium for risk. The formal calculation is:

$$ERs = Rf + \beta(ERm\text{-}Rf)$$

where *ERs* is the expected return on the equity share, *Rf* is the risk free rate and *ERm* is the expected return on the market; β (beta) is a measure of the shares' sensitivity to market movements. A company whose shares move up or down in line with market movements has a β of 1. If the price of its shares tends to move up or down 2 per cent for each 1 percent change in the market, its shares have a beta of 2 and would be considered risky. If the shares move up (or down) only ½ per cent for market increase (decrease) of 1 per cent then the company's shares have a beta of 0.5. The capital asset pricing model enables company executives to calculate the return investors expect on their shares. This is of course the cost of equity which is a major input into the calculation of the weighted average cost of capital. For example, suppose the risk free rate is 6 per cent, the expected return on the market 13 per cent and the estimated β, 1.2, we would expect the share to give us a return of:

$$ERs = 6 \text{ per cent} + 1.2(13\%\text{–}6\%)$$

or 14.4 per cent.

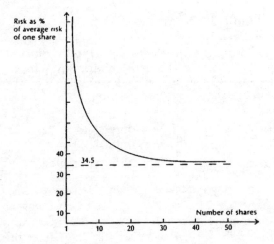

The effect of risk of the number of securities in the portfolio

Source: Solnik (1974). By permission of the *Financial Analysts' Journal*

Figure 3.3 Diversification and risk

We are left with a striking result. The expected return on a share depends only on a single measure of risk, its beta. All other factors, such as the risk of the failure of a production process, of the next marketing campaign not capturing customers' attention, are not of themselves, important. Investors should hold diversified portfolios. If they do, all these risks, as far as they are not captured in the company's beta, will be eliminated by diversification.

How is β calculated? Excess returns on the share are regressed against the excess return on the market. (Excess returns are measured by deducting the risk free rate from the return on the share or the return on the market, as appropriate). The beta factor is simply estimated by least squares regression. Alternatively, a line can be fitted through the points on a scatter chart as shown in Figure 3.4. Usually about 60 observations of monthly data are used to compute beta. This is thought to be a good compromise between basing the β on a long but possibly dated series, which captures the companies' fortunes through the business cycle, and a shorter but more up-to-date series which only reflects business conditions in part of the cycle.

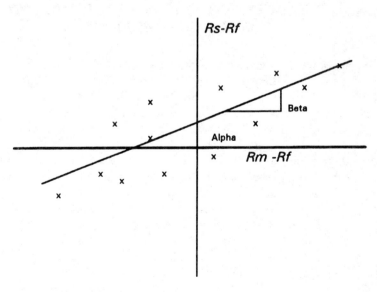

Rm   is return on the market

Rf   is the risk free rate of interest

Rs   is the return on the share

Figure 3.4 The market model

The Market Model

Figure 3.4 is known as the market model and can be defined formally as:

$$Rs - Rf = \alpha + \beta(Rm - Rf) + e$$

where α or alpha represents the excess return of the share in an unchanged market. We would expect this to be zero. However most shares will have performed either better or worse than predicted and α will frequently be statistically significant. The error term e should conform with the normal assumptions of linear regression.

In 1977 Roll made a major challenge to the capital asset pricing model. One problem he pointed out was that the market portfolio should include all assets and not just stock market investments. So the value of economically significant assets such as housing, should be included. While there has been academic recognition for the theoretical strength of Roll's position, the CAPM model in practice provides a useful way of dealing with risk in the market.

HOW EFFICIENT IS THE STOCK MARKET AT PRICING SECURITIES?

So far we have discussed two notions. Firstly that the stock market is efficient, ie it incorporates all available information in its prices, and secondly a simple model which states that the expected return on a security depends on the risk free rate plus a premium for risk which is measured by beta. The two hypotheses of market efficiency and of the capital asset pricing model are very closely related. Many of the tests of market efficiency depend on the model specifying equilibrium returns in the market place, the capital asset pricing model.

All three forms of market efficiency have been extensively tested. Most of the early tests seemed to confirm that the market efficiently prices securities. Some of the later tests provide evidence of anomalies while other tests appear to refute the hypothesis. As the literature has been extensively summarised elsewhere (Dobbins, Witt and Fielding, 1994) we will give only the briefest outline.

Tests of the Weak Form

The reader will recall that the weak form of the hypothesis stated that excess returns could not be made from analysing the historic sequence of prices. Early tests showed that the serial correlations of returns of 30 large shares in the US were virtually zero when measured over lags of 1 to 16 days (Fama, 1965). In other words, share price movements seemed to be random and future returns could not be predicted by using the returns of periods ranging from 1 to 16 days. Fama also confirmed, what Mandelbrot (1963) had previously found, that stock returns did not seem to be normally distributed. Their distribution had much fatter tails than expected. In fact they seemed to belong to a class of stable paretian distributions whose variance is infinite. This has had a profound effect on stock market research since most statistical tests depend on normally distributed data. In particular we have already mentioned that Markowitz's portfolio theory depends on risk being measured by the standard deviation of expected returns. Fama (1965) discounts the problem. Nevertheless, it is one that has continued to concern researchers and further reference to this point will be made in the section on excess volatility.

In further tests of the weak form, researchers examined a number of techniques used by chartists to select winning shares. The results again support the weak form and none of the chartists' methods show the ability to earn excess returns consistently.

Tests of the Semi-strong Form

The semi-strong form states that all public information is incorporated in share prices. Tests of this form of the hypothesis (known as event studies) have examined the speed at which events whose effect can be predicted are assimilated into share prices. For example Ball and Brown (1968) studied the impact of 261 earnings announcements on share prices. Their sample of companies was divided into two. The first sub-sample included companies returning higher earnings than expected and the second, companies with earnings lower than expected. How did the share prices of these companies react before and after the announcement? The share prices of the companies reporting favourable earnings increased in the 12 months before the announcement but not much following the announcement. The market anticipated the good news and there was little opportunity for an investor to make excess returns by buying the shares following the announcement. In a similar way the share prices of companies reporting poor results fell in the 12 months before the announcement and there was only a small fall after the announcement. All this is consistent with a market which is continuously examining companies' prospects and anticipating the news included in annual accounts.

There have been hundreds of other event studies and they all have virtually the same result. A surprise announcement leads to an immediate adjustment and thereafter the share price seems to follow a random walk.

Tests of the Strong Form

The strong form of the hypothesis asserts that even private information is quickly incorporated into share prices. Researchers have tested this form by examining the performance of professionally managed funds. Academics argued that investment analysts may become privy to private information which they incorporate into their investment recommendations. Shares are purchased and the share price increases towards fundamental value. Michael Jensen (1968) in his pioneering study of 115 mutual funds in the US found that after allowing for risk, as measured by beta, only half the mutual funds beat the market. When expenses were deducted, most funds underperformed. It seems that few investment professionals consistently beat the market.

However despite this evidence, the claim that the market is strong form efficient is clearly weak. The assumption that investment analysts have access to large amounts of private information is questionable and there is considerable evidence, both anecdotal and also from academic studies, that insiders do consistently beat the market.

On the other hand, however, there are some *a priori* grounds for believing the market to be strong form efficient. Directors who conclude that their shares are undervalued have an obligation to their shareholders to argue for a higher value. They frequently employ public relations experts to present their case. If the directors believe shares of their companies to be overvalued they should promptly warn the market of possible future difficulties.

So far the evidence seems to support the EMH, except perhaps in its strong form. To many investment professionals and even to some academics the EMH fails to reflect what they observe taking place in the market. How can the stock market represent a rational view of investment fundamentals, ie future dividends discounted at a risk adjusted rate, when it fell by one-third in three days in the October 1987 crash? An alternative explanation is that stock prices are influenced to a very considerable extent by fashions and fads. We must now examine the evidence against market efficiency.

EVIDENCE AGAINST MARKET EFFICIENCY

Introduction

The idea that the stock market may be influenced by fashions and fads is certainly not new. As early as 1936 Keynes had suggested that picking winners on the stock market was like newspaper competitions where the reader was invited to choose the prettiest face from a selection. The game was not to choose who had the prettiest face but to guess which face the judges would select as the prettiest. In the same way an investor might base their investment decision on which stocks the market favours rather than on their views of the fundamental worth of the companies.

Shiller (1984) argued that fashions and fads might be as prevalent in the stock market as they are in many other aspects of life. He cites the fashion for jogging which became popular only in the mid-1970's despite the beneficial effects of exercise for health being understood for many years. Enthusiasm for a share may cause its price to rise. Other investors see that their colleagues have made money through owning that share and they also buy it, forcing further price rises. Some investors may even believe the share to be already fundamentally overvalued. However they think that it is worth buying because of the enthusiasm of others. In this way the upward movement of the price will continue until the bubble bursts.

The notions of market efficiency found little favour with the vast majority of investment practitioners, whose livelihood depended on persuading investors that they were able to outperform the market, either by selecting winning stocks or by judging the movements of the market. It was not however until the late 1970s that the first serious academic attacks were made on the EMH. In an important paper Summers (1986) simulated a volatile series of stock prices characterised by fads. He tested whether the early serial correlation tests and the event studies were sufficiently powerful to detect departures from randomness implied by his series. The answer was strongly, no. In fact, as he went on to argue, 5000 years of stock market data would be necessary to discriminate between his and a random series. In other words, while the early tests were all consistent with market efficiency they were unable to test an important alternative to efficiency. It is well known that the test of any hypothesis is whether the data support *it* better than any competing hypotheses. (A discussion of what it means to establish evidence in favour of a scientific hypothesis may be found in Hempel (1965).) It is therefore clear that the evidence quoted previously in favour of market efficiency is very much weaker than originally thought. At this stage we must turn our attention to the evidence that appears to refute the efficient market.

Anomalies

In the early 1970s a number of studies were published which cast doubt on whether the EMH held for all stocks and over all time periods. These have been described in the literature as anomalies. It will be left to the reader to decide whether they provide minor exceptions to the EMH, or whether they represent a major failure of the hypothesis.

Banz (1981) found that US firms with a small market capitalisation had provided investors with higher excess returns, capital gains and dividends, than larger firms. The reader will recall that the capital asset pricing model predicts that returns should depend only on the company's beta which measures systematic risk. Unsystematic risk can be eliminated by diversification. There was thus no reason why small firms should perform better than large firms. Levis (1989) found a similar but rather less pronounced effect in the UK market.

Other researchers have detected a number of seasonal effects in the stock market. For example Rozeff and Kinney (1976) found in the US that returns in January were much higher than in other months. The average return in January on the New York Stock Exchange from 1904 to 1974 amounted to 3.5 per cent while the average return in the remaining 11 months was less than 1 per cent per month. In the UK there is a seasonal effect which appears to run from January until April. The January effect been found in a number of stock markets around the world.

The availability of large databases of share prices has enabled researchers to test extensively for a number of other calendar effects. Regularities related to time of the day, day of the week, and time of the month, have all been found. However many of these regularities are small and only market professionals can be expected to profit from them.

For many years analysts believed that the shares of companies with low price earnings ratios were undervalued relative to companies with high price earnings ratios. Basu (1977) found this to be the case in his study of 1400 firms on the New York Stock Exchange. It seems that excess returns could be earned by buying companies with low price earnings ratios.

A major anomaly that has been difficult to explain is the premium or discount at which the shares of investment trusts trade from the value of their underlying net assets. It would be expected in an efficient market that the dividend stream arising from the underlying portfolio would have the same value as the dividends from the trust itself. Interestingly the amount of the premium or discount varies both between trusts and over time. While management expenses and levels of gearing may explain a part of this anomaly, it still remains a puzzle.

RATIONALITY AND THE STOCK MARKET

The economist's model of an efficient market assumes that rational, profit maximising individuals or institutions dominate the market. Any departure from rational fundamental values leads to profit opportunities for traders. However since the difficulties of valuing a company are well known it may not be clear when a share has departed from its fundamental value. Black (1986) has argued that there are two types of traders in the market, information traders and noise traders. Noise is irrelevant or meaningless information. Noise traders, trade on noise and may cause a share to move from its fundamental value. The effect of these traders is cumulative and over time the price of a share may wander further and further from its intrinsic value. Given the uncertainties in the world it may be difficult to detect when a share has departed from fundamental value. An information trader may buy the share hoping that its price will move towards fundamental value. Noise traders may continue trading, forcing further departures from fundamental value. Black speculates that a share may vary from its intrinsic value by a factor of two before it becomes obviously too cheap or too expensive.

A number of studies by psychologists have found that decision makers behave far from rationally. For example Kahneman and Tversky (1973) asked subjects to predict the exam results of a number of students from a variety of sources of data. Some good predictors were given to the subjects as well as predictors that ought clearly to have been of very little help. When given useless predictors it is sensible for the subjects to base their forecasts on the mean overall score of the class and when given good predictors the subjects should give a wide range of predictions. What Tversky and Kahneman found was that the subjects gave just as wide a range of predications with the useless predictor as with the good predictor. There are numerous other studies that also illustrate apparent lack of rationality in decision making. The current craze for gambling on the National Lottery would suggest that many ordinary people do not seem to be rational wealth maximisers. It is possible, however, that the psychological thrill of the game provides sufficient recompense for expected losses.

De Bondt and Thaler (1985) argued that investors overreact to both good and bad news. Thus, shares of companies which had performed well, tend to be overvalued, while shares of companies which performed poorly are undervalued. If this was true, it could be expected that shares of successful companies might eventually fall while those of unsuccessful companies might rise. This is exactly what De Bondt and Thaler found. Portfolios of shares of looser companies outperformed the market on average by 19.6 per cent over a three-year period while winner portfolios earned about 5 per cent less than the market over a similar period. Interestingly the majority of the gain for looser companies occurred in January. Supporters of the EMH have been quick to challenge these findings. They argued that the betas of these shares, which were calculated from historical data, were understated, since these companies were falling on increasingly hard times. In such circumstances their earnings may have been very volatile and their gearing rising. Both these factors increase beta. If the betas truly reflected the situation of the companies immediately before the test period they would have been considerably higher than the betas which De Bondt and Thaler had calculated and the CAPM would have required higher returns. EMH supporters therefore argued that much of the apparent overperformance of looser companies was illusory.

Many economists are unimpressed by the arguments of psychologists that market participants do not act in a rational manner. Robert Merton (1987) has argued that few of the tests properly replicate the conditions of organised securities markets. In these, analysts and fund managers have to interact as a group in repeatedly making important investment decisions. Merton believes it is unlikely that, in real world conditions, they would make the same mistakes as the subjects made in the experimental tests.

THE VOLATILITY OF THE STOCK MARKET

To the casual observer the stock market often seems irrational and its large day-to-day fluctuations too large to be explained by changes in investment fundamentals. We have already mentioned the huge fall in the market that occurred in three days in October 1987. In an efficient market, stock prices are optimal forecasts of the present value of future dividends discounted at an appropriate rate (see the equation on page 74). If it were otherwise, investors could buy undervalued shares, hold them until they rose to their fundamental value and realise excess returns. In an efficient market such gains do not exist.

How can share price indices be so volatile when, in an efficient market, they represent the present value of future dividends? It is well known that dividends are a relatively smooth series when compared with share prices. Shiller (1981) computed what he described as the perfect foresight price by discounting the actual series of dividends on an index of US stocks from 1871 to 1979, by a constant discount rate. He compared the volatility of the series he calculated with the volatility of the actual share index representing the same series of dividends. He found that share index was over five times more volatile than his test allowed.

A number of researchers criticised this study on grounds of econometric shortcomings. Shiller later repeated his work using econometric techniques which had only very recently become available. He again found excess volatility but at a level much lower than in his original study.

The reader will have noticed that in his original study Shiller used a constant discount rate. Advocates of the EMH argued that the apparent excess volatility could be caused by changes in the rate of interest at which investors discount dividends. Thus when business conditions are poor, forecasts of future dividends may be low. At the same time the high uncertainty in the market place causes investors to increase the risk premium that they require from their investments. In reply Shiller and others have argued that the necessary changes in discount rates needed to explain excess volatility are much too large to be plausible.

Bulkley and Tonks (1989) also found excess volatility in the UK share indices and they developed a trading rule which, when tested on sample data, gave them excess profits of 1.5 per cent per annum.

Excess volatility implies that sometimes the stock market is too high and at others it is too low. If so, then it should be possible to forecast the market. The dividend model shown on page 74 gives a good starting point since stock prices are argued to represent the present value of future dividends. It is well known that dividends are a relatively smooth series and that directors are extremely reluctant to reduce them. Fama and French (1988) used dividend yields to predict returns on the New York Stock Exchange for periods from one month to four years. They argued that if dividend yields were high then either market prices were too low and reflected undue pessimism among investors or discount rates were high reflecting considerable uncertainty in the marketplace. If dividends were low then stock prices might be unrealistically high or alternatively investors had reduced their discount rate to reflect the confident market conditions. Fama and French's model was poor at forecasting returns over short periods such as one month but improved rapidly with longer horizons. For periods of four years they were able to predict as much as 49 per cent of nominal returns in the period 1941–86. The reader may think that Fama and French had found the road to riches. Sadly this was not to be. Again their results were challenged on the grounds of alleged econometric shortcomings. When technical deficiencies were remedied the forecast power of their models was significantly reduced. Furthermore other researchers have found that the forecast power may be very good in some periods but very poor in others. Our own researches on the UK stock market suggest that dividend yields forecast annual returns extremely well in the period from 1964 to 1977 but nil in the period 1978 to 1992. A major problem with some of the attempts to forecast returns is that if long horizons, say up to four years, are used, then there are only 10 independent observations in a 40 year period. This is not much on which to base reliable statistics.

THE CURRENT STATE OF PLAY

The reader will have seen that the academic argument centred on whether excess volatility could be explained by rational shifts in the rate at which investors discount cash flows. Unfortunately it has proved difficult to test this proposition empirically although a number of attempts have been made. Therefore whether shifts in discount rates explain excess volatility must remain an unresolved question.

MORE ON THE VOLATILITY OF THE STOCK MARKET

It has been recognised that the variances of stock returns change over time and that this reflects uncertainty over either future cash flows or over discount rates. The stock market crash in 1987 has already been mentioned. In the UK there was a dramatic fall in share prices in 1974 and a recovery in 1975 and 1976. Engle (1982) developed a method of modelling volatility named ARCH (autoregressive conditional heteroscedasticity*) which captured the tendency for large (small) price changes to be followed by large (small) price changes but of an unpredictable sign. In Engle's set-up, the variance of stock returns depended on a linear function of the past squared values of the process. Any number of past values of the process could enter the formulation and some researchers have modelled the volatility of a series with as many as 12 past values. An alternative and more flexible lag structure was provided by Bollerslev (1986) which he named GARCH (generalised autoregressive conditional heteroscedasticity). As in Engle (1982), the variance could depend on a linear function of the past squared values of the process but he added a moving average term. This effectively corresponds to an infinite order linear ARCH model with geometrically declining parameters. Researchers have found that simple GARCH models with just one autoregressive term and one moving average term have usually performed as well as models with a more complicated lag structure. Readers familiar with statistical time series and Box Jenkins methods will recognise the similarity of GARCH in modelling the volatility of a series to ARMA in modelling its mean.

Stock price changes have been shown to be unpredictable in the short term. While researchers have had some success in being able to model longer term returns their work has been criticised on econometric grounds. On the other hand, attempts to predict the volatility of stock prices and of other speculative assets have been rather more successful. The amount that can be forecast is generally modest but may be economically important.

The development of ARCH has led to a proliferation of research and a recent review refers to over 300 papers in academic journals. The reader will appreciate that it is impossible to do justice to this vast academic effort in the few paragraphs which are available. Much of the research is relatively recent and it is possible that its conclusions may be overturned.

A number of authors have shown that there is a positive relationship between volatility and subsequent returns. This seems to be consistent with the idea that excess returns can be explained by investors increasing their discount rates to reflect risks in volatile markets and may provide an explanation for the predictability of long term returns found in Fama and French (1988).

Some limited success has been achieved using the GARCH processes in modelling the fat tails of stock return distributions. The reader will recall that Markowitz's portfolio theory depends on stock returns being normally distributed and on the usefulness of standard deviation as a

---

*Regression analysis assumes that residuals are homoscedastic. In time series analysis this means that the variance is constant and does not vary through time. Where the variance of the residuals is not constant it is said to be heteroscedastic.

measure of dispersion. The quest for a satisfactory distribution which adequately describes the statistical properties of stock returns, is currently an active area for research.

Currently there is an interest in applying ideas from chaos theory to the stock market. In chaos theory, a hidden pattern is found in apparently random events. Chaos theory questions analytical methods that tend to leave out extremes, to assume normal distributions, and to rely on linearity. A number of tests have shown some evidence of deterministic chaos in stock prices. However when ARCH effects are removed very little evidence of non-linear dependence remains.

Increasingly sophisticated research into the behaviour of speculative prices is being undertaken by the large broking firms. Frequently this is carried out by mathematicians or others trained in the physical sciences rather than in econometrics which forms the discipline of most academic research in recent years. It is difficult to evaluate the success of this work since, if any models do show promise of generating excess returns, they remain carefully guarded proprietary secrets. However, given the mobility of labour within financial markets, it is interesting to speculate how long any firm will be able to protect a secret model.

CONCLUSION

For Investment Management

As we have seen, the early research into market efficiency provided much evidence that new information is rapidly assimilated into stock prices. Later research, together with casual observation, suggests that the market is more volatile than can be attributed to investment fundamentals. Attempts, however, to derive rules for forecasting the market over periods of three months to four years, met with only modest success. While the market rapidly incorporates new information, this does not necessarily imply that share prices correctly reflect all information. The difficulty in formulating decision rules which consistently outperform the market cannot, on its own, be taken as conclusive evidence of market efficiency. The market might well mis-price securities but it may be both difficult and risky for speculators to identify the resultant profit opportunities. Many of the anomalies such as the size or the January effects are unlikely to repeat themselves given the amount of publicity they have received. The best hope for achieving excess returns is by identifying major under-or over-valuations of the market. However there are probably only one or two times in an investment analyst's career when the market seems obviously incorrectly valued. The market collapse in 1974 might be considered to be one of these times.

The disappointing performance of professional investors has led to greater interest in passively managed portfolios which aim to track the market. The launch of Virgin Direct is a recent example of such a fund.

Portfolio theory developed by Markowitz still lays the mathematical foundations for building portfolios by balancing risk and return. The capital asset pricing model, despite having recently been shown to be an incomplete description of risk and return (see Fama and French, 1992), is still a useful tool for creating portfolios of the desired risk characteristics.

The more recent work in modelling the short term volatility of the stock market does show promise and this is likely to be of direct relevance to traders in derivatives.

For Financial Management

The capital asset pricing model has been, for many years, the standard tool for financial executives to estimate the cost of their equity. Despite recent research which has shown its shortcomings, it is still simply the best measure available.

In an efficient marketplace, prices reflect all available information. This means that financial executives have about a 50:50 chance of guessing whether the market is correctly valued. If they believe the market is about to rise, they may be sensible to delay a rights issue. As we have already seen, there have only been a few times in the last 30 years when it may have been possible make this judgement with any degree of confidence. For most of the time it is sensible to raise equity simply when it is needed. Of course, some would argue that directors have insider information regarding the prospects for their firms. If they believe their shares are underpriced, they clearly should do all that is possible to improve investors' perceptions of their business. If this fails, they may decide to delay a rights issue pending an increase in their share price. It is quite possible however, even after the publication of favourable results, that the market fails to respond as expected.

One of the explanations for apparent excess volatility of the stock market is that discount rates change with business conditions. In times of an economic downturn when uncertainty is high, they increase, and in boom times, they decrease. If this is so, then the discount rates for evaluating projects should alter through time. Financial texts, in general, are silent on this point. Perhaps, as seem likely, the business community makes implicit adjustments through a general risk aversion in recessions. This could be by lowering expected cash flows, by requiring higher rates of return, or even by disbelieving the results of any attempts at investment analysis. Is it possible that businesspeople overreact to bad news in the same way that De Bondt and Thaler suggested investors overreact? Further research into cognitive psychology may give us greater insights into how both investors and businesspeople react as groups in repeatedly making important investment decisions. It may even result in an improvement to the decision making process.

References

Ball, R and Brown, P (1968) 'An Empirical Evaluation of Accounting Income Numbers', *Journal of Accounting Research*, Autumn, pp 159–178.

Banz, R (1981) 'The Relationship between Return and Market Value of Common Stocks', *Journal of Financial Economics*, Vol 9, pp 3–18.

Basu, S (1977) 'Investment Performance of Common Stocks in Relation to their Price Earnings Ratios: A Test of the Efficient Markets Hypothesis', *Journal of Finance*, Vol 32, No 3, June, pp 663–682.

Black, F (1986) 'Noise,' *Journal of Finance,* Vol 41, No 3, pp 529–554.

Bollerslev, T (1986) 'Generalised Autoregressive Conditional Heteroscedasticity', *Journal of Econometrics*, Vol 31, pp 307–327.

Bulkley, G and Tonks, I (1989) 'Are UK Stock Prices Excessively Volatile? Trading Rules and Variance Bounds Tests', *Economic Journal*, Vol 99, pp 1083–1098.

De Bondt, W and Thaler, R (1985) 'Does the Stock Market Over React?', *Journal of Finance*, Vol 40, No 3, July, pp 793–805.

Dobbins, R Witt, S and Fielding, J (1994) *Portfolio Theory and Investment Management*, 2nd edn, Blackwell.

Engle, R (1982) 'Autoregressive Conditional Heteroscedasticity with Estimates of the Variance of United Kingdom Inflation' ,*Econometrica*, Vol 50, No 4, pp 987–1008.

Fama, E (1965) 'The Behaviour of Stock Prices', *Journal of Business*, Vol 38, January, pp 34–105.

Fama, E (1970) 'Efficient Capital Markets: A Review of the Theory and Empirical Work', *Journal of Finance*, Vol 25, No 2, pp 383–417.

Fama, E and French, K (1988) 'Dividend Yields and Expected Stock Returns', *Journal of Financial Economics*, Vol 22, pp 3–25.

Fama, E and French, K (1992) 'The Cross-Section of Expected Stock Returns', *Journal of Finance*, Vol 47, No 2, pp 427–465.

Hempel, C (1965) *Aspects of Scientific Exploration*, The Free Press, New York.

Jensen, M (1968) 'The Performance of Mutual Funds in the Period 1945–1964', *Journal of Finance*, Vol 23, May, pp 389–416.

Jensen, M (1978) 'Symposium on Some Anomalous Evidence Regarding Market Efficiency', *Journal of Financial Economics*, Vol 6, pp 95.

Kahneman, D and Tversky, A (1973) 'On the Psychology of Prediction', *Psychological Review*, Vol 80, pp 237–251.

Keynes, J (1936) *The General Theory of Employment, Interest and Money*, Harcourt Brace.

Levis, M (1989) 'Stock Market Anomalies: A Reassessment Based on UK Evidence', *Journal of Banking and Finance*, Vol 13, Nos 4–5, September 1989, pp 675–696.

Mandelbrot, B (1963) 'The Variation of Certain Speculative Prices', *Journal of Business*, Vol 36, pp 394–419.

Markowitz, H (1952) 'Portfolio Selection', *Journal of Finance*, Vol 7, pp 77–91.

Merton, R (1987) 'On the Current State of the Stock Market Rationality Hypothesis', in *Macro Economics and Finance: Essays in Honour of Franco Modigliani*, ed Stanley Fisher et al, MIT press, Cambridge, pp 93–124.

Roll, R (1977) 'A Critique of Asset Pricing Theory's Tests: Part 1: On Past and Potential Testability of the Theory', *Journal of Financial Economics*, Vol 4, pp 129–76.

Rozeff, M and Kinney, W (1976) 'Capital Market Seasonality: The Case of Stock Market Returns', *Journal of Financial Economics*, Vol 3, No 4, pp 379–402.

Sharpe, W (1964) 'Capital Asset Prices: A Theory of Market Equilibrium under Conditions of Risk', *Journal of Finance*, Vol 29, September pp 425–442.

Shiller, R (1981) 'Do Stock Prices Move too Much to be Justified by Subsequent Changes in Dividends?', *American Economic Review*, Vol 71, No 3, June, pp 421–436.

Shiller, R (1984) 'Stock Prices and Social Dynamics, *Brookings Papers on Economic Activity*, Vol 2, pp 457–489.

Solnik, B (1974) 'Why not Diversify Internationally rather than Domestically?', *Financial Analysts Journal*, Vol 30, No 4, July-August, pp 48–54.

Summers, L (1986) 'Does the Stock Market Rationally Reflect Fundamental Values', *Journal of Finance*, Vol 41, No 3, July, pp 591–601.

Tobin, J (1958) 'Liquidity Preference as a Behaviour Towards Risk', *Review of Economic Studies*, Vol 25, pp 65–85.

4

INVESTMENT RETURN REQUIREMENTS AROUND THE WORLD

Adrian Buckley

In capital budgeting, whether domestic, foreign or international, one of the early pieces of analysis concerns the determination of the required rate of return from investment. Nowadays, many firms use the capital asset pricing model (CAPM) to specify the cost of equity capital. If we are to use the CAPM methodology in establishing the value of the cost of equity through the formula:

$$k_e = R_F + \beta \, (R_M - R_F)$$

We need to be fairly clear about the magnitude of $(R_M - R_F)$. If we are looking into the future, as is the case in investment appraisal, we would ideally wish to be using a future-oriented value for the excess return (that is, $R_M - R_F$). We would be in a position to make a fortune were we to have this knowledge of the future for certain for every year. In its absence, we are able to lay our hands on past outturns. If there were a good chance that history would repeat itself, past data would provide a reasonable proxy for future returns. In the long run, this may be the best approximation that we have. But the underpinning caveat that it is based upon history repeating itself has to be borne in mind.

93

What is available from empirical work is information on US and UK equity returns, and similar returns from many other countries too. In this chapter we will present the evidence for the US, Britain and various other economies too. We will also ask whether there is any consistent pattern of realized excess returns from one country to another. These are the two key objectives of this chapter. We begin our analysis in terms of examining the evidence for US equity capital markets.

US EVIDENCE

There are two or three classic studies of US equity returns and there is now an annual update of such outturns and there are numerous other studies too. Let us look at these classic investigations. Fisher and Lorie (1968) analysed common stock returns for the period from 1926 to 1965. The before tax return, including dividends and capital gains, over the whole period was 9.3 per cent using annual compounding. The real before tax rate of return – that is, the rate adjusted for inflation – was about 7.7 per cent per annum over the 40 year period. For an investor in a relatively high tax bracket, post-tax returns fell to 7.1 per cent compounded annually and to 5.6 per cent per annum after adjusting for inflation. Note that the above data relate to total shareholder returns and not to the excess return.

Of course, the base year and the end year can have a critical impact on realised returns. Indeed Ritter and Urich (1984), measuring equity yields over the period 1968 to 1983, obtained starkly different results. US equities yielded a real return of only 1 per cent per annum in their study.

Given the need to take a long-term view in measuring equity investor returns, Ibbotson and Sinquefield publish annual data in their *Stocks, Bonds, Bills and Inflation Yearbooks*. They use 1926 as a base year and produce figures for US returns since then in respect of:

- common stocks (that is, ordinary shares)
- small company stocks
- long-term corporate bonds
- long-term government bonds
- intermediate-term government bonds
- US treasury bills (that is, three month government securities)
- inflation rates.

They present their findings in terms of an arithmetic average and a geometric average of returns – the difference between the two is significant, over 2 percentage points for US large firm common stocks. So, how does the problem arise? The arithmetic average involves the calculation of an annual return based on the end of year value of the portfolio plus dividends versus the beginning year value. Over a long period, the arithmetic mean is given by the average of such returns based on the formulation:

$$\text{Arithmetic deviation} \quad \overline{R}_a = \frac{1}{n}\sum_{t=1}^{n} R_t$$

where Rt is the annual rate of return in year t. Also, the standard deriva-tion of returns can be calculated according to the formula:

$$\text{Standard deviation} = \sqrt{\frac{1}{n-1}\sum_{t=1}^{n}\left(R_t - \overline{R}_a\right)^2}$$

The geometric mean is calculated differently. It is rather like a discounted cash flow rate of return. Over a long period – certainly longer than one year – we take into account the starting value of a portfolio of shares or securities, we allow for annual receipt of dividends and we take cog-nizance of the terminal stock market value of the portfolio. Calculating the internal rate of return gives us the geometric mean. Thus, the follow-ing formulation would be used:

$$\text{Geometric mean} \quad \overline{R}_g = \left[\sum_{t=1}^{n}\left(1 + R_t\right)\right]^{\frac{1}{n}} - 1$$

Of course returns, whether measured by arithmetic or geometric means, will be affected by start and end periods used in measurement and this potential source of difference must be borne in mind. A discussion on the relative merits of the two means follows later in this chapter.

So what is the evidence from other US studies? And, in particular, from the Ibbotson and Sinquefield research? Obviously the achieved returns, calculated according to the above definitions of arithmetic and geometric mean, will vary according to which year is chosen as an end year. Immediately following the 1987 stock market crash would yield a lower return than immediately prior. Remember that Ibbotson and Sinquefield always start their calculations from 1926. Interestingly enough, whether the end of the period is chosen as 1986, 1988, 1990 or whatever, there is a fairly persistent outturn – see recent publications of the Ibbotson Associates *Yearbooks*. Their results are summarised in Table 4.1. This exhibit shows a range of returns for the simple reason that returns vary over the period. Note that the US data reproduced show returns based on capital gains plus dividends – but such dividends are expressed gross of shareholder dividend taxes.

Investment in a broad range of US equities over the last 65 years or so has yielded real returns of around 9 to 9¼ per cent per annum on an arithmetic mean basis and 7 per cent per annum on a geometric basis (gross of shareholder taxes on dividends). The excess return is the differ-ence between the return achieved from investment in equities compared with the return achieved from investment in riskless securities, such as

Table 4.1 *Total annual returns from US investment over long run from 1926*

	Geometric mean (%)	Arithmetic mean (%)	Standard deviation (%)
Ordinary shares	9.75 to 10.0	12.0 to 12.5	21.0
Small company ordinary shares	12.0 to 12.25	17.5 to 18.0	35.5
Long-term corporate bonds	4.9 to 5.1	5.2 to 5.7	8.5
Long-term government bonds	4.3 to 4.5	4.6 to 5.1	8.5
Intermediate-term government bonds	4.6 to 4.8	4.9 to 5.4	5.5
US treasury bills	3.5 to 3.9	3.5 to 3.9	3.4
Inflation	2.8 to 3.0	3.0 to 3.2	4.75
$R_M - R_F$ (R_F based on long term government bonds)	5.6	7.2	
$R_M - R_F$ (R_F based on US treasury bills)	6.2	8.5	

Source: Ibbotson and Sinquefield

interest-bearing government borrowings and is often referred to as ($R_M - R_F$). Its value is around 8½ per cent per annum if an arithmetic mean is used and about 6.2 per cent per annum if a geometric mean is used – in this instance R_F is based on three month government securities. If R_F were measured in terms of the yield on long-term government securities, the value of ($R_M - R_F$) would approximate 7.2 per cent per annum and 5.6 per cent per annum respectively measured by arithmetic and geometric means. Note from Table 4.1 that the standard deviation of equity returns is substantial. Given this fact, the use of our evidence in *ex ante* estimates of the excess return needs to be treated with caution.

The question of whether an arithmetic or geometric mean should be used is another issue demanding caution. Leading financial textbooks differ in their prescription. Brealey and Myers (1991) opt fairly strongly for the arithmetic mean; Levy and Sarnat (1990) propose a geometric mean. As Brigham and Gapenski (1993) point out, the arithmetic average is more consistent with CAPM theory since one of its key underpinning assumptions is that investors are supposed to focus, in their portfolio decisions, upon returns in the next period and the standard deviation of this return. (Is this 'next period' one year? If so, the preference for the arithmetic mean which derives from a set of single one year period returns follows). It is worth mentioning that Jensen (1972) specified the assumptions inherent in the pioneering CAPM article by Sharpe (1964) as embracing the following:

- All investors are single-period expected utility of terminal wealth maximisers who choose among alternative portfolios on the basis of each portfolio's expected return and standard deviation.
- All investors can borrow or lend an unlimited amount at a given risk-free rate of interest, R_F, and there are no restrictions on short sales of any asset.
- All investors have identical estimates of the expected values, variances, and covariances of returns among all assets – that is, investors have homogeneous expectations.
- All assets are perfectly divisible and perfectly liquid – that is, marketable at the going price – and there are no transaction costs.
- There are no taxes.
- All investors are price takers – that is, all investors assume that their own buying and selling activity will not affect share prices.
- The quantities of all assets are given and fixed.

Several of the above assumptions are patently untrue in the literal, real world sense but the CAPM has been shown to be robust enough to stand up despite relaxation of many of them. Using apparently more realistic reflections of the world – such as the incorporation of taxation and so on – does not materially affect the implications of the model. On this topic van Horne (1995) presents an excellent analysis.

In terms of use of an arithmetic or geometric mean, it should be noted that the first of the above bullet points seems to argue in favour of an arithmetic mean. Investors undoubtedly use single periods to assess performance, but are such periods 12-month periods? That investors patently hold shares for longer periods may cast some doubt upon this assumption. This conclusion is reinforced in a paper by Blume (1974) who proposes that the arithmetic average should be applied in discounting one year cash flows, while the geometric mean is an unbiased estimate for very long periods for which it is more appropriate.

But there is evidence favouring the use of a geometric mean. In essence, it derives from ideas of mean reversion of share prices to a trend. If share prices were expected to revert to a trend, then this would tend to suggest the use of a geometric mean since the geometric mean is, by definition, an estimate of a smoothed long run trend increment. There is now a significant body of research which seeks to identify mean reversion in share prices. While some studies have found evidence of mean reversion in stock prices, it is quite weak. Furthermore, the findings of many of these studies have been criticised on statistical or methodological grounds in follow-up papers. Three well-known articles indicating some mean reversion are by Fama and French (1988 and 1992) and Poterba and Summers (1988). But they have their critics. For example, Kim, Nelson and Startz (1991) point out that the earlier Fama and French study does not show mean reversion estimates in the post war period which differ significantly from zero. And Poterba and Summers' study only finds evidence of mean reversion by relaxing the statistical significance test from 5 per cent to 40 per cent, which casts doubt on its findings. If mean reversion were shown to exist, then the arithmetic mean would be an upward biased estimator of the market risk premium.

The other idea suggesting the use of a geometric mean flows from the view that both it and the Internal Rate of Return (IRR) are essentially based on compound interest calculations over a longish term. The argument that one should compare like with like might militate in favour of comparing a geometrically derived IRR with a geometrically derived mean in capital budgeting.

But the strongest argument favouring the arithmetic mean flows from looking at the outturn, year by year, as annual draws for a stable distribution of returns. Thus, suppose that a two-period investment has equally likely outcomes of a 40 per cent return and a minus 20 per cent return. Average returns might be computed thus:

$$\text{Arithmetic mean} \quad \frac{\left[40\% + (-20\%)\right]}{2} = 10\%$$

$$\text{Geometric mean} \quad \sqrt{(1.4)(0.8)} - 1 = 5.8\%$$

But which is the more realistic measure?

The expected result at the end of the two year period can be computed thus. Assume $1000 is invested and that the returns conform to the expected frequency distribution below:

$1000 × (1.4) × (1.4) × (0.25)	=	£490
$1000 × (1.4) × (0.8) × (0.25)	=	$280
$1000 × (0.8) × (1.4) × (0.25)	=	$280
$1000 × (0.8) × (0.8) × (0.25)	=	$160
Expected value	=	$1210

Clearly we are looking at an expected outturn at the end of year two of $1210. This expected return is the arithmetic average return given by:

$1000 × (1.10)^2 = 1210

The incorrect argument is that the expected outturn at the end of the investment period is given by:

$1000 × (1.4) × (0.8) = 1120

To be sure, the latter figure of $1120 may accrue but, as shown above, it only has a 50 per cent probability of occurrence. What is ignored is the *ex ante* possibility of outturns amounting to $1960 (given by $1000 × 1.4 × 1.4) and $640 (given by $1000 × 0.8 × 0.8). Each of these has a 25 per cent probability of occurrence. Allowing for these probabilities, we obtain an expected value at the end of two years amounting to $1210. Note that the false return conforms to the geometric return. In the context here, its falsity relates to the fact that it does not take into account the binomial-type distribution of potential outturns.

Viewed from a standpoint before the event, we are aware that, by undertaking a risky investment, we are exposed to a broad spread of potential results. And we require a higher return on this risky investment, compared to an investment with a certain return, to compensate for the spread of possible outturns. Thus, the arithmetic mean would seem to be the better and more logical figure to use from an *ex ante* standpoint taking into account, as it does, the full distribution of potential results. The question that follows is what is the appropriate time interval to use. Is it one year? Or are investors single period expected wealth maximisers, given a two year period? Or a three year period? Lengthening the time interval increases the precision of the estimate of the mean return. But lengthening the time interval also strains the plausibility of the assumption that returns are drawn from a stable distribution. Indeed, the use of a geometric mean covering the period 1926 to date implies that investors are single period maximisers over a span of 60 years plus. Most would agree that this is hardly a realistic assumption.

If the problem about the *ex ante* value of $(R_M - R_F)$ to be used in capital budgeting looks tricky already, the story so far is only the tip of the iceberg of evidence. For example, Mehra and Prescott (1985) suggested that the historical returns from common stocks were too high when compared to the rates of return on short-term government securities. They point out that the difference in returns – the market risk premium for equity – implies a high degree of risk aversion on the part of investors. The high historical equity risk premium is intriguing compared to the low historical rate of return on treasury securities – see Table 4.1. On this very topic, Siegel (1994) has shown that the historical risk premium may be lower than previously thought. He points out that while the risk premium averaged 8.2 per cent per annum from 1926 to 1992, it averaged only 2.9 per cent per annum from 1802 to 1870, and 4.6 per cent per annum from 1871 to 1925 – see Table 4.2. The trend has been rising over the past two centuries or so, especially since 1926. The figures quoted above and in Table 4.2 represent an upward revision compared with the earlier paper – see Siegel (1992) – but the conclusion on either set of data remains the same – a rising pattern. The risk premium from 1926 onwards arrived at by Siegel (1994) differs slightly from the Ibbotson and Sinquefield data in the earlier table in this chapter because

Table 4.2 uses a single finishing date of 1992 whereas Table 4.1 figures are based upon a range using various terminating dates.

Perhaps the rising pattern apparent in Table 4.2 might be explained by reference to the long-term trend from the mid-1920s towards higher inflation. This rising inflation rate would increase long-term interest rates and lower bond prices resulting in realised real yields on long-term bonds at a level below the *ex ante* expected yield. If realised bond yields were below expected yields, then the risk premium as measured by

$$k_{shares} - k_{bonds} = RP_{market-}$$

will overstate the true required risk premium. If this were correct, then the 7.2 percentage points market risk premium of stocks over govern-

Table 4.2 *US returns since 1802*

Figures in percentages per annum	1802–1870	1871–1925	1926–1992	1802–1992
Common stocks (nominal)				
• arithmetic return	8.1	8.4	12.0	9.5
• geometric return	7.1	7.2	9.9	8.1
Common stocks (real)				
• arithmetic return	8.3	7.9	8.6	8.3
• geometric return	7.0	6.6	6.6	6.7
Short-term government securities				
• arithmetic return	5.2	3.8	3.8	4.3
• geometric return	5.2	3.8	3.8	4.3
Long-term government securities				
• arithmetic return	4.9	4.4	5.2	4.9
• geometric return	4.9	4.3	4.8	4.7
$R_M - R_F$ (R_F based on short-term government securities)				
• arithmetic return	2.9	4.6	8.2	5.2
• geometric return	1.9	3.4	6.1	3.8
$R_M - R_F$ (R_F based on long-term government securities)				
• arithmetic returns	3.2	4.0	6.8	4.6
• geometric returns	2.2	2.9	5.1	3.4

Source: Siegel (1994)

ment bonds on an arithmetic mean basis as reported in Table 4.1 would be too large for use in the CAPM unless inflation were to continue at comparable levels in the long run.

So where does all this leave us in terms of estimating the value of the excess return, that is (R_M minus R_F), in the US? We have to confront the significant problem of the use of geometric or an arithmetic mean. According to the most recent long run evidence, from 1926 to date, the figure of 6¼ per cent or 8½ per cent depending upon which of the respective means is used looks like the appropriate amount, given that R_F is measured by reference to treasury bills – or 5½ per cent to 7¼ per cent if R_F is measured against long-term government bonds. But are these fair figures due to the problem of rising inflation referred to above? Are these returns sustainable in the future? Humbly, we have to admit that we are not quite sure.

When we ask ourselves about future returns, the first thought that occurs is that past excess returns, or equity premium as it is often referred to, are high. In thinking about what the future level of the equity premium is likely to be, there are at least two hypotheses offering themselves. One is that the past level of return will continue in the future. The other is that the past 70 years of returns have been abnormal and future outturns will be different – perhaps lower.

If we look at the former hypothesis – that this level of equity premium will persist – the basic problem is how it is possible for the economy to go on generating rewards to shareholders of this magnitude. The least risky asset that an investor can purchase is a government security. At the time of writing, a long-dated US dollar government security would yield a nominal return of between 6 and 7 per cent with long run inflation assumed to be between 2 and 3 per cent or so. Assuming an excess return on long-term government bonds of 7¼ per cent this would suggest a potential equity yield of between 13 and 14 per cent. With a dividend yield of 3 to 4 per cent, it can be seen that a growth in dividend and share price of some 10 per cent nominal, or 7½ per cent real, would be implied to sustain an excess return in line with past results. With Western economies growing at between 2 and 4 per cent, US companies will surely have to seek substantial growth outside their home country if past excess returns are to be repeated.

If the view is taken, that it is doubtful that the 7¼ per cent excess return is likely to be sustained in the future, how have we been able to earn these equity returns in the past? Some would claim that there have been special factors impacting on equity markets. Corporate shares have been rerated relative to other assets – seventy years ago investors sought higher yields on equities versus government bonds than they do today. Inflation over this period has, with great regularity, exceeded expectations, so that investors holding assets which were not a hedge against inflation did less well compared with those holding assets that were – such as corporate shares. Dividend pay-out ratios increased.

If this account is to be believed, there have been special factors in almost every decade this century that might be cited to explain why equity returns were unexpectedly high relative to those on government bonds – rerating of the equity market, higher than expected inflation, productivity gains. Each aspect of this explanation sounds credible, but are these gains likely to be repeated? If not, American business may be hard pressed to deliver comparable shareholder returns.

In truth, in confronting problems of future calculations, we cannot really be completely certain as to whether arithmetic or geometric means should be used in valuation exercises – although, as indicated above, we prefer the arithmetic mean. Vendor and purchaser, regulator and regulated can continue their discussions. Certainly, using more than one single discount rate in valuation is probably realistic. Of course, such a methodology will result in a range of value – once again, this is realistic.

The same kind of problems apply whether we look at US, British or Japanese evidence. So the following section has the same methodological problems. In this next section we offer the evidence on excess returns for the UK.

BRITISH EVIDENCE

There have been various studies of achieved rates of return from equities and government securities in Britain. These include work in the 1960s and early '70s on ordinary share investment by Merrett and Sykes (1963, 1966, 1973), investigations of achieved excess returns on UK equities up to the late '70s by Dimson and Brealey (1978) and Dimson and Marsh (1982), a similar study of long run returns from investing in government securities and ordinary shares up to the mid-1980s by Allen, Day, Kwiatowski and Hirst (1987) and, like the Ibbotson Associates' annual update of US returns, BZW (the London-based stockbrokers) produce an annual update of returns earned from investment.

The Merrett and Sykes studies focused upon real returns accruing from UK equity investment in net of tax terms. They focused upon R_M net of tax and in real terms rather than upon $(R_M - R_F)$. They found fairly substantial standard deviations in outturns over different holding periods. However, in geometric mean terms, their results over the period from 1919 to 1971 suggest a real, net of tax return of just over 7¾ per cent, more than 1 per cent higher than compatible returns from US investment. But the lion's share of this UK return accrued in the early years of this holding period. This is shown in the summary of Merrett and Sykes' findings which appears in Table 4.3. If these findings were to perpetuate in the future, it would be logical to expect that a British company with a beta of 1.0 would yield a real, net of tax, return of between 7½ and 8 per cent to shareholders in the long run. The caveats suggested in the latter

Table 4.3 UK and US equity returns in real terms and net of shareholder tax, 1919–71

	UK Returns (%)			USA Returns (%)	
Period	Tax exempt	Tax at standard rate (capital gains tax excluded)	Period	Tax exempt	Tax at 25% (capital gains tax excluded)
1919–29	16.5	15.1	1919–29	14.0	13.1
1920–30	12.2	10.9	1920–30	15.2	13.9
1921–31	19.2	17.2	1921–31	14.1	12.4
1922–32	18.8	16.5	1922–32	6.6	4.7
1923–33	12.4	10.9	1923–33	9.6	7.9
1924–34	13.3	12.0	1924–34	10.2	8.5
1925–35	13.1	11.9	1925–35	8.1	6.7
1926–36	7.7	9.6	1926–36	9.4	8.2
1927–37	11.7	10.6	1927–37	6.6	5.5
1928–38	8.1	7.0	1928–38	1.1	0.1
1929–39	4.7	3.6	1929–39	-1.0	-1.8
1949–59	6.2	4.2	1949–59	17.8	16.5
1950–60	11.6	9.7	1950–60	14.4	13.1
1951–61	11.1	9.2	1951–61	14.0	12.9
1952–62	11.8	9.6	1952–62	12.9	11.7
1953–63	13.2	10.7	1953–63	14.3	13.1
1954–64	13.6	11.3	1954–64	12.8	11.8
1955–65	8.1	6.2	1955–65	9.6	8.8
1956–66	8.0	5.9	1956–66	7.4	6.6
1957–67	9.7	7.1	1957–67	8.9	8.0
1958–68	13.3	10.7	1958–68	9.2	8.3
1959–69	11.2	9.1	1959–69	6.1	5.3
1960–70	4.0	2.1	1960–70	5.5	4.6
1961–71	2.8	0.8	1961–71	5.2	4.3
1962–72	6.0	4.0			
1919–39	12.1	10.5	1919–39	7.8	6.5
1926–39	10.6	6.4	1926–39	7.0	5.7
1949–66	7.3	5.4	1949–66	14.1	12.7
1949–71	6.6	4.5	1949–71	12.4	10.8
1949–72	7.4	5.3			
1926–66	6.2	4.5	1926–66	7.5	6.5
1919–71	10.2	7.8	1919–71	7.7	6.5

Source: Merrett and Sykes (1973)

paragraphs of the section devoted to US returns would be equally applicable to British corporate returns.

Dimson and Marsh (1982) computed returns to investment in UK equities in a similar manner to Ibbotson Associates in the US. In other words, they calculated an arithmetic average of the risk premium ($R_M - R_F$) based on equity returns minus the treasury bill rate for individual years. For relatively long periods, beginning in 1919 and ending at 1 January 1980, the value of ($R_M - R_F$) appears to be around 8¾ per cent gross of taxes and about 8 per cent on an after tax basis. Dimson and Marsh did their computation on a net of tax basis because the structure of UK corporate tax makes this the relevant rate, under the imputation tax system, to build into calculations of the required equity cost of capital. This contrasts with the classical tax system, adopted in the US, Netherlands and a number of other countries, under which required returns should, most logically, be specified gross of shareholder taxes. Of course, in the DCF calculations, cash flows should be specified net of corporate taxes under both the imputation and classical tax systems. For a thorough analysis on this corporate tax point, see Buckley (1995a, b and c).

The difference of less than 1 per cent between gross and net, rather than 25 per cent of 8¾ per cent (25 per cent being the basic rate of UK tax), arises because the excess return comprises capital gain and dividend and these sources of increment have been taxed differently. Given that the magnitude of dividend yields in many countries is fairly close, a conversion from gross to net would frequently involve a difference of a similar absolute amount.

Using an example incorporating a beta of 0.6 and an after tax short-term risk-free interest rate of 10 per cent, and further, assuming that history will repeat itself, Dimson and Marsh (1982) state that:

> The annual net return on equity has averaged a premium of about 8 per cent above the after tax short-term interest rate. Thus our required rate of return (after personal tax) is given by:
>
> | Required rate | = | After tax interest | + | Beta | × | After tax market risk premium |
> |---|---|---|---|---|---|---|
> | | = | 10 | + | 0.6 | × | 8 |
>
> = 15 per cent

This formula... tells us the net return which can be expected from a comparably risky investment in the capital market.

Dimson and Marsh's findings on the value of the UK excess return for periods up to 1980 are summarized in Table 4.4

Allen, Day, Kwiatowski and Hirst (1987) reported UK returns in a format fairly similar to Ibbotson Associates' US studies. And BZW publish annual returns for UK investment over the long run from 1919. Most of these data are presented in arithmetic mean terms. Findings for the UK

Table 4.4 *The excess return in the UK 1919–80*

Period to 1.1.80	$(R_M - R_F)$	
	Gross %	Net %
1919–	8.7	8.1
1930–	8.3	7.7
1940–	8.8	8.3
1950–	9.6	9.6

Source: Dimson and Marsh

are summarised in Table 4.5. It should be mentioned that the data in Table 4.4 and in Table 4.5 show slightly different excess returns from 1919 onwards. This is because the former table shows returns with 1980 as a terminating date whilst the latter table derives its excess return from a range with various terminating dates.

Note that if we compare the two exhibits of US and UK returns, we find that the total return, the real return and the value of $(R_M - R_F)$ is higher for the UK. As pointed out towards the end of the section on the US evidence, rising returns may be due to an increased risk premium related to increasing unexpected inflation. The same kind of explanation may apply to the level of UK returns versus US outturns – but we really cannot be sure that this is the ultimate explanation. Suffice to say that the risk premium is higher in the UK than in the US.

THE EXCESS RETURN IN OTHER PARTS OF THE WORLD

Unfortunately, we do not have a complete picture of excess returns from world stock markets for 70 or 80 year periods. Officer (1989) reports an excess return of 7.9 per cent per annum on an arithmetic basis as accruing to equity investors in Australia for the period from 1882 to 1987 – see Table

Table 4.5 *Total annual returns from UK investment over long run from 1919*

	Geometric mean	Arithmetic mean	Standard deviation (%)
Ordinary shares	11.4 to 11.8	13.5 to 14.4	26
Long term government bonds	5.2 to 5.6	5.7 to 6.1	8.2
3 month government bills	4.6 to 5.3	4.6 to 5.3	4.4
Inflation	4.1 to 4.4	4.3 to 4.6	
$R_M - R_F$ (based on long term government bonds)	6.2	8.4	
$R_M - R_F$ (based on 3 month government bills)	6.6	9.0	

Source: BZW and Allen, Day, Kwiatowski and Hirst (1987)

to equity investors in Australia for the period from 1882 to 1987 – see Table 4.6. But note that Officer uses the yield on 10 year government bonds as representing the risk-free rate. Wydler (1989) looked at long run returns for investment in stocks and bonds in Switzerland; Hamao (1991) has undertaken a similar exercise based on Japanese returns; Frennberg and Hansson (1992) have presented data on long-term returns from investment in Sweden. The Ibbotson and Sinquefield approach has largely been followed in these studies. Investment in equities in the Netherlands is reported (Beursplein 5, Saturday 26 November 1994, page 4, Table 2) as having achieved a 6.8 per cent per annum real return from 1947 to 1993. This figure is a total return and is derived from a nominal return for a first line Dutch equity portfolio amounting to 11.45 per cent per annum less average inflation for the period. The return includes capital gains and dividend income. The latter is allowed for by assuming its reinvestment. The comparison of the value of the portfolio at the beginning of the period and at the end of the period, duly allowing for compound interest, produces the return indicated.

Copeland, Koller and Murrin (1994) refer to a figure of just below 4 per cent as the excess return, on a geometric basis, accruing to investors in German equities. But their figure is based upon much shorter investment periods than 70 or 80 years. As the academic study of financial management expands, we can expect a complete picture of long run returns around the world to emerge. In truth, such a picture, over a reasonably long period, is probably not available as of now. However, vast differences in return should not be evident because the potential for arbitrage would eliminate substantial divergences. As Copeland, Koller and Murrin (1994) state:

> Our point of view is that there is no difference in the costs of capital among developed countries after adjusting nominal costs of capital for differences in expected rates of inflation, risk, and taxation. If the cost of capital is really lower in Japan, for example, then the world would rush to borrow from Japanese lenders until supply and demand imbalance was eliminated and the cost of capital was the same across borders.

Copeland, Koller and Murrin (1994) correct their initial point of view in the quotation above by subsequently stating that 'government regulations or taxes could serve as barriers to the flow of capital and lead to differences'.

On the question of world returns, we do have various sets of data which are interesting. Ibbotson and Brinson (1993) present a useful summary of returns and a number of these have been adapted for inclusion in various parts of the remainder of this chapter. The first one presented here relates to returns achieved from equity investment in various markets over the last couple of decades and derives from figures computed by Morgan Stanley Capital International. Table 4.7 reports annualised returns and standard deviations for 18 of the world's most developed

Table 4.6 *Australian returns, 1882–1987*

| (Time period | Arithmetic average | | Geometric average | | Average 10-year government bond yields | Equity premium over bond yields (arithmetic mean) |
	Nominal	Real	Nominal	Real		
1882–1987	13.06	9.56	11.76	8.26	5.21	7.94
	(17.02)	(16.31)			(2.86)	(16.86)
1882–1887	14.45	15.17	10.82	12.16	3.76	10.68
1888–1897	9.52	10.65	6.19	7.90	3.46	6.06
1898–1907	12.34	11.23	11.33	10.23	3.46	8.87
1908–1917	10.35	5.48	7.97	3.47	4.05	6.30
1918–1927	17.16	15.74	15.81	15.32	5.53	11.64
1928–1937	12.78	13.77	9.81	11.36	4.33	8.45
1938–1947	8.96	5.33	8.83	5.41	2.94	6.02
1948–1957	11.99	4.09	9.20	2.38	4.15	7.83
1958–1967	14.52	12.04	11.49	9.20	4.92	9.60
1968–1977	7.68	−0.85	0.85	−7.04	7.32	0.36
1978–1987	24.45	14.79	18.52	10.24	12.58	11.87

Note: All the above figures are in percentage terms. Figures in parentheses are standard deviations
Source: Officer (1989)

stock markets for the period 1970 to 1990. These returns and standard deviations are tabulated in local currency terms, and in US dollar terms, and in Japanese yen, in German mark and in pound sterling terms. All the returns reported are before transaction costs and all taxes, including dividend taxes. The returns themselves are calculated in compound terms. Essentially, an IRR is derived based on the initial market value in 1970, the closing market value in 1990 and dividend receipts in between. Table 4.7 expresses these returns in nominal terms. Note that the Hong Kong market produced highest returns and a standard deviation above most other markets – the Singaporean market recorded a higher standard deviation. The least volatile market, in local currency terms, was the US stock market itself.

Plotting rewards from investment in equity markets against risk, as expressed by the standard deviation based on the data reported in Table 4.7, appears not to show too good a correlation – see Figure 4.1 in which returns and standard deviations are plotted in US dollar terms. One could debate about the best way to look at the risk/return trade-off. And, probably, it is not in terms of nominal US dollar outturns versus standard deviation. Maybe a superior view would involve looking at real returns in local currency versus the standard deviation. To this end, Table 4.8 takes the data in the previous table for local currency returns and expresses them in real terms. This is done by extracting local inflation from the local currency return. We believe that Figure 4.2 expresses a far more logical view of the risk return trade-off in equity markets over the couple of decades to 1990. The figure plots real returns in local currency against risk as measured by standard deviation. And even then no neat correlation appears evident.

Table 4.7 *Nominal returns in developed equity stock markets, 1970–90*

(First line refers to compound annual return; line in brackets refers to standard deviation)

Country	Local (%)	US$ (%)	¥ (%)	DM (%)	£(%)
			Currency		
Australia	9.6	7.7	2.9	3.2	8.8
	(29.4)	(28.5)	(29.9)	(34.7)	(30.7)
Austria	10.4	15.3	10.1	10.4	16.5
	(32.6)	(44.1)	(41.4)	(32.6)	(38.7)
Belgium	13.2	15.8	10.6	10.9	17.0
	(24.6)	(26.1)	(22.7)	(22.6)	(26.3)
Canada	10.5	10.1	5.1	5.4	11.2
	(17.7)	(17.9)	(25.5)	(23.1)	(21.9)
Denmark	14.1	15.5	10.3	10.6	16.7
	(37.6)	(32.9)	(34.5)	(38.2)	(39.2)

France	11.9	12.4	7.3	7.7	13.6
	(29.4)	(33.3)	(30.5)	(30.5)	(33.2)
Germany	7.4	12.1	7.0	7.4	13.3
	(27.6)	(33.8)	(29.5)	(27.6)	(30.6)
Hong Kong	20.7	19.2	13.8	14.2	20.5
	(53.8)	(53.9)	(55.5)	(56.8)	(59.9)
Italy	9.4	6.4	1.6	1.9	7.5
	(39.3)	(44.8)	(34.8)	(38.9)	(38.7)
Japan	13.7	19.1	13.7	14.1	20.3
	(31.8)	(38.7)	(31.8)	(37.8)	(37.5)
Netherlands	11.2	15.3	10.1	10.5	16.6
	(23.6)	(20.7)	(22.9)	(23.8)	(26.4)
Norway	14.9	14.9	9.7	10.1	16.1
	(52.0)	(54.8)	(66.1)	(52.2)	(52.8)
Singapore	12.0	15.1	10.0	10.3	16.4
	(54.8)	(55.3)	(54.4)	(57.3)	(62.3)
Spain	10.1	8.5	3.6	3.9	9.6
	(28.5)	(35.5)	(29.2)	(30.0)	(36.4)
Sweden	15.9	15.5	10.3	10.6	16.7
	(30.4)	(26.3)	(27.0)	(30.1)	(31.6)
Switzerland	5.3	11.6	6.6	6.9	12.8
	(24.2)	(27.4)	(23.7)	(22.8)	(25.7)
United Kingdom	14.7	13.5	8.4	8.7	14.7
	(37.5)	(34.7)	(33.2)	(37.8)	(37.5)
United States	10.0	10.0	5.1	5.4	14.7
	(16.6)	(16.6)	(21.9)	(23.7)	(24.8)

Source: Morgan Stanley Capital International

Were one to compute returns from stock markets in emerging and developing countries, the pattern appears equally weak in terms of any clear reward/risk relationship. Table 4.9 shows some returns of over 50 per cent per annum compound and standard deviations of very high amounts. Remember that the table expresses returns in US dollar terms. Should a developing country with high inflation defer a devaluation, this factor alone would dramatically affect the reported outturns. The conclusion that not too much should be read into the data in Table 4.9 cannot be avoided.

COUNTRY RISK

The fact that Table 4.9 fails to give us a clear lead in terms of helping us assess a discount rate for a project in a developing country is not the end of the story. The issue of whether we should add in a country risk premium is a vexing one. The answer depends upon an assessment of whether

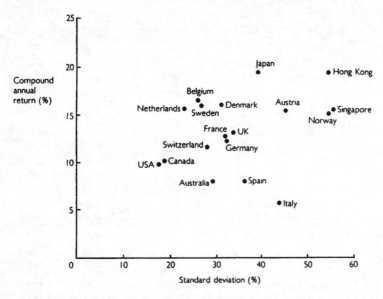

Figure 4.1 Risk and rewards from equity investment 1970–90
(expressed in US dollar terms)

Table 4.8 *Real returns in developed equity stock markets 1970–90*

	% annual real return in compound terms
Australia	0.7
Austria	5.5
Belgium	7.7
Canada	3.7
Denmark	6.3
France	4.1
Germany	3.6
Hong Kong	12.4
Italy	(1.5)
Japan	8.2
Netherlands	6.5
Norway	6.8
Singapore	7.8
Spain	(2.0)
Sweden	7.6
Switzerland	1.1
United Kingdom	4.7
United States	3.8

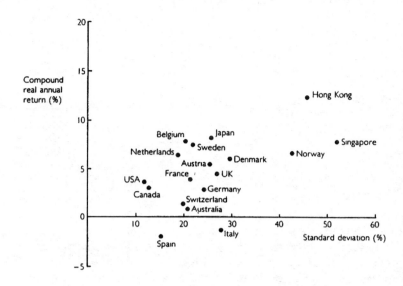

Figure 4.2 Real returns in developed equity stock markets, 1970–90
(expressed in local currency terms)

country risk is systematic or unsystematic. If the risk is unsystematic, it should not be included in the cost of equity. If, on the other hand, the risk is systematic and is not captured in the beta of the cross-border project some adjustment would be warranted.

For a company operating primarily in an advanced European country or the US, it may be argued that investment in less developed countries would provide greater diversification benefits than investment in developed countries because the economies of less developed countries are less closely linked to those of industrialised nations. However, the systematic

Table 4.9 *Risk and reward in equity markets in emerging and developing countries in US dollars over various periods to 1990*

Country	Compound annual return US$ %	Standard deviation %	Period covered
Argentina	22.6	121.2	1978–88
Brazil	0.0	60.2	1976–90
Chile	31.1	60.2	1976–90
Colombia	33.5	64.7	1985–90
Greece	5.4	56.9	1976–90
India	17.7	29.1	1976–90
Jordan	9.2	36.3	1979–90

Malaysia	12.0	20.5	1985–90
Mexico	17.4	58.4	1976–90
Nigeria	–5.3	34.1	1985–90
Pakistan	12.8	5.7	1985–90
Philippines	50.5	149.9	1985–90
Portugal	28.3	134.9	1987–90
South Korea	30.6	46.2	1976–90
Taiwan	44.5	79.0	1987–90
Thailand	22.9	53.1	1976–90
Turkey	157.7	522.9	1987–90
Venezuela	35.3	235.2	1985–90
Zimbabwe	14.3	64.7	1976–90

Source: World Bank

risk of projects in less developed countries is unlikely to be too far below the average for all projects, since such countries are still ultimately tied in to the world economy. According to this view, the systematic risk of projects in less developed countries might be only marginally below that of comparable projects in industrialised countries. A Zambian copper mine may represent a capital project in a less developed country but its systematic risk will be near to that in industrialised countries because the world demand and the world price of copper are functions of the state of economies in industrialised countries.

If stock markets take cognisance and are influenced by domestic and international operations of firms, then it follows that it is reasonable for foreign operations to be set required rates of return based upon systematic risk. Many researchers have attempted to test the hypothesis that investors take account of the foreign involvement of multinational firms. Severn (1974) found that the greater the foreign involvement of a firm, the lower the covariance of its earnings per share with the earnings of the Standard and Poor's index. But multinationals are larger than most domestic corporations and the reduction in earnings variability found by Severn might have been due to size and greater product diversification rather than to foreign earnings. Consistent with this view, Haegele (1974) showed that, while multinationals' systematic risk is lower than for domestic corporations, these differences disappear once the results are adjusted for firm size. In this area, Agmon and Lessard (1977) examined the stock market behaviour of US multinational corporations. If investors recognise and reward international diversification, they argued, price movements of multinational shares should be more closely related to a world market factor and less to a domestic US market factor, and this should be more pronounced the greater the degree of international operations. While their regression analysis, based on portfolios of US multinationals with an increasing proportion of their sales outside the US, supports this hypothesis somewhat weakly (see Table 4.10), their results

Table 4.10 *Relationship between foreign involvement and risk for multinationals according to Agmon and Lessard (1977)*

Portfolio based on multinationals with the following level of sales outside US	Beta
%	
1–7	1.04
7–10	1.06
10–13	0.98
13–17	0.82
17–21	0.98
21–25	0.98
25–28	0.82
28–35	0.99
35–42	0.86
42–62	0.88

are very low on statistical significance. Similarly, Aggarwal (1977) failed to locate any statistical relationship between multinationality and the cost of equity capital.

Perhaps, then, investors do not recognise the portfolio effects of a multinational corporation's foreign activities. Perhaps international diversification has an insignificant effect upon systematic risk. But maybe there is a defect in the approach to the analysis. Beta calculations use the market return, R_M. But R_M already contains the impact of a large number of US multinationals. Corrections for this have been undertaken by Hughes, Logue and Sweeney (1975), who developed indices using portfolios of solely domestic and multinational firms. Their results suggest that the performance of the multinational is clearly superior to that of its purely domestic counterpart.

Interesting pieces of work on portfolio diversification have been undertaken by Solnik (1974) and Jacquillat and Solnik (1978). Comparing the results achieved in terms of reduction of variance by an international portfolio versus a portfolio of internationally diversified companies, they concluded that, while multinational firms do provide diversification for investors, international portfolio diversification is a far superior source of elimination of variance – and investors are able, in the absence of restrictions on portfolio investment, to action this superior diversification on their own. This seems to suggest that the required returns on foreign projects are unlikely, all other things being equal, to be much below the required returns on comparable domestic projects. A study by Doukas and Travlos (1988) indicates significant and positive abnormal returns to shareholders of multinationals pursuing overseas takeover strategies; the gains that they identified were greatest with respect to investment in Less Developed Countries (LDCs).

There is, then, conflicting evidence as to whether we should use different required rates of return for comparable international and domestic projects, given ultimate measurement in home currency terms. The empirical evidence gives us little more than a partial answer.

If country risk were unsystematic it would not, in the context of a CAPM approach, be included in the cost of equity. Recent work by Roll (1993) suggests, in an arbitrage pricing theory (APT) framework, that the systematic country factor is significant in the case of many emerging, as opposed to industrialised country, equity markets.

Rather than attempting an adjustment to beta, some firms, including some City of London and Wall Street bankers, add on a risk premium derived from adjusting for the basis points spread of the country's bonds against UK government bonds or US treasuries of similar maturity and other terms. The more explicit way of dealing with country risk is to make adjustment in the numerator of the present value calculation, that is in the cash flow forecast for the project itself. Clearly, using both of these approaches in a particular case would be double counting, something to be avoided at all costs.

THE INTERNATIONAL CAPITAL ASSET PRICING MODEL

We now turn to another approach in terms of looking at excess returns achieved from equity investment around the globe. Let it be stated at the outset of this section that the findings here are, as readers will see, by no means conclusive – indicative is certainly the best that can be said. They concern evidence of an international capital asset pricing model (ICAPM). Essentially what we are looking at concerns the nature of international capital markets. Two extreme views are possible. These are that:

- international capital markets are integrated, and risky assets are priced according to their undiversifiable world risk, that is, a world (or inter national) capital asset pricing model applies, or
- international capital markets are segmented and risky assets are priced relative to domestic assets only, that is, domestic systematic risk is the basis of asset pricing.

Solnik (1973) tested an international capital asset pricing model and found that national factors were of importance. When these were diversified away with an international portfolio, a strong relationship existed between actual returns and international systematic risk. Stehle (1977) sought to establish whether international capital markets were integrated or separated by testing the hypothesis that US capital markets are isolated against the null hypothesis of integration. The findings suggested that neither hypothesis could be rejected in favour of the other. But he did find some empirical support for an ICAPM.

Cumby (1990) tested whether real stock returns are consistent with a model of international asset pricing. Equity market indices for the US, the UK, Japan and Germany were investigated. Cumby's tests of integration required that the conditional covariance of real stock returns and the rate of change of real consumption should move together over time. This was rejected for the 1970s but could not be rejected for the 1980s. These results do not necessarily demonstrate integration in these four key equity markets. But they are consistent with increasing integration of international capital markets during the 1980s.

Howe and Madura (1990) assessed international capital market integration in a study of international listings. They showed that Euroequity listings by US corporations do not yield shifts on various risk-related measures. Companies' domestic betas did not seem to alter with international listings. And there was no evidence that the overseas listing affected a security's sensitivity to the overseas security market. This, they claim, is evidence that these markets are integrated and that listing has no risk-related impact on the firm's securities. This evidence points in the opposite direction to that suggested in a study by Alexander, Eun and Janakiramanan (1988) who hypothesised that if markets are segmented, the foreign listing of a security should increase demand for that security, hence raising its price and reducing its expected rate of return. They found evidence of a lower expected return (thus, a higher price) for firms obtaining a foreign listing, which indicates some market segmentation.

Solnik (1974) and Lessard (1976) both present evidence that national factors have a significant impact upon security returns relative to that of any world factor. They also found that returns from different national equity markets had relatively low correlations with one another – a factor which may be less true nowadays – see Table 4.11 later in this chapter. Solnik's 1974 study demonstrates the potential benefits from international portfolio diversification following inclusion of foreign securities therein. Other studies tend to confirm this point. Looking at data from the period 1970 to 1986, Hunter and Coggin (1990) find in favour of risk reduction via international portfolio diversification. Bailey and Stulz (1990) found that, for the period 1977 to 1985, a US investor could achieve similar returns, while lowering the standard deviation of a portfolio by a third, through the optimal use of Pacific Basin plus US equities. And, according to a number of empirical studies, diversification gains are not just limited to risk reduction. For example, Solnik (1988) reports that from 1971 to 1985, the average annual returns of the world stock index in US dollars outperformed the US stock index by 13 per cent versus 9.95 per cent with a volatility of only 13.85 per cent versus 15.41 per cent for the US index,

Table 4.11 *Correlations of interest rates and stock market prices in four major markets*

	Overnight interest rates		Long-term interest rates		Stock prices	
	1970s	1980s	1970s	1980s	1970s	1980s
US versus:						
UK	0.03	0.36	0.07	0.76	0.73	0.98
Germany	0.54	0.87	−0.37	0.91	0.67	0.93
Japan	0.22	0.60	−0.25	0.79	0.66	0.97
Japan versus:						
UK	0.16	0.48	0.69	0.86	0.91	0.97
Germany	0.44	0.71	0.72	0.87	0.70	0.89
Germany versus:						
UK	−0.35	0.48	0.29	0.88	0.81	0.94

and the Morgan Stanley Capital International EAFE (Europe, Australia, Far East) stock index outperformed the US stock index by 17.09 per cent to 9.95 per cent and its rate of return per unit of risk – or return/standard deviation – was 0.99 per cent versus only 0.65 per cent for the US index.

On the bond front too, Barnett and Rosenberg (1983) showed that, based on 1973–83 evidence, investing in an internationally diversified bond portfolio lowered risk and increased return. Similar findings have been supplied by work by Cholerton, Pieraerts and Solnik (1986) drawing evidence from the period 1971–84 and by Thomas (1989) whose database covered the years 1975 to 1988.

The combination of equity shares and bonds, in an appropriate portfolio optimising manner so that return is maximised for any given level of risk, was investigated by Solnik and Noetzlin (1982) in the context of international diversification effects. They concluded that international stock diversification yields an improved risk-return pay-off, and international diversification involving stock and bond investments results in substantially less risk than international stock diversification alone. Furthermore, substantial improvement in the risk-return trade-off may be realised by investing in internationally diversified stock and bond portfolios whose weights do not conform to relative market capitalisations. This would be consistent with the various market indices used to measure world stock and bond portfolios not lying on the efficient frontier. Certainly, it has to be said that Solnik and Noetzlin had the advantage of hindsight in constructing their model. But they concluded that the potential for increased risk-adjusted returns are very large indeed.

A study by Cochran and Mansur (1991) examined the interrelationship between yields on the US and foreign equity markets over the period 1980–89. They identified, using advanced statistical techniques, the existence of significant unidirectional and bidirectional causality suggesting that international equity markets are not completely integrated. These causality effects seemed to vary from time to time, indicating that market integration may be unstable and vary over time.

Lest it be thought that increased integration is an established fact, let it be said that Artis and Taylor (1990) find no significant shifts in the correlation of monthly stock returns after 1979 and they found little to suggest that the European stock markets of Germany, the Netherlands and the UK are converging. Fraser, Helliar and Power (1994), using data from 1974 to 1990 for France, Germany, Italy, the UK and the US, find greater convergence of excess returns on shares traded in London and New York as opposed to those in the UK and their European neighbours. Reporting on European stock returns, Drummen and Zimmermann (1992) analysed local currency returns for 105 stocks in 11 European countries over the period 1986 to 1989. They found that the country factor explained 19 per cent of the average stock variance, world stock market movements accounted for 11 per cent while European market trends explained 8 per cent, industry factors accounted for 9 per cent and currency movements accounted for 2 per cent. These factors appeared to explain 49 per cent of the risk of European stocks, leaving over 50 per cent of the variance as specific.

If, overall, the evidence tends to suggest some increasing integration of world capital markets, it is certainly not an issue that has been resolved. Having said this, the next part of this section, which is based upon ideas of equity market integration, is essentially consistent with an ICAPM. It derives from a reasonable correlation between world financial markets. Some evidence to this effect is suggested by Table 4.11 which shows correlations of both interest rates and stock prices for the four major international financial markets of the world in the 1970s and 1980s. Note that the correlations of interest rates and stock prices on a monthly average basis have shown substantial increases over time.

Despite evidence for and against, if it is accepted that major stock markets around the globe have some tendency to move in sympathy with one another, we might think of a world excess return relationship in which the monthly excess returns for a particular market, for example the UK equity market, might be related to the monthly excess return on the world index. In algebraic terms, we might be thinking of a relationship of the following kind:

$$(R_C - R_F) = \alpha_C + \beta_C (R_W - R_F)$$

In the above equation, R_C represents the monthly return in, for example, US dollar terms for the equity market in country C, R_F represents the monthly riskless rate of return, again, to ensure consistency, expressed in US dollar terms, proxied by the return on US treasury bills, α_C is the monthly excess return for country C, β_C is the beta for country C and R_W

represents the monthly return, expressed in US dollar terms, from equity investment in the world index.

How does the model stand up when tested empirically? Excess returns for 18 leading equity markets around the world were compared with the excess return on the world index for the period 1960 to 1980 and for the period 1980 to 1990. In Tables 4.12 and 4.13 their monthly alphas and betas are recorded. Note that a monthly alpha, for a particular country, which is positive indicates that the market in the country concerned has beaten the world market on a risk-adjusted basis. Countries with negative alphas have been beaten by the world index after allowing for risk. For an alpha to be statistically significant at 95 per cent confidence levels, its t-statistic would have to be greater than 2 or less than minus 2. Note that all of the alphas recorded in Tables 4.12 and 4.13 are between +2 and –2 implying that none is statistically significant at the 95 per cent confidence level. Given that alphas appear not to be significantly different from zero, this in itself would be suggestive of some integration of world stock markets.

In interpreting the alpha results shown in Tables 4.12 and 4.13 caution is advised. Many of the smaller European markets have beaten the world index in both periods but remember that returns in the two tables have been restated in US dollar terms and the excess returns might be indicative of currency strength more than big portfolio gains in local currency terms. The UK market has outperformed the world market, and Hong Kong and Japan are big winners against the risk-adjusted world index. The performance of the latter two may owe a significant amount to currency strength. The Singaporean and Norwegian markets have alphas with different signs for the two periods – their colossal outperformance in the first period has been reversed in the second.

When we look at the betas in Tables 4.12 and 4.13 we see a somewhat inconsistent picture. If we believe the evidence of greater correlation of

Table 4.12 *Equity return in dollar terms regressed on world equity portfolio, 1960–80*

	Excess return regressions of country equities on world equity portfolios		
	Monthly alpha %	Monthly alpha t-static	Beta	R^2
Australia	0.13	0.42	1.02	0.52
Austria	0.41	1.15	0.01	0.01
Belgium	0.20	0.82	0.45	0.22
Canada	0.23	0.95	0.77	0.49
Denmark	0.24	0.53	0.60	0.11
France	0.01	0.04	0.50	0.10

Germany	0.20	0.53	0.45	0.08
Hong Kong*	1.71	1.88	2.81	0.70
Italy	−0.16	−0.31	0.41	0.02
Japan	0.79	1.36	0.81	0.12
Netherlands	0.05	0.25	0.90	0.64
Norway	1.12	1.16	−0.27	0.01
Singapore*	1.52	1.16	2.59	0.48
Spain	0.39	0.96	0.04	0.01
Sweden	0.14	0.48	0.51	0.20
Switzerland	0.22	0.58	0.87	0.31
United Kingdom	0.15	0.31	1.47	0.47
United States	−0.06	−0.63	1.08	0.93

*Regression run for the period 1970 to 1980
Source: Morgan Stanley Capital International

Table 4.13 *Equity return in dollar terms regressed on world equity portfolio, 1980–90*

	Excess return regressions of country equities on world equity portfolios		
	Monthly alpha %	**Monthly alpha t-statistic**	**Beta**	**R^2**
---	---	---	---	---
Australia	−0.08	−0.12	0.96	0.27
Austria	0.49	0.74	0.52	0.09
Belgium	0.31	0.65	0.91	0.37
Canada	−0.40	−1.04	0.96	0.51
Denmark	0.52	1.12	0.67	0.25
France	0.04	0.08	1.02	0.40
Germany	0.06	0.11	0.87	0.33
Hong Kong	0.29	0.36	0.93	0.18
Italy	0.45	0.74	0.89	0.26
Japan	0.38	0.88	1.17	0.55
Netherlands	0.33	0.97	0.92	0.54
Norway	−0.09	−0.15	1.05	0.33
Singapore	−0.12	−0.19	0.94	0.27
Spain	0.36	0.67	0.84	0.28
Sweden	0.77	1.54	0.90	0.35
Switzerland	−0.28	−0.77	0.90	0.49
United Kingdom	0.23	0.59	1.09	0.56
United States	0.07	0.25	0.82	0.63

Source: Morgan Stanley Capital International

markets over more recent years, we would feel happier to draw conclusions from the latter table rather than the former. Having stated this, what conclusions can we draw from the two tables? It seems that Canada's beta has been less than 1.0, the Netherlands' appears to be around 0.9, the UK beta was above 1.0 and the US beta approximates 1.0. A high R^2 is recorded by all the aforementioned countries. Although the R^2 is lower, Australia's beta has been approximately 1.0, Denmark's beta has been around 0.6 to 0.7, betas for Germany and Sweden have been well below 1.0 as, surprisingly, has Italy's. Switzerland's beta has been stable at 0.9. Otherwise, there have been some big reversals in betas – take Hong Kong and Singapore. Although the reservations are obvious, the empirical facts on country betas may be helpful for company executives in estimating excess returns for international capital investment appraisal. How might this be done?

For a country with a beta of 0.8, assuming an excess return for the US of 8 per cent per annum based on a beta of around 1.0, the excess return for the country concerned might be estimated using the formulation below:

$$(R_C - R_F) = \alpha_C + \beta_C (R_W - R_F)$$

Since alphas have been found empirically not to be significantly different from zero we can rewrite the above equation as:

$$(R_C - R_F) = \beta_C (R_W - R_F)$$

Assuming that the beta for the US is equal to unity – and this is one of the things that Tables 4.12 and 4.13 tell us – the value of $(R_W - R_F)$ would be equal to $(R_{USA} - R_F)$. This has been found, for long periods, to approximate 8 per cent. If past outturns are to be repeated, this figure may be taken as the value of the excess return on the world portfolio. Thus, for a country with a beta of 0.8, its excess return might reasonably be estimated by:

$$
\begin{aligned}
(R_C - R_F) &= \beta_C (R_W - R_F) \\
&= 0.8 \ (8\%) \\
&= 6.4\%
\end{aligned}
$$

In using this approach to estimating a country's excess return, the big problem is assessing the country beta. Perhaps Tables 4.12 and 4.13 may help, although the reservations that we have about them have already been highlighted. Having said all this, maybe this route to solving the problem of the approximate excess return requirement for investment in, for example, Germany or the Netherlands, may be useful. That it can be criticised is not denied.

Now that we have specified a method of determining the excess return for various developed countries, we can feed this into our cost of capital equations specified at the start of this chapter and thence determine the return requirement for investments in the usual way.

CONCLUSION

The capital asset pricing model derives a method of estimating the cost of equity using a formula which adds to the risk-free rate of return the product of the appropriate beta and the excess return. This excess return is given by the difference between the return expected to be earned by a market portfolio of equity shares minus the risk-free rate of return. This chapter is intended to act as an aid in deriving the value of the excess return around the world. Evidence is presented from various countries and this is followed by a survey of the international capital asset pricing model, from which ideas about determining an excess return for various developed countries around the world flow. The use of the capital asset pricing model around the world presupposes that we are able to access values as to the magnitude of the excess return in different parts of the globe. It is the pursuit and identification of these amounts that was this chapter's objective. It is, as far as we are aware, the first study to set out historic returns for such a broad spectrum of countries.

References

Aggarwal, R (1977) 'Multinationality and stock market valuation', *Financial Review,* summer, pp 45–46.

Agmon, T and Lessard, D R (1977) 'Investor recognition of corporate international diversification', *Journal of Finance,* Vol 32, pp 1049–1056.

Alexander, G J, Eun, C S and Janakiramanan, S (1988) 'International listings and stock returns: some empirical evidence', *Journal of Financial and Quantitative Analysis*, Vol 23, No 2, pp 135–151.

Allen, D E, Day, R E, Kwiatowski, J and Hirst, I R C (1987) 'Equity, gilts, treasury bills and inflation', *Investment Analyst,* January, pp 11–18.

Artis, M and Taylor, M P (1990) 'International financial stability and the regulation of capital flows', in G Bird (ed) *The International Financial Regime,* Surrey University.

Bailey, W and Stulz R M (1990) 'Benefits of international diversification: the case of Pacific Basis stock markets', *Journal of Portfolio Management*, Vol 16, No 4, pp 57–61.

Barnett, G, and Rosenberg M (1983) 'International diversification in bonds', *Prudential International Fixed Income Investment Strategy*, Vol 2.

Blume, M E (1974) 'Unbiased estimators of long-run expected rates of return', *Journal of the American Statistical Association*, September, Vol 69, No 346, pp 634–638.

Brealey, R and Myers, S (1991) *Principles of Corporate Finance,* 4th edn, McGraw-Hill, New York.

Brigham, E F and Gapenski, L C (1993) *Financial Management: Theory and Practice,* 7th edn, The Dryden Press, Forth Worth, Texas.

Buckley, A (1995a) *From Domestic to International Investment with Real Operating Options,* VU University Press, Amsterdam.

Buckley, A (1995b) *International Capital Budgeting*, Prentice Hall, Englewood Cliffs, New Jersey.

Buckley, A (1995c) 'The classical tax system, imputation tax and capital budgeting', *European Journal of Finance*, Vol 1, No 2, pp 113–128.

Cholerton, K, Pieraerts, P and Solnik, B (1986) 'Why invest in foreign currency bonds?', *Journal of Portfolio Management*, Vol 12, No 4, pp 4–8.

Cochran, S J and Mansur I (1991) 'The Interrelationships between US and foreign equity market yields: Tests of Granger causality', *Journal of International Business Studies*, Vol 4, pp 723–736.

Copeland, T E Koller, J and Murrin, J (1994) *Valuation*, 2nd edn, John Wiley, New York.

Cumby, R E (1990) 'Consumption risk and international equity returns: some empirical evidence', *Journal of International Money and Finance*, Vol 9, No 2, pp 182–191.

Dimson, E and Brealey, R A (1978) 'The premium on UK equities', *Investment Analyst*, December, pp 14–18.

Dimson, E and Marsh, P (1982) 'Calculating the cost of capital', *Long Range Planning*, Vol 15, No 2, pp 112–120.

Doukas, J and Travlos, N G (1988) 'The effect of corporate multinationalism on shareholders' wealth: evidence from international acquisitions', *Journal of Finance*, Vol 43, pp 1161–1175.

Drummen, M and Zimmermann, H (1992) 'The structure of European stock returns', *Financial Analysts Journal*, Vol, 48 No 4, pp 15–26.

Fama, E F and French, K R (1988) 'Permanent and temporary components of stock prices', *Journal of Political Economy*, Vol 96, pp 246–273.

Fama, E F and French, K R (1992) 'The cross-section of expected stock returns', *Journal of Finance*, Vol 47, pp 427–465.

Fisher, L and Lorie, J H (1968) 'Rates of return on investments in common stock: the year by year record, 1926–65', *The Journal of Business*, Vol 41, No 35, pp 291–316.

Fraser, P, Helliar, C V and Power, D M (1994), 'An empirical investigation of convergence among European equity markets', *Applied Financial Economics*, Vol 4, pp 149–157.

Frennberg, P and Hansson, B (1992) 'Swedish stocks, bonds, bills and inflation (1919–1990)', *Applied Financial Economics*, Vol 2, pp 79–86.

Haegele, M J (1974) *Exchange Rate Expectations and Security Returns*, PhD dissertation, University of Pennsylvania.

Hamao, Y (1991) 'A standard data base for the analysis of Japanese security markets', *Journal of Business*, Vol 64, pp 87–102.

Howe, J S and Madura, J (1990) 'The impact of international listings on risk: implications for capital market integration', *Journal of Banking and Finance*, Vol 14, No 6, pp 1133–1142.

Hughes, J S, Logue, D E and Sweeney, R J (1975) 'Corporate inernational diversification and market assigned measures of risk and diversification', *Journal of Finance and Quantitative Analysis*, Vol 10, No 4, pp 627–637.

Hunter, J E and Coggin, T D (1990) 'An analysis of the diversification benefit from international equity investment', *Journal of Portfolio Management*, Vol 17, No 1 pp 33–36.

Ibbotson, R G and Brinson, G P (1993) *Global Investing: The Professional's Guide to the World Capital Markets,* McGraw-Hill, New York.

Ibbotson, R G and Sinquefield, R A, *Stocks, Bonds, Bills and Inflation Yearbook*, Ibbotson Associates, Chicago, Illinois.

Jacquillat, B and Solnik, B H (1978) 'Multinationals are poor tools for diversification', *Journal of Portfolio Management,* Vol 4, No 2, pp 8–12.

Jensen, M C (1972) 'Capital markets: theory and evidence', *Bell Journal of Economics and Management Science*, Vol 3 No 2, pp 357–398.

Kim, M J, Nelson C R and Startz, R (1991) 'Mean reversion in stock prices: a reappraisal of the empirical evidence', *Review of Economic Studies,* Vol 58, pp 515–528.

Lessard, D R (1976) 'World, country, and industry relationships in equity returns: implications for risk reduction through international diversification', *Financial Analysts Journal*, Vol 32, No 1, pp 32–38.

Levy, H and Sarnat, M (1990) *Capital Investment and Financial Decisions,* 4th edn, Prentice-Hall, Englewood Cliffs, New Jersey.

Mehra, R and Prescott, E C (1985) 'The equity premium: a puzzle', *Journal of Monetary Economics,* Vol 15, pp 145–161.

Merrett, A J and Sykes A (1963) 'Return on equities and fixed interest securities, 1919–1963', *District Bank Review,* December.

Merrett, A J and Sykes, A (1966) 'Return on equities and fixed interest securities, 1919–1966', *District Bank Review,* June, pp 29–44.

Merrett, A J and Sykes A (1973) *The Finance and Analysis of Capital Projects,* 2nd edn, Longmans, London.

Officer, R R (1989) 'Rates of return to shares, bond yields and inflation rates', in *Share Markets and Portfolio Theory: Readings and Australian Evidence,* 2nd edn, University of Queensland Press, St Lucia, Queensland.

Poterba, J M and Summers, L H (1988) 'Mean reversion in stock prices: evidence and implications', *Journal of Financial Economics,* Vol 22, No 1, pp 27–59.

Ritter, L S and Urich, T (1984) *The Role of Gold in Consumer Investment Portfolios, Monograph Series in Finance and Economics*, Salomon Brothers Center for the Study of Financial Institutions, Graduate School of Business, New York University.

Roll, R (1993) 'Work in Progress Paper', Whittemore Conference on the international capital acquisition process, May, The Amos Tuck School, Dartmouth.

Siegel, J J (1992) 'The equity premium: stock and bond returns since 1802', *Financial Analysts Journal,* Vol 48, No 1, pp 28–38.

Siegel, J J (1994) *Stocks for the Long Run: A Guide to Selecting Markets for Long-Term Growth,* Richard D Irwin, Burr Ridge, Illinois.

Severn, A K (1974) 'Investor evaluation of foreign and domestic risk', *Journal of Finance*, Vol 29, pp 545–550.

Sharpe, W F (1964) 'Capital asset prices: a theory of market equilibrium under conditions of risk', *Journal of Finance*, Vol 19, pp 425–442.

Solnik, B (1973) 'A note on the validity of the random walk for European stock prices', *Journal of Finance*, Vol 28, pp 1151–1159.

Solnik, B (1974) 'Why not diversify internationally rather than domestically?', *Financial Analysts Journal*, Vol 30, No 4, pp 48–54.

Solnik, B (1988) *International Investments*, Addison-Wesley, Reading.

Solnik, B and Noetzlin, B (1982), 'Optimal international asset allocation', *Journal of Portfolio Management*, Vol 9, No1, pp 11–21.

Stehle, R H (1977) 'An empirical test of the alternative hypothesis of national and international pricing of risky assets', *Journal of Finance*, Vol 32, No 2, pp 493–502.

Thomas, L R (1989) 'The performance of currency hedged foreign bonds', *Financial Analysts Journal*, Vol 45, No 3, pp 25–31.

van Horne, J C (1995) *Financial Management and Policy*, 10th edn, Prentice-Hall, Englewood Cliffs, New Jersey.

Wydler, D (1989) 'Swiss stocks, bonds and inflation, 1926–1987', *Journal of Portfolio Management*, Vol 15, pp 27–32.

Part Three

STRATEGIC MANAGEMENT ACCOUNTING

5

ACCOUNTING FOR COMPETITIVE ADVANTAGE

Keith Ward

INTRODUCTION

Two irresistible forces are creating either a major opportunity for, or a serious challenge to, the role fulfilled within most commercial organisations by the management accounting function. First, the dramatic developments in technology are relieving management accountants and their clerical staff of much of their traditional recording and routine analytical processing duties. Second, the increasing degree of competition in most industries is forcing businesses to make more frequent, and much more fundamental, reviews of their competitive strategies.

These forces could, and should, enable the management accounting function to play a much more important strategic role within their organisations as the important strategic decisions which follow from these reviews require sound financial evaluation and control. However, the financial analysis required for one-off strategic decisions is very different from that produced for the regular, repetitive operational reviews which have been the focus of most management accounting systems. The consequent need for change is proving to be a major problem for many management accounting departments with the result that, in some companies, the strategic management accounting role is being carried out in other parts of the organisation. If such a trend was to become widespread, the potential consequences for the future role of management accounting would clearly be very serious.

STRATEGIC MANAGEMENT ACCOUNTING

The widely agreed, key objective for competitive strategies in modern corporations is to develop a sustainable competitive advantage. As discussed in Chapters 1 and 2, it is only through achieving such a sustainable competitive advantage that companies can create shareholder value, since earning a rate of return which is merely equal to that *required* by the shareholder does not create added value. It is also now widely generally accepted that, given the rapidly changing competitive environment, no single competitive advantage is infinitely sustainable. Hence while any current competitive advantage is being exploited, the business should be developing its replacement!

These statements highlight the key aspects of any strategically focused approach to management accounting. If the key objective for any competitive strategy is to develop a sustainable competitive advantage, the corresponding key focus for strategic management accounting should be 'accounting for that competitive advantage'. This means that the management accounting system should be tailored to the competitive strategy of the business and, further, that it should be appropriately modified if and when the competitive strategy is changed.

Indeed the *best* strategic management accounting system would indicate, in advance, when the competitive strategy should be changed, and would then assist in the financial evaluation of the appropriate alternatives which would already be under consideration. This is because the accounting information *should* be analysing whether the existing competitive advantage is still sustainable or needs replacing. Thus a major element in such a strategic approach to accounting is financially justifying the expenditure required first *to develop* the competitive advantage and then *to maintain* it during the period when it is capable of delivering 'added value'.

Added value is created by achieving a return which is greater than the risk adjusted required rate of return and can also be described, in economic terms, as a 'super profit'. Strategic management accounting is therefore focused on the sources of such super profits and concentrates on their financial valuation and management.

However a super profit is clearly created by developing and maintaining a sustainable competitive advantage and any competitive advantage is, by definition, a relative statement. In other words, having a 'good' product is not a competitive advantage if competitors have a 'better' product. This necessitates that strategic management accounting must have an external focus if it is to have any real strategic value.

It is a valid criticism of much of traditional management accounting that it is too internally focused – the classical 'budget, actual, variance' analysis where the budget, or financial plan, is regarded as a completely fixed tablet of stone. Any financial plan is based, as shown in Figure 5.1, on a wide range of assumptions concerning the external business environment. Most of these factors are outside the control of the business and yet they fundamentally affect the objectives and strategies selected by the management of the company.

Figure 5.1 External environmental factors

If these assumptions are subsequently proven to be wrong or a competitor modifies *its* strategy, the company will quite logically reconsider its own competitive position and make appropriate decisions. These decisions may result in resetting its objectives or in a significant change in its own competitive strategy. Unless these changes are reflected in an amended plan, the management accounting system will subsequently be comparing the company's actual performance against a set of targets towards which it is no longer aiming. Hence the management accounts could become largely irrelevant to the strategic management of the business. This can be avoided by incorporating the changing external environment into the management accounting process, as shown in Figure 5.2.

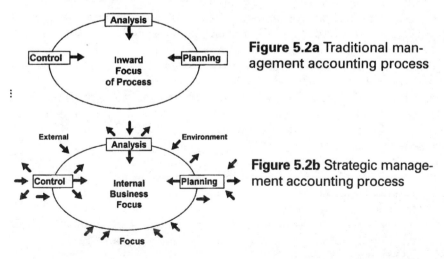

Figure 5.2a Traditional management accounting process

Figure 5.2b Strategic management accounting process

THE DEVELOPMENT OF STRATEGIC MANAGEMENT ACCOUNTING

The concept of this more strategic approach to management accounting has been around since at least 1981 when the phrase was used by Professor K Simmonds. He defined strategic management accounting as 'the provision and analysis of management accounting data about an organisation and its external environment (including stakeholders, competitors, suppliers and customers) for use in developing and monitoring the business strategy' (Simmonds, 1981).

While considerably longer than our preferred definition of 'accounting for competitive advantage', the key elements are the inclusion of the 'external environment' and the specific reference to the 'strategy' of the business. Since this definition (which has been adopted by the UK's Chartered Institute of Management Accountants) in 1981, the area of strategic management accounting has been developed with a variety of focuses and titles. However the common linkages are the consistent emphasis on a strategic orientation and the resulting requirement for the inclusion of factors external to the organisation.

In the US, this area is generally described as 'strategic accounting' (see Shank and Govindarajan, 1989), with a focus on strategic cost management (see Govindarajan and Shank, 1992, and Kaplan et al, 1990). The emphasis on strategic cost analysis has been followed by several researchers in the UK (notably Wilson, 1990) while others have concentrated on the formulation of strategy and evaluation of specific competitive advantages (see, for example, Bromwich, 1990; Palmer, 1992; Rickwood et al, 1990; Tricker, 1989). This area is also considered by Allen (1985), but he prefers the title, strategic financial management.

Many researchers and leading authors have expressed great concern over the potential decline in the perceived value of management accounting if it fails to confront the major challenge presented by the new sophistication in strategic management. This is perhaps most clearly reflected in the title of Johnson and Kaplan's book, *Relevance Lost: The Rise and Fall of Management Accounting* (1987), but many other works have attempted to link techniques from other functional areas into the management accounting area. These include value chain analysis (see Hergert and Morris, 1989) and the PIMS (profit impact of market strategies) database (see Buzzell and Gale, 1987).

The rest of this chapter attempts to highlight the ways in which strategic management accounting can be utilised within a company both to develop and to modify competitive strategies in order to create enhanced shareholder value. While drawing on the work of others, the main emphasis will be our own specific research; this work is dealt with in greater depth in *Strategic Management Accounting* (Ward, 1992).

SOURCES OF SUPER PROFIT

As already stated, the main objective of competitive strategies is to create a sustainable competitive advantage so that the company can achieve a better than required rate of return. In a perfectly competitive environment, such a super profit would be unsustainable; new entrants would be attracted into this marketplace by these above normal rates of return. The resulting increase in supply within the industry would force down the rates of return until all the opportunity to earn super profits was removed.

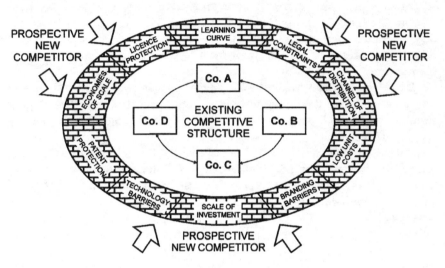

Figure 5.3 Use of entry barriers

In other words, super profits are generated by identifying or creating, and then subsequently exploiting, market imperfections; these market imperfections are really 'barriers to entry' which stop potential competitors from coming into this very profitable and hence attractive market. Figure 5.3 shows a broad range of such entry barriers, but these are meant to be illustrative rather than exhaustive. Three issues relating to these entry barriers are very important.

First, none of these entry barriers occurs without the investment of funds by the company; this investment should be rigorously financially evaluated and controlled. A patent is clearly a highly valuable entry barrier, as it will enable its owner to earn a potentially high level of super profit for the remainder of its life. However the company would have had to spend money on high-risk research and development activities to create the breakthrough which led to the registration of the patent.

Second, many of these entry barriers require significant maintenance expenditure if they are to be kept as effective deterrents to potential competitors. Well-developed brands (such as Marlboro and Coca-Cola) can generate for their owners very high levels of super profit, but the critical brand attributes (such as awareness, propensity to purchase and effective distribution) will rapidly decline unless the company carefully maintains them. In many cases, the brand attributes will be changed gradually over time as the dynamics of the competitive environment alter. If managed properly, this may enable the brand to outlast the life-cycle of the original product with which it was associated.

Third, none of these entry barriers has an infinite life; competitors will eventually find a way of breaking down the barrier to this attractive market. In the case of the patent, the economic life of the entry barrier is clearly the remaining period of the patent, but with a brand the original life can be extended several times over by carefully managing the brand positioning.

Thus the financial objective for any particular source of competitive advantage is clear: the company should seek to maximise the net present value of the cash flows generated by the competitive advantage over its economic life. This demonstrates that a key strategic role for the finance function is in the valuation of competitive advantages and in translating entry barriers into perceived added value for shareholders. The positive net present value which is predicted represents the value of the entry barrier, ie the source of the super profit.

Looked at the other way round, it means that for any major strategic investment where the discounted cash flows predict a large positive net present value, it should be possible to identify the source of that positive net present value – ie what is the competitive advantage which is capable of producing a sustained level of super profit. In many projects, there is no such identifiable entry barrier and the high projected cash flows cannot in reality be maintained when new competitors enter the market.

Another strategic role for management accounting can also be identified in this area. As already mentioned, the business should be trying to develop the next source of competitive advantage while it is exploiting the existing one. Thus if *some* of the super profits generated by the current entry barrier are successfully reinvested in creating its replacement, competitors will still be kept at bay even at the end of the current competitive advantage's life. The financial challenge is to evaluate and justify the reinvestment of the current profit stream; this requires a clear understanding of what really constitutes the present competitive advantage and what will represent an effective entry barrier in the quite distant future. A practical example may help to make this clearer.

Pharmaceutical companies can create very effective entry barriers to certain market segments through the development of patented drugs. Thus Glaxo has been able to generate a very strong stream of profits from its patented anti-ulcer drug, Zantac. However it knows very well that its competitors will be ready and waiting to launch their own versions of this drug as soon as the patent expires, having analysed and reverse engineered the existing drug. Therefore the management of Glaxo have to decide whether they should reinvest some of these high current profits in trying to create new entry barriers for the period following the expiry of Zantac's patent. They have a number of potential choices but these individually build on different sources of competitive advantage, and consequently have significant implications for an appropriately tailored strategic management accounting system (Figure 5.4).

a) Competitive Position - during the life of the Patent

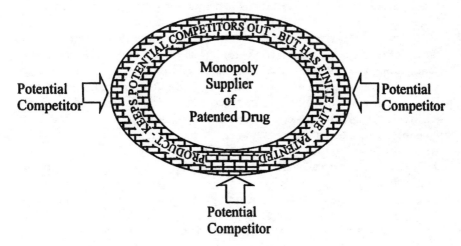

b) Competitive Position - after the expiry of the original Patent

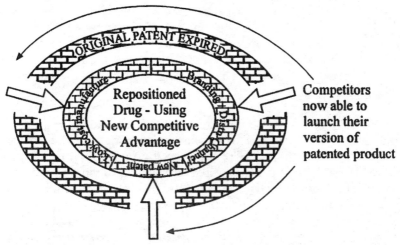

Figure 5.4 Replacing an existing competitive advantage

If they do not believe that they have any ongoing competitive advantages, they should, of course, pay out the current high levels of profits as dividends to the company's shareholders; companies should only reinvest where the expected return is greater than the shareholders' required return (as discussed in Chapter 2). This would imply that finding Zantac was a lucky break and that the company is unlikely to make a similar breakthrough in the future.

However if the company believes that it is actually very good at research and development, it may reinvest some of the existing super profit stream in this area in an attempt to develop the follow-on product to Zantac. The competitive advantage is the effectiveness with which the company is capable of carrying out research and development. This should therefore be the main focus of a strategic management accounting system, and is discussed in more detail later in the chapter.

Alternatively management may believe that the company is better than its competitors at exploiting the commercial potential of a patent. In this case it may make sense to buy the registered patents of other pharmaceutical companies, or even to buy the companies themselves, rather than to reinvest super profits in their own fundamental research programmes. If this is seen as the main source of competitive advantage, the main focus of the strategic management accounting system should be the financial evaluation of the potential acquisitions, with a rigorous analysis of why the products are worth more to them than they are to their current owners.

Yet other potential sources of super profits could relate to Zantac itself in its post patent period, where three options at least are available. Zantac could be developed into a strong brand so that, even when competitors are able to launch their own versions of the drug, the existing users will stay loyal to Zantac and may even be willing to pay a premium price for a product which they trust. In this specific example, this competitive strategy would necessitate changing the channel of distribution as well, as Zantac was originally a prescription-based drug. It is assumed that doctors would not be as easily affected by a branding strategy and, as they are under severe cost pressures, they would want to prescribe the cheapest drug which had the same medical properties.

If the product was made available in the over-the-counter market, the consumer loyalty could be used to retain a significant market share even after the end of the patent period. It would be most logical to launch the product into this new channel of distribution shortly before the expiry of the patent. However competitors would probably be unable to get permission to sell their new versions through this channel at launch, because of the lack of track record for their product (ie they cannot demonstrate substantial sales for over 10 years with no significant adverse side effects). In this case the management accounting focus should be on the financial justification of the development marketing expenditure needed to build the brand and to develop the new channel of distribution. Clearly this expenditure is not required during the initial patent period although the money will be spent then. The financial evaluation is based on the additional profits which will be generated after the initial entry barrier has been removed. The key strategic question is whether the company has the skills required to develop and then sustain a competitive advantage in the marketing area (Figure 5.4).

Another way of continuing to use the existing product is by trying to find ways of extending the patent for Zantac. In the pharmaceutical industry one way of doing this can be to develop new delivery mechanisms for the drug, such as changing a powder into a liquid or an aerosol format, or producing a controlled-release tablet/pill formulation. This area of development is quite specialised and therefore the company may decide to sub-contract the research work; their added value comes from the continuing sales of Zantac at above required rates of return. The decisions as to whether to attempt such research and, if so, where the work should be done require clear financial evaluation.

Also by the time the original patent expires, the company should have acquired substantial expertise in the manufacturing processes involved. If a significant experience curve is involved, the company should be well down it, whereas the potential competitors, which are considering coming into the market, are starting right at the top of their cost curve. Consequently the existing producer may regard its lower cost base as another potential source of competitive advantage. In order to create an effective entry barrier, it needs to launch its own generic version of the drug slightly before the patent expires (ie before competitors can enter the market). It may then be able pre-emptively to take control of this channel of distribution, as wholesalers, etc will probably only want to stock one version of the generic product. It should also price the newly launched product at a level which makes it financially unattractive to competitors to make their own required investment. This would require a very clear analysis of the potential competitor's investment needs, required rate of return and cost structure. An evaluation can then be done of the financial returns which are likely to be achieved given the pricing strategy shown to be required by this focused competitive analysis.

This example is designed to indicate that these very different potential second stage competitive strategies require significantly different management accounting emphases. The strategic management accounting system must be specifically tailored to the needs of the business and there are several potential fundamentally different types of competitive strategy for a pharmaceutical company: a patented product's strategy based on a high level of Research and Development (R&D), a marketing based business built around brands and a low-cost producer of generic products for which the patents may have expired long ago. Their tailored management accounting systems should have much more in common with companies following similar competitive strategies in very different industries than with each other. There is no such thing as a strategic management accounting system for an industry.

EXIT BARRIERS

It should be remembered that, under the assumptions for perfect competition, it is impossible to sustain a super profit; new entrants will be attracted into the industry and force down the rate of return to normal levels. Thus entry barriers represent a market imperfection which can be exploited to the company's advantage. Conversely, under the theoretical rules of perfect competition it is impossible for an industry to continue to produce rates of return which are below those *required* by investors. Some companies should leave the industry and thus reduce the total supply level; this should improve the financial returns to the required rates, when no one else should want to leave (Figure 5.5).

Of course, in the real world, this does not always happen and many industries continue for many years to make losses or to generate uneconomically low rates of return. The companies in these unattractive industries face exit barriers which can severely affect their willingness to leave the industry despite the current losses or low rates of return. Clearly therefore a good understanding of the exit barriers affecting a business and its competitors is critical if competitive responses to particular strategic initiatives are to be predicted correctly. This analysis should not be left until the industry is facing a severe over-capacity problem as it is then often very difficult to resolve the situation. If the industry is identified at an early stage as having high exit barriers, it is even more important than usual to erect very high entry barriers to keep out potential competitors. Once competitors enter the industry, they will be very, very difficult to force out due to the high exit barriers.

Figure 5.6 illustrates the types of exit barriers which are often faced, and it can be seen that several of them are by no means mutually exclusive. Indeed, it is quite possible for companies to have very high fixed costs with a high investment in very specialised, long-life fixed assets and also to face high costs to close down and leave (such as for extractive industries like mining) or to have long-term supply contracts (such as raw material processing industries like paper making or petrochemicals) or to have significant shared costs (such as refining, etc). Companies in these types of industries need very specific financial information before they implement strategic decisions, and the financial information should be primarily focused on their competitors.

A very common competitive strategy in industries with excess capacity is to start a price war in an attempt to gain market share and to achieve a

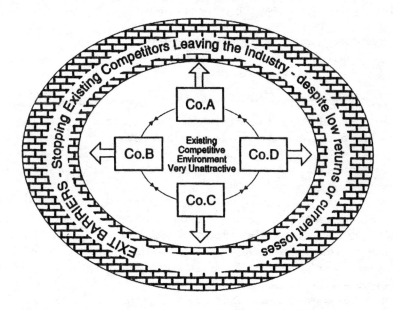

Figure 5.5 Maintaining the unattractive *status quo*–exit barriers

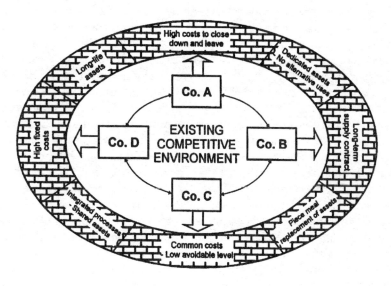

Figure 5.6 Exit barriers

better total contribution, through high sales volumes, towards the high fixed costs. This may work if the lower selling prices create a much higher level of total demand so that the whole industry is potentially better off; but such a result requires an unusually high level of price elasticity of demand for the goods or service. The success is also primarily caused by changing the overall financial position of the industry and not by gaining market share.

If the overall level of demand does not increase, it is most likely that competitors will respond by dropping their selling prices (possibly even further!), as they will be equally keen to retain their existing sales volumes. All that has been achieved therefore is to reduce the overall profitability of the industry.

In this type of situation, any competitive strategy should concentrate on pushing one or more competitors through the exit barriers so that the future profitability for the remaining companies can be significantly enhanced. Thus a price reduction strategy should be used by the lowest cost suppliers in the industry, and even then only if they can reduce (and afford to hold down) prices to a level which is below the exit price for the highest cost competitors in the industry. This clearly requires a very good assessment of competitors' cost structures from an 'avoidable' viewpoint.

Another key point for implementing a successful 'force out' competitive strategy in these situations is the timing of such an initiative. It seems immensely rational to try to force a competitor through the exit barriers when the exit barriers are at their lowest. Yet, in many cases, companies seem to attack when the exit barriers have just been increased. A good example of this would be in an asset intensive industry, where one competitor has just made a major reinvestment in plant and machinery. Quite often other companies in the industry will start a price war based on hurting the competitor immediately after its significant commitment of capital. This may cause considerable pain but is very unlikely to force the competitor to leave; it will logically regard the new investment as a sunk cost and will probably use its more efficient, newer plant to retaliate very aggressively.

A much more rational competitive strategy would be to attack the competitor just *before* it makes the reinvestment; importantly, the attack must be launched before the investment funds are *committed* by the competitor. If this is done, the competitive environment will look significantly less attractive as the competitor is financially evaluating its reinvestment proposal, and it may decide not to go ahead with the reinvestment. This type of strategic initiative clearly requires other kinds of financial information about competitors: which competitors are potentially facing major investment decisions, what are their commitment lead-times and how do they make such investment decisions?

OTHER STRATEGIC THRUSTS OF BUSINESSES

As well as using entry and exit barrier analyses, there are other very useful competitive strategy techniques which require a very tailored approach to strategic management accounting. One such approach is based on the marketing planning tool known as the Ansoff matrix. As shown in Figure 5.7, the Ansoff matrix (named after its inventor, Igor Ansoff) distinguishes only four ways of growing a business; other versions have more bases by introducing related products and customers, etc in between existing and new, but they all use the same basic concepts.

Thus a business can grow by selling more of its existing products to its existing customers, which is normally described as a market penetration strategy. This type of strategy has been well researched over the years (particularly using the already mentioned PIMS database) and a clear conclusion is that a market penetration strategy generates the greatest added value when the market is itself growing strongly. This is not surprising, as any attempt to gain market share in a static or declining industry is likely to be resisted very strongly by competitors, as they would physically lose sales volumes as a consequence. However, in a rapidly growing market, these same competitors may still be expanding

Figure 5.7 Ansoff matrix

quite well, even though they are actually losing market share. Key elements therefore for a strategic management accounting system for this strategic thrust would be assessments of the future rate of market growth, existing competitor reactions to a loss in market share and the strength of entry barriers to keep out potential new competitors.

At the other end of the spectrum is the 'diversification' strategy, which involves selling 'new products in new markets'. Diversification is normally justified by companies as a 'risk reducing' strategy, but it is very difficult to see how a company can claim to have a sustainable competitive advantage in selling 'products it doesn't currently have to customers which it has never dealt with before'. It should come as no surprise, therefore, that most of the research into diversification strategies shows that they destroy shareholder value, rather than creating it. A critical issue is that the 'risk reduction' is largely from the perception of management rather than the shareholders; shareholders can achieve a diversified investment portfolio very easily and do not need any individual company to try to achieve this for them. 'Diversification' strategies therefore need to be based on some sustainable competitive advantage; this could be thought of as a third dimension to the matrix, so that the strategic thrust is no longer into an 'all new' box. The challenge for the strategic management accounting system, therefore, is to identify, as clearly as possible, the specific competitive advantage which can be developed into other areas of activity (for example, the competitive advantage may be brand management, management of high technology, or management of mature businesses, etc).

The remaining two bases represent the major strategic thrusts for future growth in most companies and yet the titles given to them in the Ansoff matrix can be misleading. Hence in the modified version shown as Figure 5.8 they are renamed to highlight the competitive advantages on which they are based.

If a company is basing its strategy on developing new products to sell to its existing customers, this must be regarded as an existing customer-led strategy. All the new products must have attributes which are appropriate to the target group of existing customers on which the strategic thrust is based. Hopefully it should by now be obvious that the strategy should be built around those existing customers which generate a super profit for the company. Trying to sell more new products to the existing, biggest or most loyal customers may not build a long-term financially successful business. Existing customers may be loyal because they are getting such a good deal that the company is actually losing money by dealing with them; no doubt they would be equally loyal to any new loss-making products introduced by the company. Equally it is very unusual to find that the largest customers are the most profitable; normally they have

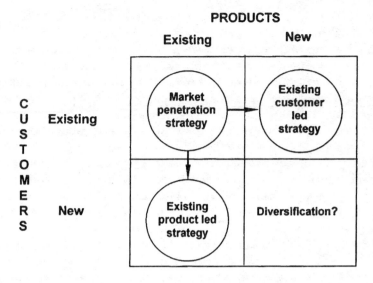

PRODUCTS

Figure 5.8 Potential strategic thrusts of businesses (based on Ansoff matrix)

used their considerable buying power to negotiate a very good deal for themselves, at the cost of reduced profitability to the supplier.

Thus a fundamental requirement for any customer-led strategic thrust is a soundly based customer account profitability (CAP) analysis. This CAP analysis should not attempt to apportion the net profit of the company among the different categories of customers. Rather it should be designed to indicate the cost, and resulting profit, differences caused by the different ways in which various classes of customers are dealt with. Thus the relative profit contributions from customers are highlighted and any subsequent decisions to reallocate resources so as to focus on the more profitable areas of business can be based on a sensible financial analysis. The importance of designing the CAP analysis as a decision support aid cannot be overemphasised, as is the case for any part of a strategic management accounting system.

The alternative to a customer-led strategy is obviously to build the future growth of the business around finding new markets in which to sell existing products. Clearly such a product-led strategy should be based on the existing products which generate super profits in their existing markets. Thus a direct product profitability (DPP) analysis is needed to show the relative profitability of the different product groups.

It is important that the company sets up the analytical system in an appropriate way for its key strategic focus, as many companies try to extract both customer-based and product-based profitability analyses from one system. This will inevitably provide false and potentially very misleading information because some costs are directly attributable to customers but are indirect to products and vice versa for other costs. Most costing systems within companies are still based around products and, despite an increasing number of mission statements which espouse customers as the 'most important asset of the business', many customer-based profitability analyses are extracted from these products oriented costing systems by reapportioning the costs in some pseudo-scientific way.

Another important element for these segment profitability analyses is that, if they are to serve a strategic focus of the business, they should be carried out on a long-term basis. Any competitive advantage only adds real value if it is sustainable, and therefore the comparison of customers and products should identify whether sustainable levels of super profit can be achieved. This involves carrying out relative profitability analyses over the life-cycle of the product or the customer. Life-cycle profitability analysis can be used to evaluate which customers and products are worth investing in; the initial investment has to develop some kind of entry barrier which can be used to generate a more than required return over the economic life of the investment.

The concept of relationship marketing is gathering momentum in many industries but, unfortunately, many of these customer focused investment strategies are being implemented in the absence of suitably tailored strategic management accounting systems.

TAILORED FINANCIAL CONTROL SYSTEMS

So far, the need to tailor the strategic management accounting system has been indicated in a number of ways, eg to the specific competitive environment and the ensuing entry and exit barriers, and to the specific strategic thrust of the business. However it is also important that the financial control measures used by the business are also appropriately tailored.

It is very disappointing that the vast majority of companies still use some form of accounting return on investment as the principal financial measure of performance. As will be demonstrated in this section, this type of financial control measure is only appropriate for businesses which are mature; if applied to businesses which are at other stages of development, they will tend to behave as if they are mature, in order to comply with the control measure to which they are subjected.

As products move through their life cycles, the critical focus of their competitive strategies will change and as these change, so should the financial control measures against which their performance is assessed. Figure 5.9 shows how the overall level of business risk reduces as the product progresses over time, but it also highlights where the competitive strategy should be focused at each stage of development.

Thus at the launch stage the critical success factor in many industries is 'time to market', in terms of getting products established in the market before competitors. This can be seen very clearly in the case of the

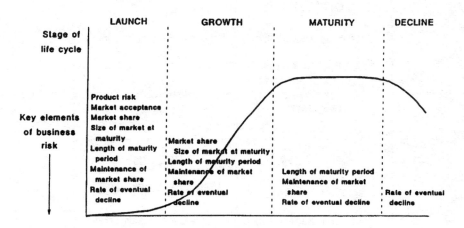

Figure 5.9 Changing business risk profile over the product life-cycle

patented drugs used as an earlier example. As soon as the patent is registered, its time as a competitive advantage starts to expire; therefore, if the company spends too long getting the product tested and approved, it is limiting the time in which it can generate a super profit.

Once successfully developed and launched, the competitive strategy changes its focus to building market share and developing the market to its full long-term potential. As previously stated, it is well established that a competitive strategy designed to increase market share is most likely to be successful while the market is, itself, growing strongly. Hence during the growth phase, the company should be both taking share off its existing competitors and building entry barriers against prospective new competitors. These strategic aims have a long-term time-scale as they are designed for the maturity stage of the life-cycle.

It is during the maturity stage that the company should reap the benefit of its previous investments both in R&D (during the launch stage) and marketing (during the growth stage). If these have been implemented successfully, the company should now be well positioned against all competition and thus should be able to maintain its strong market share with a reasonable level of support activity. The company should now be highly profitable but should not try to reinvest these high profits in growing this business; now is a time for maintenance not growth.

GROWTH	LAUNCH
Business Risk - High	Business Risk - Very High
CSF - Growth in Market Share and Development of Total Market	CSF - Development and Launch of New Product
MATURITY	DECLINE
Business Risk - Medium	Business Risk - Low
CSF - Maintenance of Market Share at Minimum Cost	CSF - Cost Minimisation and Asset Realisations

Figure 5.10 Changing critical success factors (CSF) over the product life-cycle

Eventually these very high profits will become unsustainable as the market goes into decline. The competitive strategy must now focus on managing the decline of the total market and the company's own market share so as to maximise the value generated over the remaining life of the product. Many people see this decline stage as very depressing, but some industries can be in decline for a very long time and the successful companies in such industries can be highly profitable. (For example, the US cigarette industry has been in volume decline for several years but Philip Morris, as discussed in Chapter 1, generates over $5 billion per year in operating profits from this declining market!)

It should now be clear, as shown diagrammatically in Figure 5.10, that the focus of the competitive strategy will change over time. In a strategically oriented management accounting system, the financial control measures applied to assess the success of the competitive strategy should also change during this life-cycle. The important word here is 'control' as strategic decisions, being long term in nature, will normally be *evaluated* using discounted cash flow techniques.

Thus the initial decision to invest in the development and launch of a new product will be financially evaluated by a full discounted cash flow analysis of the expected future cash flows resulting from the decision. Unfortunately the range of outcomes (which may well be from zero income to 'lots and lots' if the project is successful) make the *expected* value used for the project evaluation completely useless as a financial *control* measure. All that would be certain is that there would be a large variance; what is not known is whether it will be favourable or unfavourable. Also the final outcome of financial success is often too far away to be used as an ongoing measure of financial control.

As shown in Figure 5.11, the company needs a decision focused set of controls which can be applied prior to the commitment of the next tranche of expenditure (ie during the development and launch stage). These control measures should indicate whether the project is on target

GROWTH FCM - DCF Evaluation of Investments in Growth in Market and Market Share	LAUNCH FCM - R & D Milestones, Decision Focused Reviews Probability Assessments
MATURITY FCM - Accounting Return on Investment or Residual Income	DECLINE FCM - Free Cash Flow from Operations

Figure 5.11 Tailored financial control measures (FCM) over the product life-cycle

and hence R&D milestones and probability estimates can be used as useful indicators of progress.

Once the product is launched and sales are being made, the range of outcomes narrows considerably. The major expenditures are now being made in the marketing area in order to grow both market share and the total market. As already stated, these investments are made for the long term and so should be controlled by long-term measures such as discounted cash flows. The focus of the strategic management accounting system is on the development of entry barriers (such as branding, channels of distribution, customers etc), which can be sustained into the maturity stage.

During the maturity stage, the company is trying to hang on to what it has while making a good rate of return. It does not want to run down the business, so the idea of maintenance expenditure predominates. Accordingly a measure of profit relative to the required investment is now quite logical. Residual income is widely accepted as being superior to return on investment, but most businesses prefer to use some form of accounting return on investment. Unfortunately, as previously mentioned, it is not only applied to businesses which are at this stage of development.

When the product moves into decline, there is no longer a logical assumption that maintaining the business is financially worthwhile. Thus the financial controls should revert to a cash based measure (accounting profit can be used during the maturity stage as it is a reasonable approximation for cash flow, since depreciation will be close to new investment while the business is in a maintenance mode), but now this should not be a long-term based measure. Free cash flow is a good financial control measure for a declining business as it allows management to make a conscious decision as to the rate of reinvestment, if any, which they wish to make in this business. If the rate of decline in the overall market accelerates, they may wish to accelerate the rate of cash withdrawal even though this further increases the rate of decline of their company.

Far too many companies have destroyed considerable amounts of shareholder value on the assumption that any single company automatically should have an infinite life!

DESIGNING AND OPERATING A STRATEGIC MANAGEMENT ACCOUNTING SYSTEM

It is obviously very important that any strategic management accounting system has tailored financial controls which are appropriate to the specific competitive strategy which it is implementing. The previous section considered this issue in the context of the product life-cycle. This has also been considered by other researchers (see Shields and Young, 1991, and Susman, 1991). It has the very important implication that companies with many products (or businesses) at different stages of development *must* use different financial control measures for their different products and businesses.

The implications for organisational structures are quite profound as it can change the role of the centre and should affect the way in which businesses' units are grouped for financial control purposes. The idea of linking control systems to business strategy has also received some consideration elsewhere (see Govindarajan and Gupta, 1985, and Simons, 1987), but in practice far too many companies apply a single financial control measure to all their business units. As all successful conglomerates are based around a mature, cash-producing business, it is not too surprising to find that the dominant financial control measure is accounting return on investment, as this is appropriate to the original, core business, even if not the rest of the group.

Strategic management accounting systems themselves must be justified in terms of their own costs and benefits, and these benefits come from improving the quality of the strategic decision making within the business. Strategic decisions are particularly difficult to support as they are normally unique (ie one-off, non-repetitive) decisions in areas where the company has little or no relevant experience. Also, these decisions are often made under severe competitive pressure and hence the financial analysis is subject to strict time limitation.

This means that the accounting system should try to predict the type of strategic decision which the company is likely to face, and then to build up supporting information for such decisions. Such a proactive approach will not only increase the amount of information available, but also will reduce the lead time in supplying it so that a better decision can be taken more quickly.

Competitive strategies are successful if they achieve the objectives set for them and this requires their *effectiveness* to be measured. Unfortunately most traditional accounting measures and techniques concentrate on measuring *efficiency* rather than effectiveness. The differences may appear subtle, but they are important. Efficiency can be paraphrased as 'doing things right' as it measures relative levels of inputs to outputs; it makes no comment on whether these 'things' should have been done at all. Effectiveness, on the other hand, is exclusively focused on 'doing the right things' and reflects how well the stated objectives have been achieved – clearly very relevant to any assessment of competitive strategies.

It is quite possible for a company to be very efficient and totally ineffective (because it was doing the wrong things very efficiently), and being very effective yet inefficient is to be preferred. The optimum, of course, is to be both effective and efficient which means that a strategic management accounting system should contain appropriately tailored measures of both effectiveness and efficiency.

The overall financial success of a competitive strategy is reflected in the creation of shareholder value, but this is also determined by the competitive environment in which the business is operating. If the competitive environment is particularly attractive, all the companies in the industry may be earning super profits (these super profits will only be sustainable if there are significant entry barriers). This makes the industry very attractive from an economic investment perspective but says little about the relative performance of the management team (except that they were in the right place at the right time). Their relative performance as managers can only be assessed by comparing them against other managers working in a similar environment (eg direct competitors) or by only using measures over which they can exercise control. It is generally accepted that managerial performance measures should only take into account things over which managers can exercise control; yet economic decisions are based upon all the relevant factors whether they are controllable or not.

Thus in a very depressed industry with high exit barriers, it may well be that none of the companies is earning anything like a normal required rate of return. From an economic perspective, this is very bad news and the investor will be looking either for an exit route or at worst to minimise further losses. This does not mean that all the managers involved in the industry are poor and the best management team may have done a very good job of reducing the losses as far as possible; however, even they can only make a smaller loss rather than generate a super profit.

The implications of this for any strategic management accounting system are that the financial performance measures should distinguish between economic and managerial performance. Unfortunately in many companies there is no separation between these types of measures and many managers have their performance assessed by reference to purely economic measures over which they can exert no control. At the top of the company this may be of limited significance but, at lower levels of management, there is a much greater gap between what influences economic performance and how much of this is actually controlled by the managers. It is therefore even more important that separate managerial performance measures are devised which focus on what the different levels of management really do control.

COMPETITOR ACCOUNTING AND ANALYSIS

Everything in this chapter has tried to emphasise that a competitive advantage is a relative concept and that this requires an external focus in the strategic management accounting system. Even more specifically, the development and maintenance of a competitive advantage can only be assessed by comparison against a specified set of both actual and potential competitors.

This necessitates the collection and analysis of financial information on these competitors, but this must also be tailored to the specific competitive strategy being followed by the company and by these competitors. Thus, if a company is trying to position itself as the lowest cost supplier in its marketplace, it should carry out in-depth cost comparisons against its competitors. However, such detailed cost benchmarking is of limited value if the competitive strategy is to differentiate its product offering through a much higher level of service and customer responsiveness. Indeed, competitive benchmarking may be counter productive because it may well highlight a cost disadvantage in the customer service area; a cost cutting initiative to remove the apparent disadvantage could, of course, destroy the real competitive advantage. Competitor accounting and analysis is considered in much more detail in Chapter 6.

The important focus for strategic management accounting should be on maximising added value by developing and then maintaining entry barriers. Any excessive emphasis on cost reduction can be detrimental to the long-term success of many types of competitive strategy. This has proved a problem for many business process re-engineering initiatives, as these have become driven primarily as cost reduction exercises. In many industries, the easiest areas to attack for cost savings are actually those which generate the greatest added value; reducing cost levels by 10 per cent and destroying over 50 per cent of the value added by the business is not a sensible way to re-engineer any business.

CONCLUSION

Management accounting faces a period of considerable change and resulting challenge. Provided that accounting professionals rise to this challenge, they can establish a pivotal role in the strategic management of their organisations. However, there can be little doubt that the emphasis placed on creating added value from the development and implementation of competitive strategies will continue, and that the need for sound, strategically focused financial information will also therefore increase. Should the management accounting function fail to supply such strategic decision support, it is likely that other areas of the business will do it themselves. This would leave management accountants with an operationally based, score-keeping role, but even this function is increasingly being computerised and almost completely automated as a result.

The future for management accounting is very bright, as long as it has a strategic focus.

References

Allen, D (1985) 'Strategic management accounting', *Management Accounting*, March, pp 25–27.

Bromwich, M (1990) 'The case for strategic management accounting: The role of accounting information for strategy in competitive markets', *Accounting, Organisations and Society*, Vol 15, No 1/2, pp 27–46.

Buzzell, R D, and Gale, B T (1987) *The PIMS Principles: Linking Strategy to Performance*, The Free Press, New York.

Govindarajan, V and Gupta, A K (1985) 'Linking control systems to business unit strategy: impact on performance', *Accounting, Organisations and Society*, Vol 10, (No 1), pp 51–66.

Govindarajan, V and Shank, J K (1992) 'Strategic cost management: Tailoring controls to strategies', *Journal of Cost Management*, Autumn, pp 14–24.

Hergert, M and Morris, D (1989) 'Accounting Data for Value Chain Analysis', *Strategic Management Journal*, Vol 10, pp 175–188.

Johnson, H T and Kaplan, R S (1987) *Relevance Lost: The Rise and Fall of Management Accounting*, Harvard Business School Press, Boston, Massachusetts.

Kaplan, R S, Shank, J K, Horngren, C, Boer, G, Ferrara, W and Robins, M (1990) 'Contribution Margin Analysis: No Longer Relevant/Strategic Cost Management: The New Paradigm', *Journal of Management Accounting Research*, Vol 2, pp 1–32.

Palmer, R J (1992) 'Strategic Goals and the Design of Strategic Management Accounting Systems', *Advances in Management Accounting*, Vol 1, pp 179–204.

Rickwood, C P, Coates, J B and Stacey, R J (1990) 'Stapylton: strategic management accounting to gain competitive advantage', *Management Accounting Research*, Vol 1, pp 37–49.

Shank, J K and Govindarajan, V (1989) *Strategic Cost Analysis: The Evolution from Managerial to Strategic Accounting*, Irwin, Homewood, Illinois.

Shields, M D and Young, M S (1991) 'Managing Product Life Cycle Costs: An Organizational Model', *Journal of Cost Management*, Autumn, pp 39–52

Simmonds, K (1981) 'Strategic Management Accounting', *Management Accounting*, April, pp 26–29.

Simons, R (1987) 'Accounting control systems and business strategy: An empirical analysis', *Accounting, Organisations and Society*, Vol. 12, No 4, pp 357–374.

Susman, G I (1991) *Product Life Cycle Management, Handbook of Cost Management*, ed B Brinkler, Warren, Gorham and Lamont, New York.

Tricker, R I (1989) 'The management accountant as strategist', *Management Accounting,* December, pp 26–28.

Ward, K R (1992) *Strategic Management Accounting,* Butterworth Heinemann,Oxford.

Wilson, R M S (1990) 'Strategic cost analysis', *Management Accounting,* October, pp 42–43.

ACCOUNTING FOR MARKETING STRATEGIES

Keith Ward

INTRODUCTION

The previous chapter highlighted the need for management accounting to focus on the specific competitive strategy of the business and to tailor the financial control measures to the particular strategic thrust and stage of development of the organisation. For many businesses, the key sources of competitive advantage are in the marketing area and this means that 'accounting for marketing' must become an important element in such a company's strategic management accounting system. Unfortunately for many companies, the term 'accounting for marketing' still refers only to the recording of the financial transactions undertaken by the marketing function! This is a long way from the desired financial involvement in the evaluation and control of the strategic marketing decisions. Indeed, the ultimate level of a competitive strategy relates to a specific product (where product relates to both goods and services) sold in a specific market against specifically identified competitors. Hence, marketing accounting at this level must provide decision support in products, customers and competitors.

It is very interesting also that most modern businesses will insist on quite rigorous financial analysis, using full discounted cash-flow techniques, of all significant investments in any tangible assets such as plant and machinery, computers and office equipment, and buildings. Yet many of these businesses will carry out, at best, a cursory financial evaluation of much larger expenditures when they relate to marketing activities. This is seemingly justified by the argument that marketing expenditure is 'very difficult' to evaluate financially – for example, the very famous and undoubtedly apocryphal quote from Lord Leverhulme 'I know that I waste half the money I spend on advertising but I don't know which half!' The main objective of this chapter is to try to demonstrate that this attitude is not only very dangerous for the future financial success of the business but also outdated, because companies can now employ quite rigorous financial evaluations to all areas of marketing activity.

The research basis for this chapter is the work carried out by the Marketing Accounting Research Centre (MARC) at Cranfield School of Management. Over a number of years the centre has worked with our academic marketing colleagues and a broad spread of companies to develop and apply accounting techniques to the marketing decisions faced in the real world. It is a sad comment on the development of management accounting that over the last 30 years or so, while the marketing profession has developed a very comprehensive range of evaluation and review procedures for almost every different type of marketing expenditure, most accounting systems still only record budgeted spend, actual spend and the resulting variance.

Unfortunately, as most of the research carried out by MARC on an in-company basis has been subject to confidentiality agreements, many of the examples can only be described in general terms. However, the key issues for more general application should still be easily extracted from these examples.

The structure of the chapter flows from the strategic thrust discussion in Chapter 5, so that the detailed discussion starts by considering brand-led strategies and the key implications for marketing accounting. The next two areas to be considered are customer-led strategies and product-led strategies. All of these strategic thrusts have long-term implications if they are to be sources of *sustainable* competitive advantage; therefore, the need for an appropriately structured life cycle costing approach is dealt with together, after considering the individual areas. This leads on to the increasingly important area of relationship marketing, which now forms the main marketing focus for many companies, particularly in the service sector. The chapter then finishes by highlighting some overall implications for the design and implementation of a sound marketing accounting system, by considering the needs for competitor accounting and analysis.

However, before becoming embroiled in the detailed applications, it is sensible to take an overall look at the role of accounting for marketing and segment profitability analysis.

OVERVIEW OF ACCOUNTING FOR MARKETING

The key objective of any strategic management accounting system is to provide financial support for the major strategic decisions faced by the business. This may require the integration of non-financial information into the management accounting information system. It is an irrelevant semantic question whether the incorporation of such non-financial information and the use of non-financial performance measures means that the resulting reports should be classified as management accounts or management information! Not surprisingly in this chapter, such information will be referred to as strategic management accounting and this attitude is also taken by Kaplan and Norton (1992 and 1993) in their development and application of the balanced scorecard.

An important role for this detailed level of strategic management accounting is to highlight in advance the need for a change in the competitive strategy. In a marketing-led business, such an indicator might be the unexpected sudden fall in the market share of a main product, even though the total market was still growing strongly. Unfortunately, many companies do not incorporate this type of marketing information in their management accounting reports. The traditional comparison of budget and actual sales revenues may not indicate a major problem for the company, so that no change in competitive strategy is considered. Indeed, if total sales in the market are significantly above the levels anticipated at the time of preparing the budget, the actual sales for our business may be above those included in the budget, despite a sizeable loss in market share by the company. Any competitive strategy must be reviewed in the light of the best current information, which should be externally focused and give a relative measure of performance. This does not mean a budget which was based on what are now outdated and wrong assumptions.

Incorporating such externally based non-financial comparisons can greatly enhance the management accounting information, as it places the current levels of sales revenues, costs, profit and cash flows in their appropriate relative, strategic context. It also means that managers can be set, and subsequently be monitored against, targets and objectives which are appropriate to the long-term objectives of the business. As discussed in Chapter 5, this is particularly important in growth businesses where there is likely to be a conflict between the long-term strategic objectives of the company and its short-term profit levels. It is far too easy to achieve a short-term profit or return on investment target by reducing the development level of expenditure needed to build a long-term sustainable competitive advantage.

Most marketing-led businesses therefore need a balance of measures which reflect how successfully the long-term strategy is being implemented and shorter term indications of the financial performance of the company. (It is, of course, vitally important that the business does not run out of money while it waits for the long-term success of its competitive strategy!)

It is also important that individual parts of the business are set appropriately coordinated targets, so as to ensure goal congruence across the business. This is especially true for the sales and marketing area and yet this is often where simplistic, financial measures of performance are still applied. If sales managers are given performance targets expressed exclusively in terms of sales revenue or, even worse, sales volumes for a particular period, they cannot be expected to be overly concerned with either the profitability of these sales or, more importantly, the long term development of these customer relationships.

SEGMENT PROFITABILITY ANALYSIS

Solving these problems requires the development of appropriately tailored management accounting performance measures and reports. As with all strategic management accounting issues, the main emphasis must be in helping with the strategic decision process. This means that the information provided must be relevant to strategic decisions and the performance measures should be equally relevant.

This creates major problems for most traditionally oriented management accounting systems as they are based on the sophisticated apportionment of the actual, historic costs incurred by the organisation. The relevant costs for future strategic decisions are, of course, not the apportioned historic, actual costs but the direct incremental or avoidable costs (ie the attributable costs) which will be affected by the decision. Unfortunately, the highly complex recharging and apportionment systems in use in many very large companies make it very difficult to identify the true, direct costs involved. Most apportionment systems are designed to ensure that all of the actual cost is spread across the various categories or business segments.

Such a process can lead to management accounting analyses which look incredibly neat but which are completely useless in terms of decision making. This is particularly true where segment profitability analysis is concerned. It is very important for any company to understand where it makes its super profits and this can be highlighted by an appropriately designed segment profitability analysis. Segmented analysis within a business can be done in various ways: by customer, by product, by brand, by competitor, and at various levels or by sub-groupings, or even by a combination of these categories. The objective must be remembered and this is to aid decision making; thus the relevant costs must be charged to the segments, depending upon how they will change as the levels of activity change. The ways in which the major costs change should also dictate the way the segmentation is done.

Unfortunately this relationship differs for many costs across the different segmentation categories. Thus a cost which is direct to specific customer segments (such as sales force costs) will be indirect to particular products if the sales force sells a wide range of products to each customer. Similarly advertising costs may be directly attributable to specific products but indirect to any customer segmentation. This can create severe problems if a one-dimensional analysis (ie a customer or product-based segmentation) is subsequently used as part of a differently focused segmentation analysis. A common example would be using a product profitability analysis as the basis for a subsequent customer account profitability analysis; this is often done by simply computing the total apparent profitability generated by the specific mix of products sold to each customer grouping.

Each segmentation analysis must be produced from the correct analysis of its direct associated costs and an appropriately based apportionment of the attributable shared costs. No segmentation analysis should ever attempt to measure and report the 'net profit' earned by customers or products. Yet some companies not only attempt to do this on a one-dimensional basis but also produce a net profit apportionment by both product and customer in a single matrix. As shown in Figure 6.1, it is incredibly neat (all revenues and costs are included so that both sides of the matrix total the net profit of the business) and completely useless!

£000's		INDIVIDUAL CUSTOMERS XYZ						"Y" Product's Total Profit
			6					
I N D I V I D U A L	ABC	6	4	10	5	15	20	60
	P		5					
	R		4					
	O D		16					
	U		15					
	C T		9					
L			11					
"X"	Customer's Total Profit		70					Business Total Profit

Note: All costs are spread to a specific product and a specific customer, so that every customer's total profit (Row X) is split across each of the individual products. Similarly each product's total profit (Column Y) is spread to individual customers. This means that the sum of all the customer's individual profits will equal the sum of all the products' individual profits and both will equal the business' total profits.

Comment: Very neat and completely useless!!

Figure 6.1 The 'ultimate neat' segment profitability analysis

The appropriate decision-based level of analysis clearly depends on the type of decision which is being faced. This requires that the strategic management accounting system is flexible enough to respond to the different needs of the strategic marketing decisions facing the company. In reality, marketing decisions can be characterised generically as entry decisions (which include expansion decisions) and exit decisions (which include reduction decisions); thus the required financial costing information is, respectively, incremental and avoidable costs, as stated above.

However, these entry and exit decisions may relate to products or customers (eg closing down a particular product or starting to deal with a specific new customer), but where the decision does not impact the other dimension in the same way. Thus, exiting from one product may well mean that the company is still servicing all its existing customers. This re-emphasises the point that each different type of segmented profitability analysis has to be compiled from scratch. This has severe workload and resourcing implications in the management accounting area, unless careful thought goes into the design of the accounting coding and information system.

This issue of developing appropriate segment profitability reports highlights some of the problems encountered in trying to measure the true financial impact of marketing strategies. The following sections consider the individual marketing segmentations into brands, customers and products. There are many other issues relating to the measurement of the profitability of marketing which have been considered for many years but which space does not allow to be discussed here; for coverage of some of these areas, see Feder, 1965; Simon, 1969; Christopher, 1977; Ward, 1989; Foster and Gupta, 1994.

Brand-led Strategies

Brands are, for many companies, the key source of sustainable competitive advantage in that they are what enables the company to achieve the super profits which create shareholder value. The focus of the company will therefore be on the management of these brands and this *must* extend to the focus of the management accounting system. Yet, disappointingly, even in many highly brand oriented businesses, the management accounting system provides virtually no relevant financial evaluation or control information.

In fact the major area of discussion, with regard to brands, among professional accountants in recent years has been whether to put brand values on the balance sheet of the company in its published financial statements (see Barwise et al, 1989, Murphy et al, 1989, and Kato Communications, 1993). The brand values considered to be included as 'assets' of the business only included those brands which had been purchased rather than those which had been developed internally. This incredibly sterile and academic debate missed the key point that it is the internal, strategic decision oriented accounting for brands, whether organically developed or purchased, which is important.

Companies need to be able financially to evaluate proposed marketing expenditures on brands in advance and then to control the effectiveness of the actual expenditure, as well as the efficiency of implementation, eg how well the media buying was carried out in terms of cost per opportunity to see. This needs a very close relationship between the marketing and management accounting areas which is based on mutual respect and trust, so that both areas believe that the other is genuinely trying to enhance shareholder value through their activities. This is not achieved if, as is the case in many companies, the marketing budget is seen as the easiest area to reduce when the short-term profit target is under threat. Management accounting should be seen as a way for the marketing budget to be optimised, not reduced. Conversely the arrogant attitude within some marketing departments that they should never be required to justify their marketing spending ('we *need* to spend this much to support the brand') is hardly conducive to mutual respect and trust.

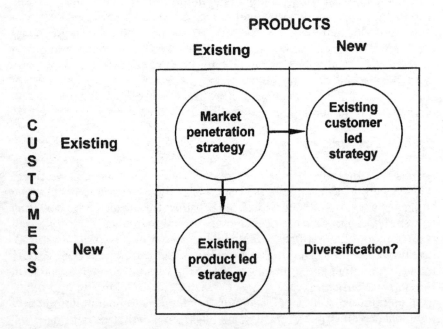

Figure 6.2 Potential strategic thrusts of businesses
(based on Ansoff matrix)

The reasons for considering brand-led strategies before the other types of segmentation are that brands illustrate most of the main problems encountered in accounting for marketing, and also that brands can be critical elements in both product-led and customer-led strategies. As shown in Figure 6.2, which was also used in Chapter 5, companies can attempt to grow by selling new products to existing customers or by selling existing products to new customers. The existing product-led strategy can be very successfully based around a branded product which is launched into new markets (such as Coca-Cola, Marlboro, McDonald's, etc). Equally, the existing customer-led strategy can be built around a brand, but this type of brand must have different attributes. A successful customer oriented brand creates a willingness by the customer to try the new products which are launched under the brand umbrella; good examples of such customer focused brands are retailer brands, such as Marks & Spencer.

In order to have future value to the business (ie to be considered an intangible asset), any brand must have developed identifiable brand attributes. Building these brand attributes requires a strategy, marketing skill, time, consistency and considerable financial investment. Thus, any brand-led strategy needs brand development expenditure to be considered as a long-term investment. This means that marketing budgets should be split between development and maintenance expenditure, as would be the case for expenditure on any of the significant tangible assets of the company. (All types of marketing assets, not just brands, require development and maintenance expenditures.)

Development expenditure seeks to increase the level of the brand attributes and accordingly should be financially justified over the life of these improved attributes. These brand building issues have been very well researched by marketing academics and professional managers; hence they are now well understood and specific marketing activities are aimed at particular brand development objectives. The gap is that these marketing evaluations are not translated into financial evaluations in most cases. Thus the marketing department may have carefully evaluated that by spending an additional £5 million on television advertising they can improve unprompted brand awareness by 5 per cent; the critical question is whether a 5 per cent improvement in awareness is worth a £5 million investment? There are obviously a significant number of variables which need to be considered in such a financial evaluation, but the important point is that, in many marketing-led companies, the marketing department will have researched most, if not all, of these relationships.

For example, the decay rate in the awareness created by television advertising will probably have been established through tracking studies, the conversion rate of awareness into potential buyers can be monitored through attitudinal surveys, and turning potential buyers into actual purchasers depends on the level and effectiveness of distribution which is normally measured and tested on a regular basis, and so on. Space does not permit a full discussion of the issues relating to brand development but, in any case, this is covered comprehensively in the academic and professional marketing literature (see, for example, Cowley, 1991, and Kapferer, 1992). What is covered much less comprehensively is the financial evaluation of these marketing investments, (Ward et al, 1992).

However, discussion of these topics is by no means a new phenomenon; in 1966, Dean raised the specific question, 'Does advertising belong in the capital budget' and this had already been more generally discussed the previous year by Tarpey (see Dean, 1966 and Tarpey, 1965). From the internal managerial perspective this discussion has not progressed dramatically during the last 30 years, as can be seen from the similarity in many of the points being made in much more recent contributions on the subject (see, for example, Guilding and Pike, 1990).

Also, what academic discussion has taken place has tended to remain at the conceptual level rather than being based on empirical and practical research. Through a number of its in-company research projects, MARC has been able to demonstrate the practicality of linking financial evaluation techniques with the marketing effectiveness measures in use within modern sophisticated marketing departments. Thus comparisons of the effectiveness of alternative marketing mixes of advertising, consumer trial incentives and effective distribution were made on the launch of a consumer product using controlled experiments. The experimental levels selected were chosen by using analyses of previous brand launches.

In another study, alternative brand awareness creation and maintenance strategies were modelled and compared for a highly seasonal product, using existing awareness decay relationships which had been developed empirically by the company. This research compared the financial effectiveness of using regular advertising throughout the year with highly seasonal advertising which was timed to coincide with the seasonal sales peak. Careful design is, of course, needed for these research studies and each one needs to be specifically tailored to a certain degree, but the outcome is to enable the company to base its investment decision on a much more rationally based, financial analysis. Even more valuable is the very steep learning curve which the company progresses along, if the actual results are carefully and appropriately monitored. In other words, the initial model will be wrong, but it can be refined rapidly as the initial results of the research are obtained.

As with any assets, not all of the expenditure on brands can be regarded as development activity. Initially with a new brand, most of the marketing effort obviously goes into developing the brand attributes. However, even when developed, brand attributes will decay unless they are maintained. Thus, over time, an increasing proportion of the marketing expenditure goes on maintaining the brand attributes at their existing levels. A key strategic marketing decision is, therefore, to identify the point at which the law of diminishing returns sets in for incremental development expenditure. As is shown diagrammatically in Figure 6.3, the relationship between development expenditure and brand attributes is not linear, with the result that understanding where the brand is on the curve prior to any new marketing is very important.

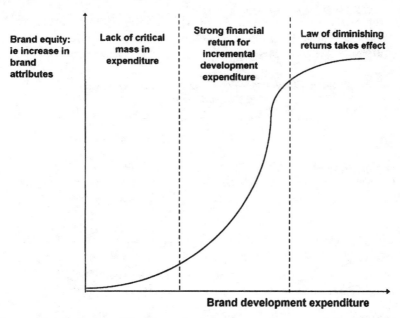

Figure 6.3 Relationship of marketing expenditure and market share

Figure 6.3 also demonstrates that it is quite possible to spend far too little on developing a brand, as well as spending too much. If less than a minimum critical mass of development expenditure is put behind the brand, the likelihood of success is minimal and all the marketing expenditure will be wasted. This critical mass is dependent upon the level of competitive marketing activity as the targeted customer is subject to all the other 'noise' that is taking place in the market at any given time. A simple ratio has been found very useful as a guide to this area (it must be emphasised that 'simple, general ratios' can be dangerous and damaging if they are not applied carefully and intelligently; hence this one is given with a substantial financial health warning!).

The relationship between share of voice (the proportion spent on marketing by one company as a proportion of the total spent in the market by this company and its competitors) and the market share held by the company is, in the absence of evidence to the contrary, a guide to the future development of the brand. Diagramatically the possibilities are shown in Table 6.1 where it becomes clear that, for a development brand, the company should ideally have a ratio (share of voice divided by share of market) of more than 1. If the strategy is simply to try to stand still in terms of market share, a ratio of around 1 may be sufficient. However, if the ratio falls below 1, the company is living off the past investment in the brand attributes and is likely to see a decline in market share over time.

This does not mean that such a strategy is necessarily unsound. It may be a very sensible, deliberate, financially based strategy to reduce the maintenance support of a brand as it reaches the decline stage of its life-cycle. The application of life cycle costing techniques to brands as well as customers and products is considered later in the chapter.

Table 6.1 *Share of voice (SOV) to share of market (SOM) relationship*

Type of	Desired ratio	Marketing strategy
DEVELOPMENT BRAND	$\dfrac{SOV}{SOM} > 1$	Outspending the competition in order to develop the attributes of the brand
MAINTENANCE BRAND	$\dfrac{SOV}{SOM} = 1$	Maintain the brand attributes at their existing level by spending at a similar rate to competition
HARVESTING BRAND	$\dfrac{SOV}{SOM} < 1$	Allowing brand attributes to decline from their existing level by reducing marketing support below the maintenance level

Customer-led Strategies

It has already been stated that brands may be built around products or customers, but customer-led strategies are, of course, not necessarily brand based. The key element of any customer-led strategy is, as is shown in Figure 6.4, that it is based around the existing customers which are regarded as the most important asset of the business. Thus, new products are developed with these existing customers in mind, with the result that it is essential that the business knows which of its customers should form the basis for its future product development strategy.

As discussed in Chapter 5, the key financial basis for selecting the key customers for future investment is an appropriately based customer account profitability analysis. Customer account profitability (CAP) analysis can be defined as 'the total sales revenue generated from a customer

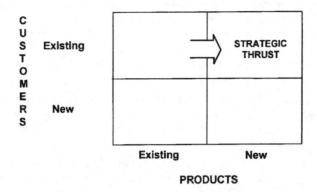

Figure 6.4 Existing customer-led strategies
– maximising value of existing customers

or customer group less all the costs that are incurred in servicing that customer or customer group'. As discussed above, the objective is to demonstrate the relative profitability of different classifications of customers, not
to spread all costs to customers so as to show the net profit of any particular customer.

An immediate impact of introducing any level of segmented financial
analysis into a company is to destroy totally any illusion that the same
level of profit is derived from all customers. Groups of customers or even
different channels of distribution can often be distinguished by the different effective selling prices achieved and variations in the mix of products
purchased. However, these factors may be much less important than the
different levels of costs incurred due to the varying levels of customer service, etc that are supplied. It may well be that the lower selling prices
charged to one such segment are more than justified by the cost savings
which are generated by the way in which these customers are serviced.
Hence these customers may be more profitable, in reality, than those in
areas where the higher selling prices achieved are more than offset by the
increased costs incurred in achieving the sales. If the business is to allo-
cate its limited resources most effectively in the future so as to achieve its
corporate objectives, it must have reliable information on which of its
potential customer groupings are its most profitable and whether there
are any existing areas in which the business actually makes a loss.

This is the major benefit to a business of carrying out CAP analysis and
indicates that, once again, relative comparative performance is much
more important than the absolute profitability levels of individual segments. Thus the financial analysis can concentrate on quantifying the
impact of the differences in the way in which the various customer
groups are dealt with by the business. As previously discussed, it is important that these resource allocation decisions are based on relevant costs.
Neither gross contribution margins, before taking account of different
servicing costs, nor net profit levels, after arbitrarily apportioning commit-

ted shared costs across the different customer groups, are therefore appropriate levels of financial analysis for this purpose.

CAP has become a major area of interest for many companies, particularly due to the increasing focus on customers as 'the most important assets which the company has'. The increasing demands from major customers for individual, tailored treatment in terms of pricing, distribution, sales support, specialised packaging, etc have accelerated the need for more accurate financial evaluations of the impact of these potential changes in competitive strategies.

It is also important that the financial analysis ensures that increasing sales to these existing customers will enhance the long-term profitability of the business. The logic of such a marketing strategy is that it is more cost-effective to build on the established loyalty of these existing customers, rather than to try to develop new markets in which to sell the existing product range. Clearly the comparative competitor analysis of related strengths should have indicated which strategy was most appropriate for the particular business.

However, this customer asset-based strategy must not be seen as risk free, even though the effective intangible asset turnover ratio is being improved as well as potentially enhancing the profit margin level through better absorption of existing fixed costs. If the new products are not well accepted by these vitally important existing customers, there is an obvious danger of a rebound effect on the sales levels of existing products. This risk needs to be taken into account when financially evaluating the benefits of such an integrated marketing strategy; it also helps to explain why some leading marketing-orientated companies insist that all their products are separately and independently branded, despite the loss of economies of scale and synergy benefits in their advertising.

When implementing a system of CAP, the business must highlight the differences in costs between two categories of customer, but the relevant size of the difference may change depending on the strategic decision under consideration. An example using sales-force costs may make this clearer. One category of customer may be considering doing away with the services of the field sales-force of its suppliers and is seeking to negotiate an appropriate discount to reflect the prospective savings to be made by the suppliers. From the supplier's perspective, the potential discount should reflect the avoidable cost of the sales-force which will be saved if the change is made. However, this avoidable cost will not normally be the same as the historic actual cost which may have been apportioned to this particular customer, as this will include some shared costs (such as sales managers) who will not change if only this customer stops using these support services. Clearly the CAP analysis must reflect increasing levels of attributable cost as the customer groupings are made more general; thus if a change is made for the whole of the distribution channel, the savings might be much greater. Also the potential cost saving may not be equal to the potential incremental cost which would be incurred if a single customer or group of customers wanted to start using the services of the field sales-force.

Unfortunately if segment profitability analysis is to be of maximum value as a decision support tool, it must be tailored to the needs of each category of decision, as was emphasised earlier in the chapter.

There has been a lot of detailed discussion of customer account profitability analysis techniques in the academic literature: for examples, see Day *et al*, 1979; Hill and Harland, 1983; Ward and Anandarajan, 1989.

Product-led strategies

Product costing has been a mainstay of management accounting for many years and many companies have developed very complex cost apportionment systems in this area. However, even for many of these apparently financially sophisticated businesses, the concept of applying an externally focused, strategic decision-based analysis to relative product profitabilities is still new and, in some sectors of industry, is as yet not widely in use. Most existing product costing systems are oriented around production technology or some other product attributes, rather than being designed from the perspective of the external marketplace and the competitive strategy of the business. Thus accounting systems often emphasise the impact of sales volumes by assuming a linear relationship between volume and product profitability. This clearly is an invalid assumption in the long-term, when all costs must be regarded as variable (see Day, 1986, for a good application of pricing strategies in an experience curve environment), but it is also unrealistic to assume that, in the short-term, sales volumes can be increased without altering the effective contribution per unit achieved on product sales. The classical profit/volume straight line graph becomes a complex set of curves when trying to assess the financial impact of alternative product-based marketing strategies.

This financial analysis of relative product profitabilities is obviously of critical importance to those businesses which have as their main strategic thrust the development of new markets in which to sell their existing products, as shown in Figure 6.5. Instead of their major strengths being based on loyal customers, these businesses have a relative competitive advantage in their existing products, and this should form the basis for their future competitive strategy. In many cases, this strength is embodied in the well-established branding of the particular product attributes and the proposed marketing strategy is to exploit this brand in other markets and with other new customers. Once again, the basis of this competitive strategy should be financially analysed to ensure both that the relative product profitability of the core brand is sufficiently strong to justify its further development and that the proposed developments into new markets will improve, rather than dissipate, this existing level of profitability.

Not surprisingly, therefore, the early developments in systems for deci-

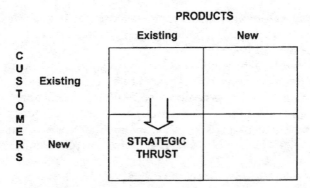

Figure 6.5 Existing product-led strategies
– maximising the value of existing products

sion-based product profitability analysis were driven by such strongly product-orientated and highly branded companies. These companies, of which Procter and Gamble (P&G) was the leader, wanted to use the analysis as a major strategic marketing tool in order to expand both their customer base and their share of the existing customer base. This strategy was based on preparing the product profitability analysis, not from the traditionally inwardly focused perspective, but from the point of view of their customers. P&G's products are principally sold through retailers (ie an intermediary channel of distribution) which are mainly concerned with the relative financial performance of the alternative products which they are asked to stock in their stores. The selling space in the stores is clearly limited and thus constitutes a critical limiting factor on which to base the relative product contribution analysis. The strategic objective of the companies introducing this innovative use of product profitability analyses was to show that their products made a relatively high rate of profit contribution when expressed in terms of the customers' limiting factor (the retail selling space in the current example). This would be particularly helpful for products which, on a more superficial financial comparison, appeared less attractive than rivals for the limited shelf space; high unit volume products with relatively low unit selling prices, such as toilet rolls and washing powders, would fit into this category. By including the higher rate of sale of these products, it was possible to show that they made a perfectly acceptable overall contribution for the space which they occupied.

The financial analysis was made more sophisticated by including other differences in relative costs across the various product categories. Thus specific financial allowances were made for ease or difficulty of ordering, delivery, handling, storage, display in-store, and the period of credit granted to the retailer, as well as the more obvious marketing promotional offers made by the suppliers. Clearly such a financial analysis focuses on relative contribution levels per unit of limiting factor and this makes the process considerably more practical.

When it was introduced, this type of direct product profitability (DPP), as it has become known, had a significant impact and it was quickly picked up and applied by the retailers themselves, using their in-depth internal knowledge of the operational cost differences among the products. It has also been applied as a positive marketing tool in many other areas of business (it has particular application where an intermediary channel of distribution is involved) and is now available in a range of tailored computer software application packages.

Indeed many companies are now linking DPP analysis and CAP analysis in order to devise financially justified, specifically tailored marketing strategies for individual customer groups purchasing a range of products. These applications indicate the potential added value which can be generated by a sound strategic application of segmented financial analysis in the area of accounting for marketing strategies.

LIFE-CYCLE ANALYTICAL TECHNIQUES

Any sound competitive strategy seeks to develop *sustainable* competitive advantages which can generate an ongoing, defendable level of super profits. This means that any focused segmentation strategy, whether based on brands, customers or products, should not consider only the short-term relative profit contributions from the different segments. The much more important concept is the long-term differences in returns which are produced by these classifications and groupings.

Thus there is a need for life-cycle profitability analyses of products, brands and customers. Life-cycle analyses take into account all the relevant cash flows over the entire economic life of the segment, rather than just concentrating on the current period. This should, of course, enable valid financial comparisons to be made across, for example, products which are at very different stages of their life-cycles. If a single period comparison was used, the newly launched product would look financially unattractive and might be closed down or starved of essential development funding.

The application of life-cycle analytical techniques should therefore assist in concentrating resources on those segments where the greatest, long-term financial returns can be generated. This concept is well developed in terms of its application to products and has been very proactively applied in some industries in the pricing strategies used by product focused companies (see Day, 1986).

However, the idea of life-cycle financial analyses are less generally applied in the areas of brands and customers. Some marketing managers still argue that brands do not have life-cycles, but the critical brand attributes do decay eventually and need refurbishment, refreshment or complete replacement. Thus, it is important that senior managers are provided with a long term financial evaluation which indicates when such a change in the brand marketing strategy is required (see Ward et al, 1989).

Where the life-cycle concept is rapidly gaining ground is with reference to customers, because it is fundamental to the increasingly common strategic thrust known commonly as relationship marketing, (see Christopher et al, 1991). Relationship marketing focuses on the customer as the key long term source of super profits to the business but acknowledges that the development of such a long term relationship requires an initial investment by the seller.

Thus there is no attempt to generate a super profit rate of return in the early periods while the relationship is being launched and developed. Indeed there may quite deliberately be a negative return generated due to the high costs involved in acquiring new customers. There may also be a low rate of return generated as the company increases its proportion of the customer's business; this is due to the reinvestment in building the relationship.

Once a relationship enters its maintenance/maturity stage when the company has a significant share of the customer's available business, it is important that an attractively high financial return is achieved. This is clearly necessary to justify the initial investments which have been made in acquiring and developing the relationship with the customer. However, the challenge is that this increase in profitability must be generated without jeopardising the long-term relationship with the customer. This is quite probable if the higher profits are generated by increasing selling prices to these well-established customers. Such a strategy would also attract other potential suppliers (ie competitors) to this customer as the potential profitability has been enhanced.

A much more logical competitive strategy is to increase the entry barriers facing potential competitors rather than reducing them through price increases. If a good long-term relationship has been developed, customer and supplier should now be doing business in a mutually efficient and cost-effective way. Thus there should be cost savings generated in the way this long-term customer is serviced relative to a newly acquired customer.

The significant management accounting challenge is to calculate these savings so that they can be *shared* with the long-term customer; such a mutually beneficial approach builds a partnership with the customer as well as creating another financial entry barrier to competitors. A long-term approach to customer account profitability analysis should also indicate which categories of customer are likely to be suitable for such a relationship marketing strategy. It is impossible to develop this type of long-term profitable relationship with customers which will always buy on price and do not place a financial value on extra service levels; the logical strategy is to be the cheapest. This requires the company to be the *lowest-cost* supplier if it is to generate a super profit from such customers. As stated throughout this section of the book, marketing strategies must be tailored to the demands of the market segment which is being addressed.

COMPETITOR ACCOUNTING AND ANALYSIS

Strategic management has already been stated as being interested in creating a sustainable competitive advantage and this can clearly only be created by direct comparison to competitors. This comparison should be as precise and as clearly identified as is practical. Therefore, the business must conduct detailed relative financial evaluations of its major competitors. In any such competitor accounting analysis, relative costs and prices are much more important than the absolute levels. This is of considerable assistance as it should be much easier to build up a picture of the relative cost structure of these competitors by using the knowledge of all the appropriate managers within the business and the wide range of potential external sources. Thus competitor accounting should not be seen as the exclusive preserve of the accounting department, but neither should it focus exclusively on relative cost comparisons. The competitor's marketing strategy must be understood and factored into the analysis – for example, if its product positioning is one of very high quality and this enables it to command a substantial price premium in the market due to the high value perceived by customers, the relative cost comparison is likely to indicate an apparent but irrelevant cost disadvantage.

The process for undertaking a competitor accounting analysis is fairly straightforward. The existing and current competition should be identified by reference to the strategic objectives of the business unit, but it is important to include other companies which satisfy similar customer needs, even if in very different ways. In other words, this stage should be done from the perspective of the targeted customers by considering which other businesses they would consider as alternative suppliers.

The most important element in the competitor analysis now is to consider what alternative competitive strategies could be implemented by each of these identified competitors. This strategic analysis clearly requires an assessment of their relative cost positions and customer value propositions, but it must also include their commitment to this particular business segment and its importance to their overall business. This should indicate their likely response both to changes in the external environment and to any possible new strategic competitive initiatives.

Clearly for many companies it is very difficult even to measure the historic level of competitors' costs, particularly when these competitors are part of very large diversified businesses which only publish overall financial results for the group. However, by using a combination of externally published figures and deductive reasoning from both direct observation and a whole series of indirect sources, such as are indicated in Figure 6.6, it is normally possible to build up a reasonable picture of the major differences in cost between the competitor and the originating business. It is important to remember that none of these analytical forecasting methods can ever produce a precisely accurate result, and an absolute snapshot of the competitor's cost level is not the objective. Consistent application of the technique on a regular basis will start to show up the trend in relative cost levels, and this can be of great value in selecting the most appropriate competitive strategy in the future.

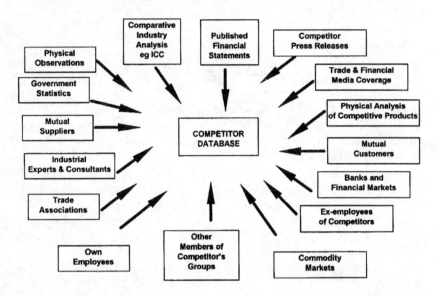

Figure 6.6 Sources of competitor information

It is not necessary also even to develop a complete cost picture in some cases, as the key relative items can be defined by the stage of development of the products and markets in which the businesses compete, as was discussed in more detail in Chapter 5. If the product is very new in the market and the market development is not yet guaranteed, a key competitive issue may be the relative strengths of the research and development teams. The relative levels of expenditure on R&D can be assessed by building up an estimate of competitive spending, if by no other means than using the size of their physical facilities and applying a normal level of space allocation per person, etc.

Where there is a high growth market, the critical competitive factor will often be growth in market share and this can be monitored over time. Forecasts can be generated by reference to estimates of relative levels of marketing expenditure, and these relationships can be tested over time and the models updated. As always, it is important to take account of possible differences in strategic thrusts for particular competitors. It is normally prudent to carry out a particularly careful review for any competitor which appears to be implementing a competitive strategy which is directly contrary to everyone else in the market – perhaps they have got it right! When the market matures and the rate of growth declines rapidly, it is quite common for price competition to become much more important. Consequently in this environment relative cost comparisons become particularly important and quite small, but sustainable, differences can make significant differences to the financial success of the mature business.

However, once again allowance must be made for competitors which successfully maintain their premium pricing strategy during this maturity phase. If their market share is retained, their customers must place an even higher premium value on their enhanced product attributes. It is important to try to assess if any cost penalty being incurred by this competitor more than offsets the pricing premium obtained in the market.

This information can be of value in assessing possible future opportunities for, and threats to, the competitive strategy of the business. It must be remembered that this is the main objective of competitor financial analysis. This should focus the analytical effort on areas which can add value to future competitive strategy decisions, rather than merely improve the detailed accuracy of the relative cost assessment for a particular competitor if the existing level of accuracy is satisfactory.

CONCLUSION

The decision focus of competitor accounting and analysis is of critical importance to all aspects of marketing accounting. The objective is to develop an appropriately tailored system of management accounting information which aids marketing managers in their major decisions. This necessitates a consideration of how the required financial information should be presented to the decision makers. Far too often, the financial function still presents its financial analyses in ways which render it almost incomprehensible to the proposed users. The marketing accounting system must provide readily accessible, user friendly, information rather than comprehensive but unintelligible, financial data; this issue is discussed in detail in Harrison, 1979, and Meldrum, et al, 1987.

References

Barwise, P, Higson, C, Likierman, A, and Marsh, P (1989) *Accounting for Brands*, London Business School and The Institute of Chartered Accountants in England and Wales.

Christopher, W F (1977) 'Marketing achievement reporting: a profitability approach', *Industrial Marketing Management*, Vol 6, pp 149–162.

Christopher, M, Payne, A, and Ballantyne, D (1991) *Relationship Marketing*, Butterworth Heinemann, Oxford.

Cowley, D (ed) (1991) *Understanding Brands*, Kogan Page, London.

Day G S (1986) *Analysis for Strategic Market Decisions*, West, St Paul, Minnesota.

Day, G S, Scocher A. D, and Srivastara, R K, (1979), 'Customer Oriented Approaches to identifying product markets', *Journal of Marketing,* Fall, Vol. 43.

Dean, J (1966) 'Does Advertising Belong in the Capital Budget?', *Journal of Marketing,* October, Vol 30, pp 15–21.

Feder, R A (1965) 'How to measure marketing performance', *Harvard Business Review,* May.

Foster, G and Gupta, M (1994) 'Marketing, cost management and management accounting, *Journal of Management Accounting Research,* Autumn.

Guilding, C and Pike, R (1990) 'Intangible Marketing Assets: A Managerial Accounting Perspective', *Accounting and Business Research*, Vol 21, No 18, pp 41–49.

Harrison, G L (1979) 'The Accounting/Marketing Interface – A Marketing Perspective', *The Australian Accountant,* August.

Hill, G and Harland, D A (1983) 'The Customer Profit-Centre', *The Journal of the Institute of Physical Distribution Management*, Vol 2, No 2, May/June.

Kapferer, J N (1992) *Strategic Brand Management*, Kogan Page, London.

Kaplan, R S and Norton, D P (1992) 'The Balanced Scorecard – Measures that Drive Performance', *Harvard Business Review*, January/February.

Kaplan, R S and Norton, D P (1993) 'Putting the Balanced Scorecard to Work', *Harvard Business Review*, September/October.

Kato Communications (1993) 'Accounting for Brands', *Financial Times Management Reports.*

Meldrum, M, Ward, K and Srikanthan, S (1987) 'Needs, Issues and Directions in the Marketing Accountancy Divide', *Quarterly Review of Marketing*, Spring/Summer.

Murphy, J ed (1989) *Brand Valuation – Establishing a True and Fair View*, Hutchinson, London.

Simon, S R (1969) *Managing Marketing Profitability,* American Management Association.

Tarpey, L X (1965) 'Advertising Theory and the Capital Budgeting Model', *Business Horizons*, Summer, pp 87–93.

Ward, K (1989) *Financial Aspects of Marketing*, Butterworth Heinemann, Oxford.

Ward, K Srikanthan, S and Neal, R (1989) 'Life-Cycle Costing in the Financial Evaluation and Control of Brands', *Quarterly Review of Marketing*, Autumn.

Ward, K and Anandarajan, A (1989) 'Customer Profitability Analysis: A New Perspective', Cranfield School of Management Working Paper Series, SWP52/89.

Ward, K, Srikanthan, S and Neal, R (1992) 'Marketing Investment Analysis: The Critical Success Factors for Financially Evaluating and Effectively Controlling Marketing Investment Decisions', Cranfield School of Management Working Paper Series, SWP 7/91.

Part Four

STRATEGIC VALUE MANAGEMENT

HOW COMPANIES CAN AVOID DESTROYING SHAREHOLDER VALUE

Tony Grundy

INTRODUCTION

Although many companies espouse the need to create shareholder value, management often conspire to destroy it rather than to create it. Shareholder value is destroyed in a variety of ways – through pursuit of strategic goals without adequate financial testing, through incremental increase in business complexity and through lower organic and acquisitive investment. It is also destroyed by managing costs which have longer-term benefits being managed with a myopic one-year budget focus. These costs are, in effect, quasi-investment decisions and should thus be managed as such (see Grundy, 1992).

The box below identifies no less than eight key areas where shareholder value is destroyed internally by management. These range from longer-term issues such as mission, creeping complexity and organic and acquisitive investment through to what appears to be shorter-term issues such as cost management and change management.

In the first part of this chapter we focus on each of these areas where value is destroyed. In the second part we examine how managers can avoid destroying shareholder value by managing value more strategically.

The second part explores a detailed framework of the links between shareholder value, corporate-level and business-level strategy and strategic investment decisions and strategic cost programmes. This part dovetails into a conceptual framework and management practice. This provides managers with a means of diagnosing their problems in linking shareholder value with strategic and financial planning.

Some key areas where shareholder value is destroyed

1 Mission and objectives-driven strategy (without adequate competitive analysis).

2 Creeping business complexity (products, markets, distribution, technology, services).

3 Tactical pricing (price wars, lower margins).

4 Business investment decisions.

5 Acquisitions (poor criteria, over-bidding, ineffective integration).

6 Cost management (last year's budget plus or minus x percent).

7 Change management (restructuring, quality, culture, process simplification).

8 Product brand and technology development.

EASY WAYS OF DESTROYING SHAREHOLDER VALUE

Mission and objectives-driven strategies

Although many writers (for example, Campbell and Tawadey, 1990) extol the benefits of having a mission, this can easily misdirect management. Invariably, the 'mission' is stretching and may often be unrealistic, yet it may still exert a powerful influence over strategic and more tactical thinking.

One example of this is the well-documented case of Dowty Communications (Grundy, 1993, and Grundy, 1994). Senior management of a telecommunications business (turnover over £100m) began a strategic review by setting a mission for (rapid) profitable growth (to be achieved by international expansion largely via existing product range). During the strategic review it became apparent that the current competitive position of the company was not as strong as was previously thought. This position provided an inadequate platform to achieve the stretching mission (and associated financial objectives).

Yet this mission continued to send the wrong signals to management during crucial stages of the strategic review. It was only by a thorough analysis of the external competitive position and of internal capability that the plan for major international expansion was arrested.

In order to avoid a mission and objectives-driven strategy, we would suggest that:

- Some analysis is undertaken of the organisation's internal capabilities before formulating a mission (or indeed a 'vision').
- It is often more advisable to work upwards to a mission, based on thoroughly analysed competitive strategy rather than formulate strategy top-down, based on a pre-set mission.
- 'The mission' should be coupled with analysis of 'the industry' which it suggests that the company should have a major position in. What makes management think that being in that particular industry (and markets) will generate adequate returns to shareholders? How is this view founded on (sustainable) industry attractiveness? If not, then what makes managers think the company has an objectively strong (and probably dominant), sustainable competitive position?

Unless managers are prepared to undergo the rigour of these tests, mission and objectives-driven strategy are likely to result in a Star-Trek-like journey to 'Explore new worlds, to boldly go where no man has gone before'. However, unlike the heroic Star Ship Enterprise crew, in the actual world of business, corporate missions are likely to founder on harsh competitive realities, destroying value through misguided decisions.

Creeping business complexity

Strategic management theory is not, as many managers believe, a single, consistent whole. On the one hand, the design school of strategy preaches that strategic analysis and choice should be pursued rationally and analytically as a systematic process. On the other hand, incrementalists highlight that strategy emerges, sometimes as a haphazard process. The approach which we take in managing – by design or incrementally – does have implications for how shareholder value is destroyed in business practice.

While the design school of strategies battle it out with the incrementalists and exponents of emergent strategy, managers are busy destroying value through creeping business complexity. While some may argue that Porter's competitive strategies are over-prescriptive and somewhat simplistic (see Grundy, 1994), Porter rightly stressed the need for a) coherent strategic analysis and b) the need to make explicit choices on how to create superior value through a particular competitive strategy. Yes, explicit choices about 'how we are going to compete' and sometimes even 'where we are going to compete' seem to be almost a rarity in practice.

Also, many businesses have still to generate even 'working notions' (or hypotheses) of 'what business we are in'. Strategic development decisions are then justified purely on a marginal and incremental basis. The effect on areas elsewhere in the business system are then peripheral and neglected.

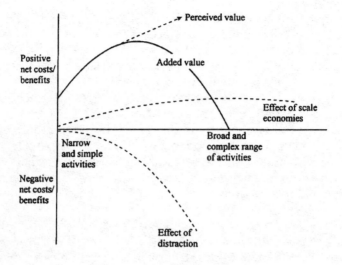

Figure 7.1 Schematic analysis of cost/benefits of narrow versus broad and complex activities

Yet Figure 7.1 highlights how increasing complexity may begin to destroy value. That complexity begins to overreach the capability of the organisation to make and manage choices, and also the learning capability of senior managers. Much of this value is destroyed by the costs of distraction – if you are pursuing 101 product/market segments, you can be forever switching your attention from one to the other and back again. This can generate additional costs and risks each time the managers change their attention, trying to make the organisation respond flexibly. Alternatively, the organisation remains rigid, set in its operational recipes of 'how to do things', again destroying value.

In a thousand different ways, business strategy can become more and more complex. This can result (as in the Dowty Communications case) not only in a need for business process re-engineering but also in the need for subsequent strategy redesign and business simplification.

What we are arguing runs against still fashionable notions of managing strategic and financial synergies. Figure 7.1 challenges notions of easy harvesting of synergies (very much along the lines of Porter's 'horizontal strategy' which tries to extract value between businesses in the same group). Unless synergies are reasonably simple, then the difficulty of managing them will easily surpass any benefits accruing.

The key lessons for practice in avoiding creeping business complexity are the need for managers:

- To subject any new business opportunity to a 'strategic screen' – probing it for the attractiveness of the market or niche, its likely competitive position, implementation capability and financial scale and attractiveness.
- To help focus managers on making a few larger-scale projects work effectively, rather than to seek to diversify risk through lots of smaller projects.
- To revisit continually 'the business(es)' we are in and in particular to define the kinds of business we are *not* in. (The most valuable part of strategic and financial choice is often to be able to say 'no' to certain kinds of opportunity.)
- To map (by drawing up a matrix of products against markets against customer groups, markets (or customer groups) against distribution channels, and also products with enabling technologies) the complexity of the business (see Figure 7.2). This highlights just how diverse and thinly spread the business is threatening to (or has) become.

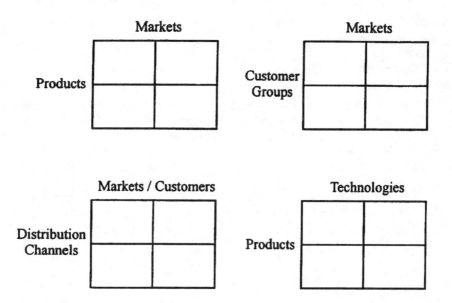

Figure 7.2 Analysing business compexity on four channels

But the toughest job is that of the top team saying 'no' to business opportunity which may seem tactically attractive but which may result in diversion, distraction and value destruction.

Tactical pricing

Tactical pricing is another way of destroying value through making decisions which may make short-term financial sense but no sense longer term. We need look no further than the retail industry to look at the perils of tactical pricing. During the UK recession, Do-It-Yourself (DIY) stores began a price war which ended up in major financial losses for several key players. Instead of any particular player gaining market share, the result was that the market became slightly more attractive to the customers through lowering prices.

The market share game is also being played with vigour in the UK supermarket trade. In mid/late 1993 in the UK the first shots of significant discounting have been fired – with Tesco and J. Sainsbury in mutual combat against each other and the discount chains, like Aldi and Cosco. Presumably the hope is that lower prices on basic lines will deter switching by customers at the same time as increasing barriers to entry. Although this lowering of price might be essential to maintain existing market position, one may speculate about the *sustainability* of this move.

Lessons on tactical pricing are:

- When considering lower pricing this must be looked at as just one of the options to meet the strategic objective of protecting or growing (profitable) market share. Other options might include: market repositioning, and enhancing customer service in ways which are known to add perceived and real value.
- Decisions to make major adjustments in price should take into account likely competitor reactions, within an interactive game played out over time. This involves working through a series of possible competitive moves – and not just as a single, one-off mechanical response. (A useful vehicle for teasing out possible reactions is to construct a 'competitive scenario' where a number of managers, armed with key data on competitors, then formulate possible intent in an informal, game-like situation. This does not have to be over-structured and can be done effectively within a workshop environment.)
- Where price reductions are contemplated, will they be big enough to secure the necessary shift in industry structure and behaviour and in competitive position? The reduction in price of *The Times* newspaper in the UK from 45p to 30p a day was sufficiently large to encourage a substantial increase in share and also in absolute circulation (but it could easily have been otherwise).

- In some cases, it may be appropriate (but counter-intuitive) to let go of market share which is less profitable or becoming increasingly difficult to defend. This runs against the heroic self-image of many management teams to fight to the death for the business they have created. However, it is just this ill-founded heroism which may destroy corporate value in the long run.

Business investment decisions

Despite the wealth of prescriptive theory on capital and related investment decisions, management practices in general are often fragmented with weak integration of financial and strategic appraisal (Barwise et al, 1988, and Grundy, 1993). This may lead to inappropriate strategic investment decisions being made.

To illustrate some of the problems posed by business investment decisions, let us consider the pitfalls of investing in a growth strategy. There is often a tendency among managers to assume that growth equates with value added. For instance, Simon Woolley, Head of Corporate Planning at BP Chemicals, relates how value based management was used at BP to counter the (implicit) mind-set that business growth was a good objective in its own right:

> Where you applied value based management (VBM) there were always surprises. For example, I was sitting with one BP manager and we were looking at a model of his business which represented his future profitability and cash flows from operations and key assumptions about the market. The manager explained that it was easy to generate additional value through business growth as profitability was increased.
>
> But we then played a 'what-if' scenario which increased the growth rate of part of the business using a cash flow model of the business' operations. The manager was shocked when the net present value (NPV) of the business strategy *actually went down.* This was because the 'growth' was not 'profitable growth' in value-based terms; although it was apparently profitable on an accounting basis, once an allowance for the time value of money had been made and particularly adjustment for additional working capital, it was not. This taught us a lot about the business as it not only raised questions about incremental value creation but also about the quality of opportunity facing this business and its competitive position.

Simon Woolley's account is by no means exceptional. In this case managers were able to link explicitly the appraisal of a growth strategy to the financial appraisal with its discounted cash flows supported by both operational *and* competitive assumptions. BP has invested for a number of years in value-based management to integrate its strategic and financial planning processes. But few managers elsewhere appear to have the tools and the time to do this in practice.

Another positive example of where value analysis techniques can become better integrated with strategic analysis is explored by Simon Hart, Corporate Planning Manager of Rolls-Royce Aeroengines:

> I like the concept of valuing a bit of business, not just a project. I mean a whole operating unit, and be able to say, what's the kind of strategy we are into, what is it worth?

> So what I did was plot what the project does, the NPV of the first five years against the NPV over the next five years [see Figure 7.3]. . . Obviously the older projects have got a pretty high NPV. I found it quite helpful, seeing whether the share price stacked up against the value of the projects. It was really a way to communicate to our own management the value of projects . . .It was quite a convenient shorthand way of marrying, certainly our corporate plan, with the underlying value of the strategy. The value of the strategy is this, plus that, plus that, plus all of those over the life. If it doesn't match up [with the share price] then we've got a problem; someone else can come in and pay more for it.

In Figure 7.3 the key projects which underpin a business strategy can be positioned according to whether their NPVs are positive or negative, and relative to their short- versus longer-term contribution to shareholder value. For Rolls-Royce Aeroengines, 'longer term' is over five years. In other businesses with shorter investment life-cycles, a split of three years for short term and over three years might be more appropriate.

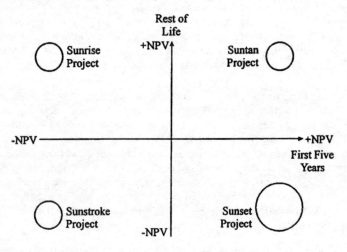

NOTE *This picture is indebted to Simon Hart, Corporate Planning Manager, Rolls Royce Aeroengines.*

Figure 7.3 Trading off long-term against short-term value

This tool for analysing value created can also be used by group to consider corporate investment decisions. The tool can be used as a stimulus to debate about whether projects really deliver assumed shareholder value. But a much simpler and more practical use is that it enables a Board of Directors to reflect on why its future projected cash flows look as they do. For instance, there may be a number of projects which we call 'sunrise' (top left) which are being fed surplus value (for the time being) by sunset projects (bottom right).

The grid also highlights the obvious benefits of having 'suntan projects' – in the top right-hand corner, where net present value is generated both during the first five years and over the rest of life. Often there is merit in investing to protect suntan projects rather than milking these to fund sunrise projects. Unless these sunrise projects are well thought through, they soon become sunstroke projects (bottom left).

Turning now to the business level, investment decisions can destroy shareholder value in a variety of ways, for instance:

- Synergies are assumed but are not fully thought through in terms of when, under what conditions and how these will be harvested.
- Less tangible value may be sought, such as improving quality, from the point of view of the customer. Yet the assumption that 'improvements to quality' actually add value as *perceived by customers* are often not tested by external research. Where value is created, this may be fully absorbed by the customer without consequent increase in price or in volumes due to customer buying power.
- Key uncertainties may exist which are not teased out. The appraisal may capture only most obvious assumptions and miss those which are both *high importance* and *high uncertainty.*
- Apparently worthwhile projects may not seem to yield a sufficient incremental return to generate a positive net present value. Yet managers do not often reflect 'Why is this?'. This deficiency might be due, for instance, to the investment project serving largely to maintain or protect the business' existing competitive scope. Incremental investment may be necessary to defend a business strategy which adds value, or one which may actually be destroying it.

There are several ways of addressing these issues so that corporate value is not inadvertently destroyed, for instance:

- Synergies need to be tested by asking how these synergies will be managed and harvested and especially *by whom.* Also, how will corporate style and management systems (especially rewards and communication) play an enabling role in capturing synergy?
- Less tangibles need to be targeted by way of indicators and by indirect measures so that it becomes easier to put *some sort* of financial value on them. This slightly softer financial value need not be pre-

cise, but sufficiently well founded so as to not infect the more tangible and accurately estimated value in the business case.

- Assumptions which are both very important and very uncertain can be surfaced through brainstorming and the use of the importance/uncertainty grid (Mitroff and Linstone, 1993) – see Figure 7.4 for an illustration. Provided that the brainstorming is sufficiently focused externally as well as internally (to capture for example competitor response, the impact of price discounting, regulation, etc), then the importance/uncertainty grid normally highlights the most critical ssumptions, provided that managers do this in an open environment like a workshop.

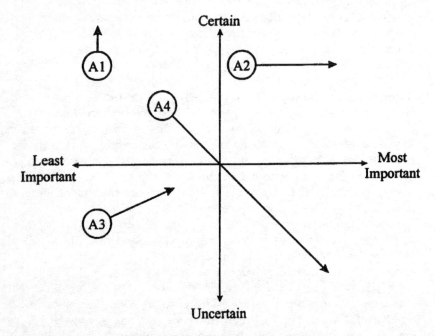

NOTE *Arrows show movement during analysis. A4-type movements can transform the bulk of the value of the decision.*

Source: Adapted from Mitroff I I and Linstone A L, p 144 (8) (1993)

Figure 7.4 Uncertainty and importance: key assumptions

Acquisitions

Acquisitions have been long recognised as a graveyard area for corporate value (Porter, 1987). Corporate strategists have pointed out that many acquisitions are divested subsequently, often in a matter of a couple of years. In the late 1980s and early 1990s, there have been some spectacular corporate collapses of companies which have made inappropriate acquisitions (for example, in the UK, Coloroll) and either have been taken over or have gone into receivership.

Financial analysts have also highlighted how an opportunistic, or alternatively visionary acquisition strategy has destroyed a substantial amount of corporate ('shareholder') value (Wenner and Le Ber, 1989). Sometimes the estimates of value destroyed are staggering: the acquisition of Case Communications (together with Dowty's organic investments in telecommunications) is claimed by one source to have destroyed tens of millions of pounds off the value of Dowty Group (now taken over by TI).

Although it is easy for these claims to be made with hindsight (with analysts poring over figures for estimated discounted cash flows before and after the acquisition), there does seem to be a clear pattern emerging. Poorly thought through acquisitions can destroy a substantial amount of shareholder value, especially where the 'strategic benefits' are not tested out operationally, organisationally and financially.

One way of avoiding 'the hindsight' problem is to deploy foresight. For instance, a scenario of the future for UK banks and building societies contemplating entry (by acquisition) to the estate agency market could easily have been constructed around 1987 to 1988 with the following ingredients:

- The UK economy overheats, moves into recession (1989–90).
- The UK housing market falters, then goes into a spiral, compounded by high interest rates and unemployment (1990–92).
- Internal synergies are then hard to realise because culture and style differences prove much harder to manage than are assumed.

This scenario ought to have been relatively easily generated by focused brainstorming and by the use of the uncertainty/importance grid. Yet so few companies use the scenario approach for managing acquisitions, both to compile an external scenario(s) and also a scenario(s) for integration. As Haspeslagh and Jemison, 1991, pointed out, value can be created (or destroyed) by acquisition at three key stages:

- Via identifying the target and evolving a clear strategy for integration/post acquisition management.
- Via the deal itself (especially through not over-paying).
- Via integration/post acquisition management itself.

Some key lessons for managers on how to avoid destroying value via acquisitions are therefore to:

- Think through the acquisition strategy in depth and integrate the strategic, operational, organisational and financial assumptions, testing these using the uncertainty/ importance grid (Figure 7.4).

- Use scenario tools and the importance/uncertainty grid to understand how value can be destroyed, then to assess riskiness and to reshape the strategy (both pre- and post-integration).
- Manage the deal-making and post-acquisition process with just as much care and attention as the pre-acquisition appraisal.
- Remember that any acquisition involves acquiring a 'business system' which may or may not be compatible with your own. It is also one which you can easily and inadvertently damage during integration.

Cost management

Costs are not only often *not* regarded as a strategic issue, but they are also often managed in a very politicised and myopic way. Almost invariably, they are managed (even in times of adversity and recession) as last year's figures plus or minus x per cent.

Many areas of cost generate longer-term financial benefits and involve lags between cash outlay and recouping the benefit. These costs should be regarded at a minimum as quasi-investment decisions. They should therefore be subjected to a full cost/benefit/risk assessment and to a business case.

Although in recent years costs seem to be becoming managed in a more coherent way (for instance, through business process redesign, re-engineering and simplification), these programmes have not permeated all companies. Nor, it would seem, are they always managed effectively. This may be due partly to the fact that many organisations are serving up re-engineering as a management fashion. But will these organisations sustain their attention to managing costs strategically (ie will longer-term cost-level targets be geared to sustaining competitive advantage)? We suggest that it is only through integrating approaches to cost management – financial, operational and competitive – as part of an overall framework of strategic cost management that improvements can be sustained.

The topic of strategic cost management is taken up at greater length in Chapter 9, so we now turn to a related issue, change management.

Change management

One of the key costs of organisational life is unquestionably the cost of change. Change programmes come in diverse forms – quality management, culture change, business process redesign, and many other interventions. These interventions are not always (often?) managed in a well-targeted way, as was forcibly highlighted by Schaffer and Thomson (1992). They are also costly, not only in a direct sense but also in absorbing time and energy which might have generated more value by alternative use.

Although frameworks for managing change as a systematic process exist (for example, see Grundy, 1993), many change programmes (often with strategic input) can be characterised in the following ways:

- Lacking clear objectives and precisely targeted financial and non-financial benefits.
- Being instigated as a result of only partial diagnosis of 'the problem'.
- Are conceived of as 'push' interventions which set up many resistances which destroy potential value and increase cost.
- Are unevenly pursued by senior management – without tenacity and continuity of attention much of the value is lost.
- Can be costly through disturbing organisational activity and routines (especially via frequent and incremental structural change).

There are a number of ways for avoiding the destruction of shareholder value through change programmes, especially:

- Change projects or programmes should be subject to a formal business case.
- This business case should define the strategic objectives of the change, how it fits with and reinforces other change programmes (to form part of a 'set' of projects or overall change thrust). The case should examine key options, not only for the scope of change but also for how the change process is conducted, and benefits, costs and risks. These should also be supported by an explicit set of assumptions – for instance, about implementation difficulty (given the degree of shift needed in 'how we do things around here', likely resistances and adequacy of resources for the intervention).
- This business case should be used actively to promote and communicate the changes, as well as to monitor both the benefits and costs.

Product brand and technology development

Investment in product, brand and technology development is crucial to long-term corporate health and thus to shareholder value. Yet this investment is often either an act of faith or alternatively is supported by spuriously accurate-looking cash flow projections. In either case, frequently 80 per cent of investment is expended on the 20 per cent of projects with *least* potential for competitive *and* financial benefit.

Where managers suspect that this is the case, they may unwittingly cut the strategic lifeblood of the company by axing the wrong projects. This problem might be avoided or minimised:

- By assessing the value of capability to exploit a future opportunity through constructing a scenario of how that opportunity might crystallise. This should be followed by managers thinking through the *conditions* under which the scenario might crystallise. They should then consider how realistic the company's assumptions are so that the opportunity can be exploited for financial advantage.

- By evaluating 'the value' of this capability again as part of a set of other organisational capabilities – for instance, in marketing, production and distribution. (For more background on the idea of a 'strategic project set' as the basis for project evaluation, see Grundy, 1992). As projects often have complex interdependencies with one another, it is often better to look at the value of an interrelated set and to assess individual projects through their contribution to that set. Capabilities only generate value if they are harvested in some business strategy or process. Also, without sufficient support from other key areas of the wider business system, value may not be yielded by a key capability, as it is offset by other disabilities.
- By applying a number of key tests. For instance, where the product, brand or technology development offers some major market breakthrough, will that market be profitable and will this profitability be sustained? Where will the company's sustainable share be? To what extent will customer value added be shared by the customer (due to high buyer-power) versus the company?

WHERE DO WE GO FROM HERE?

We have now seen that there are numerous ways in which managers (often inadvertently) destroy shareholder value. Most public companies are subject to the threat of takeover if they make obvious mistakes which harm shareholder value, or where they simply drift. However, this penalty often comes into play only where there have been extreme mistakes or complacency. Many companies manage to muddle through by achieving 'satisfactory' financial success in spite of themselves – often buoyed up by a few value-generating strategic moves which they now live on the back of. Others conceal the strategic and financial blunders through smoothing out the financial bad news in reported figures and other techniques with which we are now very familiar (see Smith, 1992).

Other managers protest that 'it is all too difficult' to manage a strategic vision for financial (and shareholder) value. In the following section, let us therefore examine how some of the issues in linking strategic vision and shareholder value can be unravelled. This is achieved by presenting a framework for integrating corporate strategy, business strategy and shareholder value.

INTEGRATING CORPORATE STRATEGY, BUSINESS STRATEGY AND SHAREHOLDER VALUE

The following framework brings together:

- Shareholder value.
- Corporate strategy and business strategy.
- Strategic investment projects and strategic cost programmes.

This framework builds from Cranfield research into corporate strategy and financial decisions (Grundy, 1992). This investigated the approaches of managers in four major companies: Grand Met (IDV), Rolls-Royce Aeroengines, London Underground and Post Office Counters Business.

This framework is presented through a number of interlinked Figures 7.5–7.10. Figure 7.5 begins by providing a top-level view of the links between corporate strategy, business strategy and shareholder value (particularly in the cost of capital, financial constraints and goals). Not only does this picture invite managers to make explicit links with *mission* but also with the more fluid idea of strategic intent. (Strategic intent may exist even when there is no formal mission as such.)

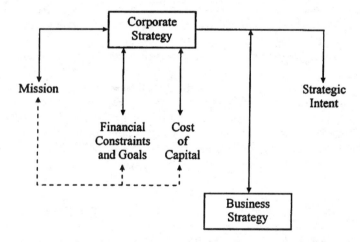

Figure 7.5 Linking shareholder value and strategy

Mission, financial constraints and goals, and the cost of capital are closely tied together with one another. They help to set the parameters for corporate performance – the goal-posts for corporate and business strategy. They are also either inward-facing (towards company staff) or are facing towards external stakeholders, particularly shareholders. Strategic intent guides internal staff activities and provides some broad parameters for external, market and *competitive* performance.

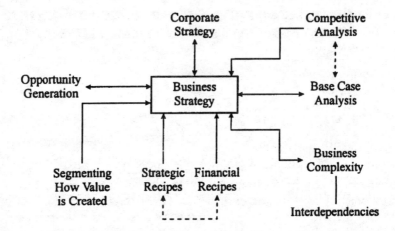

Figure 7.6 Evaluating and valuing business strategy

Figure 7.6 now brings us down a level to the business strategy. This is not only shaped by corporate strategy but also from the stream of opportunities generated at the business level (see the left of the figure).

Business strategy can be effective only if it is based on thorough competitive appraisal (see top right-hand corner of Figure 7.6). In addition, some understanding of the base case – what will happen to the business without new investment or without major business development – is needed (see the right-hand side of the figure).

The base case may also be evaluated usefully by stripping out areas of major cost programmes to develop the business – what would happen if the business was run just with basic maintenance of existing operations? The base case is thus a very useful way of exploring key strategic and financial options, helping managers to explore the impact of low-cost strategies for business maintenance and development.

Often the base case is characterised by declining, as opposed to steady-state cash flows. This may cause a variety of problems, for instance:

- The 'with investment' case for the business may not be sufficient to generate an incremental stream of cash flows (relative to present levels), although it may protect it against cash flow erosion. This feature may confuse the appraisal of new investment projects.
- The cash flows generated by the existing business strategy on a with investment basis may show a negative present value. Other options (such as reshaping the business strategy or by selective divestment) may yield a positive present value.

Figure 7.6 also highlights (see bottom of the figure) how managers' informal strategic recipes (Spender, 1980) and financial recipes may shape the kinds of investment projects and cost programmes which managers support. These 'recipes' are based on rules-of-thumb which capture what has, or has not worked in the past, and loosely define the kinds of invest-ment projects and cost programmes that managers find more comfort-able to work with.

Another important issue which is highlighted in Figure 7.6 is the diversi-ty of ways in which value is created by the business (segmenting value – see bottom left of the figure). This diversity can occur through the business:

- Adding superior value to the customer relative to key competitors.
- Then being able to harvest an increasing part of this value through prices higher than competitors'.
- Achieving operational economies and lower costs through offering additional customer value, which thus generates higher volumes.
- Avoiding value lost by making costs which might otherwise have been incurred, redundant. (For instance, having a strong brand identity like that of Marks & Spencer displaces the need for advertising.)

There are many company-specific and industry-specific ways of segment-ing how value is created. Unless these are dissected in detail it is very like-ly that investment projects and cost programmes will be ill-targeted.

Finally, Figure 7.6 highlights the links via business complexity through to interdependencies (see bottom right of the figure). The more complex the business is, the easier it is to lose value in a labyrinth of interdependencies, unless the organisation is exceedingly clever and flexible – which few are.

Turning next to Figure 7.7, additional ways of thinking about how value can be segmented are:

- Protective value versus extension value (ie, by extending the business' scope).

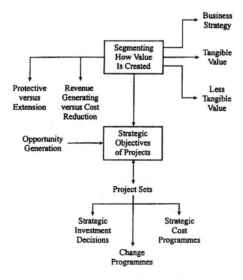

Figure 7.7 Segmenting value

- Revenue generating versus cost reduction.
- Tangible versus less tangible value.

New projects can be related to how they create value explicitly by setting strategic objectives for each one. These strategic objectives then spell out how a project adds value either directly or indirectly to the business strategy.

Figure 7.8 now links the base case analysis of a business with uncertainty and interdependencies. As we have seen already, one of the major problems of predicting the effects of the base case is that the rate and pace of decline on a do nothing/do minimum basis is uncertain. This decline is contingent upon competitive activity. For instance, in one particular environment a business may have to match competitor investment and business improvement just to stay still. Alternatively, in another case a recession may occur and a business might overshoot in its investment plans. In boom time it might have invested in servicing policies which provided superior value which can no longer be harvested through either premium prices or through additional volumes. This problem may be aggravated by competitors undertaking rigorous retrenchment and simplification of their value-adding processes.

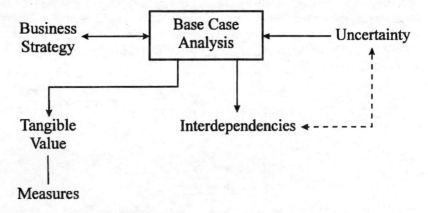

Figure 7.8 Evaluating the base case

Base case analysis (and strategic development and financial appraisal) therefore needs to be managed via a *contingency approach*. Managers often seek (but do not find) a simple panacea to the problem of evaluating the base case. They do not find it because the answer depends upon external, competitive dynamics which are fluid and non-uniform.

Figure 7.9 now focuses more specifically on the three softer areas of value:

- Less tangibles.
- Interdependencies.
- Uncertainty.

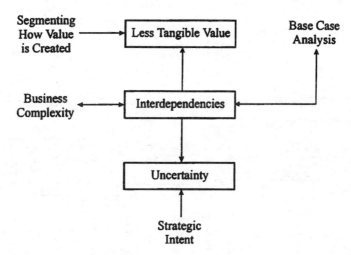

Figure 7.9 The three value curses

In many managers' minds, these three areas of value (what we might call – paraphrasing Ghemawat, 1991 – the three 'curses' of value) are often confused and overlapping. To help clarify this, less tangibles are zones of value which are hard to quantify financially because they are:

- Either concerned with adding customer value, some of which may or may not be harvested.
- Value which is future and thus, inevitably, contingent.
- Value which we just don't know enough about (due to uncertainty), whether this is external or simply due to uncertain, strategic intent.
- Value which is contingent upon a variety of internal or external interdependencies.

Less tangible value is therefore due to a variety of causes – customer value, contingent value, uncertainty and interdependency. It can be targeted, therefore, in different ways. We are therefore prescribing a *tailored* approach to targeting and monitoring less tangible value.

Figure 7.10 now integrates the whole picture, following Figures 7.5–7.9. Figure 7.10 highlights not merely the complexity of the linkages between strategy, finance and shareholder value, but also how they form part of a total system. It is hardly surprising that if key parts of this system are not there, or are not working effectively, then the whole system becomes ineffective. Yet that is precisely how many companies choose to operate, with parts of the system of how value creation is managed, missing or inoperative.

For instance, imagine if a company which has a well articulated set of financial constraints and goals, but lacks a clear mission, has a confused

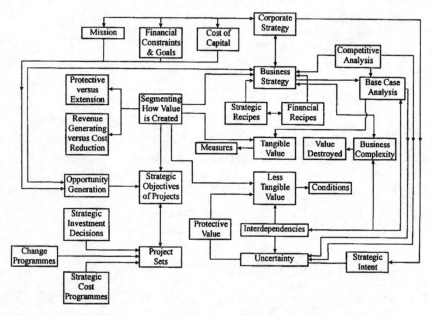

Figure 7.10 Value-based strategic and financial planning

strategic intent and exhibits overcomplexity within its businesses. Where complexity leads to a large number of internal interdependencies and where there is intense competitive activity, this leads to many planning difficulties, particularly in:

- Problems in evaluating many areas of less tangible value.
- Dilemmas of what to do about measuring and managing the inter dependencies.
- Difficulties in setting targets and indicators for value.

These problems may be further compounded where 'opportunity genera-tion' drives business development without much explicit strategic screening.

Allowing you now a pause to reflect, do these problems sound familiar in your business? Perhaps the framework in Figure 7.10 can help you to make better sense of where, how and why value is being destroyed or blocked in your organisation. The figure is therefore a diagnostic tool which can reveal where many of the conflicts and tensions exist within strategic and financial planning, helping to bring it all together.

Five key questions you may now wish to ask of your own business, using Figure 7.10, are:

1 Is there a clear fit (and consistency) between shareholder value aspira-tions and corporate strategy and business strategy, as it really is?
2 What is really driving business strategy development, is it largely

untested recipes or clear and integrated vision based on competitive analysis, and how is value being generated within the business and the base case analysed?

3 Is value being destroyed through increasing business complexity, through ill-targeted less tangibles or through poorly managed inter-dependencies?

4 Are key uncertainties identified, explored and tested out prior to making strategic and financial commitments?

5 Are strategic investment and strategic cost programmes managed as coherent and integrated project sets with clear strategic objectives?

To conclude, Figure 7.10 does not seek to prescribe a new and complex management process to crack a complex management problem. The last thing which management wants is an unwieldy, mechanistic process. The model in the figure aims to generate *insights* into gaps, inconsistencies and imbalances in existing management practice, and suggested *clues* as to how these may be overcome.

CONCLUSION

Few companies can really claim to be managing shareholder value effectively in the 1990s. Often shareholder value approaches are seized on as a way of challenging particular businesses which are merely 'ticking over'. In these kinds of situation they are typically used to tease out possible divestment targets and options. They are thus used partially rather than to drive the strategic management process across a wider front. Their application to core business and corporate strategy is much rarer, and its successful implementation rarer still.

We have clearly a long way to go before shareholder value management becomes integrated not only with strategic management but also with operational management tool. But the first steps have now been achieved in helping you to ask the right questions through laying down this initial road map of how strategy, finance and shareholder value might be closely integrated.

References

Barwise, P, Marsh, P, Thomas, K and Wensley, R (1988) 'Managing Strategic Investment Decisions in Large Diversified Companies', London Business School.

Campbell, A and Tawadey, K (1990) *Mission and Business Philosophy*, Heinemann, Oxford.

Ghemawat, P (1991) *Commitment, the Dynamic of Strategy*, The Free Press, Macmillan, New York.

Grundy, A N (1992) 'Using Strategic Planning to Drive Strategic Change', *Long Range Planning*, Vol 21, No 1, pp 100–108.

Grundy, A N (1993) 'Putting Value on a Strategy', *Long Range Planning*, Vol 26, No 3, pp 87–94.

Grundy, A N (1993) *Implementing Strategic Change*, Kogan Page.

Grundy, A N (1994) *Strategic Learning in Action*, McGraw Hill.

Haspeslagh, C and Jemison, D B (1991) *Managing Acquisitions*, The Free Press, New York.

Mitroff, I I and Linstone, A L (1993) *The Unbounded Mind*, Oxford University Press.

Porter, M E (1987) 'From Competitive Advantage to Competitive Strategy', *Harvard Business Review*, May–June, pp 43–59.

Schaffer, R H and Thomson, H A (1992) 'Successful Change Programs Begin with Results', *Harvard Business Review*, January–February.

Smith, T (1992) *Accounting for Growth*, Century Business.

Spender, J C (1980) 'Strategy Making in Business', PhD Thesis, School of Business, University of Manchester.

Wenner, D L and Le Ber, R W (1989) 'Managing for Shareholder Value – From Top to Bottom', *Harvard Business Review*, November–December, pp 52–65.

8

STRATEGIC COST MANAGEMENT

Tony Grundy

INTRODUCTION

In Chapter 7, we argued that managers inadvertently destroy value in their business through a variety of misconceived strategies and tactics. In this chapter, we shall focus on one of these issues – cost management. Although cost management is very much a traditional concern of finance, it does seem to be 'the land that strategy forgot' (Grundy, 1992a).

Perhaps strategists have found more interesting and larger subjects to concentrate on. Yet much of what counts as 'strategy' materialises in practice through the allocation of budgetary resources. Most practising managers would recognise this simply as cost management, but in reality many areas of cost have major longer-term and external competitive benefit.

The idea of 'strategic cost management' was born simultaneously on both sides of the Atlantic. In the US, Shank and Govindarajan (1993) presented a framework which integrates:

- Value chain analysis.
- Strategic positioning analysis.
- Cost driver analysis.

This framework is content-led, consisting of a variety of tools from strategic, financial and operational disciplines.

Strategic cost management (SCM) has also been developed in parallel in the UK at Cranfield School of Management. It has been applied (in varying forms) in a number of major companies including the Prudential (Grundy, 1993), Mercury Communications (Grundy, 1994) and at Hewlett Packard. Not surprisingly, many of the tools in the US version appear in the UK. However, much more emphasis is placed at Cranfield on *implementing* strategic cost management as an organisational change and learning process. It is feared that full-blown SCM, US style, would be difficult for managers virgin to SCM concepts to assimilate. What is therefore presented in this chapter is perhaps a simplified framework for SCM which is closely married to a feasible process of implementation.

In this chapter we argue that cost management needs to be managed strategically for both financial and competitive advantage (or FCA). This is accomplished by considering:

- What is strategic cost management?
- What different perspectives on cost exist?
- The strategic cost management process.
- Case illustration – Cotswold Technology.
- Lessons and conclusions.

Much of the chapter therefore gives practical guidance on how to apply strategic cost management, but it is useful to begin by exploring different theoretical perspectives to the issue of cost management.

WHAT IS STRATEGIC COST MANAGEMENT?

Strategic cost management is about managing costs for both financial and competitive advantage, longer term as well as short term. To achieve these objectives, we need to implement a number of steps simultaneously:

- Manage costs for improved financial performance, balancing longer-term against shorter-term priorities
- Achieving this by adding to, rather than subtracting from, the business strategy.
- Making explicit and continuing trade-offs between costs against value added, both externally and internally.
- Prioritising expenditure against agreed, complementary, strategic and financial criteria.
- Identifying, understanding and managing key cost drivers.

Some of the elements of strategic cost management are old and some are much newer. For instance, the problem of balancing longer-term against shorter-term priorities is a very old one. But explicitly linking to the business strategy and the competitive context in which value is created is thus newer. The fundamental difference is that strategic cost management provides a disciplined and coherent framework for managing the cost process in a strategic rather than in a purely tactical manner. This process is inseparable from that of managing organisational change. It involves managing the cost base in a way which is competitively targeted and bench-marked. It also involves appraising and minimising the costs associated with strategic change.

In order to manage costs in the round, it is necessary to explore a number of quite different but other complementary perspectives on costs.

WHAT DIFFERENT PERSPECTIVES ON COST EXIST?

This section gives an overview of perspectives on cost. These are then related to the strategic cost management process. The following are dealt with in turn:

- Strategic management.
- Financial management.
- Operations management.

Strategic management

Cost is rarely mentioned by strategic thinkers as being a key issue (with a small number of exceptions). These exceptions are however, important, as taken together they help us to build a framework for strategic cost management. A number of key strategic notions help us, namely:

- The experience curve.
- Cost leadership strategies.
- Competitor analysis.
- Differentiation strategies.
- The value chain.
- Capability building.
- Environmental shifts and scenarios.

The Experience Curve

First, cost plays a role in the *experience curve*, which extrapolates the effect of learning experiences and physical economies of scale. The experience curve works as follows: as an organisation produces a particular product or service in greater and greater volumes, its unit costs tend to fall. In some industries, particularly where the end product or service, and/or the process of production and delivery is complex, this decline in costs can be dramatic.

In some industries, the fall in costs can be so steep as to present a straight line over time against a log scale (see Figure 8.1). For non-mathematicians, this means that the costs fall over time. This rate of decline of costs occurs disproportionately over time in proportion to cumulative volume. The caveat here is that volume is not achieved at the expense of *adding complexity* – invariably dramatic cost reduction is achieved at least in part by simplification – of product, of process or of both.

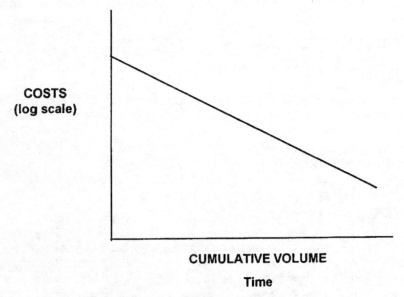

COSTS (log scale)

CUMULATIVE VOLUME

Time

Figure 8.1 An illustrative experience curve

The reduction in costs relative to cumulative volume can be dramatic, for instance when dealing with information technology (IT) or telecommunications hardware. For instance, recently the price of a modem virtually halved in the UK in just over one year mainly due to experience-curve effects.

Experience-curve effects can be of vital strategic significance. If a company is able to achieve a relative high market share early on in the development of a product or market, then it can drive down its costs using the experience-curve effect. This can be achieved by attaining a cumulative volume far in excess of its nearest competitor. Should an early lead therefore be established, then the benefits in terms of both competitive and financial advantage are also cumulative over time.

Despite early airings of the experience-curve phenomenon in strategy theory, this effect is often underplayed largely because most industries lack such dramatic gains to scale, as we saw in the IT or telecommunications industry (Ghemawat, 1985). However, it is still possible to achieve a *creeping* reduction in cost through a much more gradual but nevertheless real experience curve.

The gains in less technology-intensive industries are not so easily and precisely measurable. However, even in service industries, like professional services, there can still be pronounced experience curve effects.

An illustration

In the UK the accounting profession is currently dominated by a small number of very large players. Each of these players has a relatively 'full range' of products and services, from audit and tax and corporate finance (traditionally their core businesses) through to information and management consultancy, and also a range of more exotic, specialist services.

During the late 1980s and very early 1990s, the mid-sized players and bottom three of 'the top ten' UK accounting firms sought to expand their management consulting practices. The 1990–2 recession virtually wiped out these mid-range players who struggled to sustain small volumes of consulting work across a fairly wide range of consulting services.

Meanwhile, the more successful of the bigger firms were able to achieve profit through dominating specific product/service niches. This enabled these bigger players to:

- Reduce initial marketing and sales costs.
- Achieve much greater operational efficiencies.
- Secure more referred or follow-on work, again reducing both marketing/sales costs and time spent by consultants in between project.
- Add more value in the same time, or the same value with less time, and cost, relative to the mid-range players.

These bigger firms thus achieved a virtuous cycle compared to their weaker competitors.

Although perhaps few of these firms explicitly saw cost base as a competitive weapon, by 1993–4 (and after a shake-out of around 25 per cent of staff in some of these firms, according to some sources), cost levels were very much seen as a crucial, competitive weapon. The lessons from this illustrative case are that:

- Cost levels tend to increase when there is a proliferation of business activities relative to business size.
- During periods of major industry and competitive change, cost levels which were supportable at one time may now threaten to sink the company – this situation can crystallise very rapidly.
- Larger firms may carry more substantial overheads. However, they may be better placed to drive down unit costs through product/ser-

vice specialisation, or by achieving high relative market shares, and thus reaping the benefits of the learning curve and sheer economies of scale.

The impact of the experience curve needs to be evaluated on a case-by-case basis. Shank and Govindarajan (1993) rightly point out that managers often make decisions to expand product line or volume which assume easy-to-reap economies of scale. Often the incremental profits (and cash flow) are elusive because this incremental business is not truly profitable.

This may be because of inappropriate cost allocations through fixed or semi-fixed costs rising to sustain additional activity, or because of distraction effects. So there are some major riders to the experience curve in pursuing SCM – managers should not delude themselves that higher volume and relative market share necessarily yield lower cost relative to competitors.

Shank and Govindarajan's critique underscores the need to dissect the impact of marginal business. This needs to be achieved by unravelling the complex internal and external interdependencies which are not always self-evident when evaluating a project on a strictly incremental basis.

Cost leadership

The discussion of the experience curve above leads naturally to the topic of cost leadership. According to Michael Porter (1985), cost leadership is achieved only when a company has the lowest cost position in a particular industry. This does not necessarily mean that the cost leader has the lowest price (although low price and low cost are often closely associated in practice). This test of being the lowest cost player is a strenuous one. In practice, where an industry is made up of a number of fragmented groups of players (for instance in retailing), it is often better to define cost leadership relative to a group of competitors (or 'strategic group').

Being able to achieve the lowest cost position in an entire industry is contingent upon customers being relatively uniform in terms of their buying expectations and needs. For example, in the UK motor insurance market most customers are indifferent as to who they buy insurance from – what matters most to them is price. This means that the 'blue-chip', traditional players were not well protected against a new, low-cost player. Indeed, a cost leader – Direct Line – has now become market leader in the UK. Direct Line achieved this position in a very short period of time. In this case, it is much easier to define the cost leader than it is in a much more fragmented industry, like management consulting, where there may be a number of 'cost leaders' operating in different strategic groups.

Differentiation

The next kind of generic strategy of relevance to cost management is *differentiation*. Differentiation involves adding more real or perceived value to target customers relative to competitors – with costs slightly higher or on a par with key competitors.

Where competitive rivalry has increased substantially (for instance in a maturing industry), companies are saddled with the challenge, however, of both improving service and value and reducing costs. Strategies to sustain advantage through differentiation need to be underpinned by strong cost management.

Frequently the process of ongoing reduction in the cost base is managed in part by publishing targeted reductions in the cost base for several years, rolling into the future. While possibly unsettling to many managers, this at least creates a climate and awareness of challenging cost. But rolling cost reductions do need competitive justification. Also, they need to be made without subtracting from the business (and competitive strategy). This example also highlights that cost programmes should be managed as a central part of any strategic change process, otherwise they will damage organisational capability.

As we have already said, with a differentiation strategy the core value of the superior product or service should be delivered at a cost *not substantially out of line with competitors* – this is a message worth enforcing. Additional costs over and above those of competitors are then tolerated and, indeed, are selectively encouraged *if and only if* they add disproportionate value to customers. This incremental value must then be harvested through premium price or additional volume, or both.

This suggests that the successful differentiator needs to achieve a high value/cost leverage for the more discretionary areas of cost, particularly those associated with service and product performance. Where brand is an important means of achieving competitive advantage, a successful differentiator may also require a high relative market share to gain sufficient value/cost leverage for its advertising and promotional spend (A&P).

Few companies are in the happy situation of managing cost to achieve both differentiated and low cost at the same time. Practice appears to follow theory (Porter, 1985) by and large, but with some exceptions. These are now explored through a short case which examines Marks & Spencer (where SCM is applied intuitively, as can be inferred purely from publicly available data).

Case study: Strategic Cost Management at Marks & Spencer

Marks & Spencer's UK clothes businesses achieve differentiation over many competitors through a mix of:

- Superior service in real terms.
- Perceived quality through the M&S brand.
- High product quality.
- M&S' returns policy (customers can always return products, even if perfect – except, of course, food).

But because of a tighter product-line focus than many of its competitors, and because of its absolute market share, Marks & Spencer also achieves low cost through its restricted range of high volume products.

We would not say that M&S is differentiated relative to Harrods, but many would agree that it is differentiated relative to some other players. If differentiation is thus a relative thing, then so is cost leadership – M&S may be cost leaders within its particular group of players (or 'strategic group') but may not be so outside it. But the real point here is that the style of cost management adopted by M&S is of crucial importance to its (successful) business strategies within M&S. Costs are challenged continually through each and every aspect of the series of linked activities through which M&S adds value (this is often called a company's value chain). For instance, costs are challenged in:

- Its servicing strategy: M&S has very strong links with its suppliers and is known through many industries as a 'very strong customer' in specifying what it wants in quality terms.
- Its information systems support: M&S has invested heavily and successfully in systems to reduce stocks and to increase responsiveness through a rapid reordering facility, thus adding more value. This benefit is harvested in higher sales volumes than would otherwise occur.
- Its credit card policy: M&S refuses to accept other companies' credit cards – indeed, it now has its own, very successful card.
- Its attitude to central overheads, which have been substantially reduced in the early 1990s by systematic review of value added versus cost.
- In conclusion, Marks & Spencer highlights that costs do need to be strategically targeted and controlled, particularly in a very competitive and challenging environment, like the UK retail industry

Competitor analysis

Another key input from strategic management is that of competitor analysis. This can yield very powerful insights about relative cost levels. For example, at Dowty Case Communications (for full case, see Grundy, 1993) competitor analysis revealed that rivals were deploying much heavier sales teams on key accounts. Although at first sight this seemed to be more expensive, in fact sales costs relative to sales revenues at Dowty were higher because their hit rate was actually lower.

The value chain

Strategic cost management can also help us to identify 'what business(es) we are in', but to do this we must first explore the notion of the 'value chain'.

We have already touched on the value chain, which helps companies to define where and how they add value, for instance in:

- Procurement.
- Logistics.
- Manufacture.
- Marketing.
- Personnel, finance and administration support.

The value chain is one way of exploring 'what business(es) we are in' and also what business(es) we *should* be in – from the inside out. It should be distinguished quite clearly from the more simplistic notion of added value. The value chain involves analysing the company's value chain and its existing and potential fit with the value chains of both customers and suppliers. As Shank and Govindarajan (1993) highlight, the notion of the value chain is superior because, unlike value added, it doesn't just stop on delivery to the customer. Equally, it doesn't just begin on delivery from the supplier. SCM must consider not merely the impact of some cost option internally, but also externally, within the customer's value chain.

A linked point is that the balance of competitive power in the industry value chain is also important. A firm may invest very heavily in the quality of its service, adding value to the customer but may fail because of limited bargaining power to harvest this value through any price premium.

Porter's value chain is thus a first, albeit crude, step along the journey of identifying key business processes. Bundles of these processes can be viewed as mini-business units in their own right. For instance, a data processing centre might sell its services externally, becoming an external profit centre for a distribution or retail company.

The value chain is an unquestioningly important tool within SCM, affording a variety of comparisons – with customers, suppliers, competitors, distributors (see Figure 8.2). Figure 8.2 highlights that value chain analysis must be used on both external and internal analysis – it is not simply an internal analysis tool. However, within the SCM process it is important not to overburden managers with too much value chain analysis too soon, as they will produce learning overload.

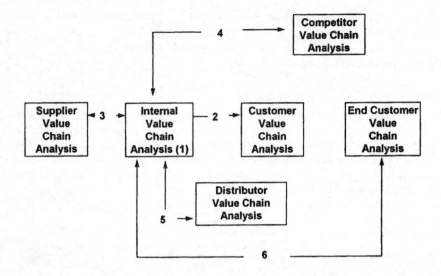

Figure 8.2 Six possible value chain analyses

Capability building

Quite often businesses find it essential to build up a key capability (like information services, distribution or R&D) and find it hard to cost justify this capability. This may suggest that the company might offer its services as a mini-business to other companies in its own right. Or, there may be a case for re-examining this business function or process to see whether it is so crucial for longer-term competitive advantage and, if this is questionable, whether there is a case for sub-contracting out.

Finally, where it is inherently costly to support a particular business unit, then this may shift its inherent financial attractiveness. This shift can come about as a result of government regulation, environmental (green) pressures, or simply shifts in customer expectations. Sometimes internal cost analysis may suggest that divestment or run-down strategic options need to be contemplated. For example, in the early 1990s parts of ICI's business were severely threatened by increased regulatory and environmental pressure. This shifted the cost base of some businesses so that it became hard to justify both new and existing investment. ICI has subsequently divested of or restructured many of the business units affected by this shift.

Scenario development

A way of helping to identify impacts of environmental change is that of scenario development. This can be used not merely to look at the impact of changes in industry conditions but also to picture the impact of shifts in competitive rivalry and thus on the cost base of players. Finally, this can also be used to shape organisational scenarios which might paint the broad shape structure and style which might deliver the cost levels, quality and flexibility to meet future competitive challenge. (This is not a particularly difficult exercise and can be accomplished through a half- to one-day workshop – see Grundy, 1994.)

We have therefore seen that cost should and often does play a major role in shaping business strategies in practice. Costs are a very important ingredient of both internal, strategic analysis and also in considering external, competitive advantage. Cost analysis may also play a role in determining which industries, markets and market segments are inherently attractive to operate in, and how sustainable this attractiveness is likely to be. This has a fundamental and ongoing input into 'what business(es) we are in'.

Financial management

Most books on cost management in any well-stocked bookshop will be found under the 'Accounting' section, probably as 'Cost Accounting'. Traditional cost accounting focuses on setting budgets and standard costs, and upon subsequent monitoring and analysis of the variances. This territory is well mapped out and it is not the purpose of this chapter to reinvent the cost accounting wheel.

Activity-based costing

More interesting from the point of view of strategic cost management is the attack on traditional cost accounting which occurred in the 1980s, principally by Kaplan (1987). Kaplan argued that traditional management accounting systems produce misleading management information. Historically, costs were allocated in relation to the physical use of production assets – both capital and labour. But as the service element grew as a proportion of the value chain of most businesses, the traditional bases of cost allocation became increasingly irrelevant.

Kaplan's argument is that there are often more important activities which underpinned the value added within the production process than those associated with physical operations. For instance, a particular customer might want to have a product or service tailored to some highly specific needs. The additional costs generated by tailoring delivery against these needs across a range of business processes (some tangible and some less tangible) would not be caught by conventional management accounting systems.

Instead, Kaplan proposed an alternative process which he named 'activity based costing' or 'ABC'. The key steps of ABC (Cooper and Kaplan, 1991) involve:

- First, managers need to understand how costs are generated (directly and indirectly) in the organisation – hence identifying the key cost drivers.
- Secondly, they then need to see whether processes can be simplified or changed in order to reduce costs or add more value (thus leading to an embryonic form of business process re-engineering).
- Thirdly, having redesigned business processes, they need to devise a method of tracking costs through monitoring the performance of a number of key performance indicators designed to measure the impact of key cost and value drivers.

Some applications of activity based costing short-circuited and became merely the redesign of the accounting systems, with at best a superficial investigation of either the cost and value system, and of business process redesign. Interestingly, Shank and Govindarajan (1993) explicitly state that ABC accounting systems can actually inhibit the challenging questioning of SCM, because they often become too bureaucratic.

In our view, ABC-type approaches should not be seen as stand-alone but should be integrated with attempts to get a clearer view of what business(es) we should be in and with business process re-engineering (Hammer and Champy, 1993). These management programmes are usefully placed under the banner of 'strategic cost management' to position them appropriately within the organisation.

Cost drivers

We mentioned above the idea of 'cost drivers'. This notion is not self evident, either in theory or in practice. In terms of theory, Porter (p 70, 1985) defines cost drivers as: 'A number of structural factors that influence cost'.

He also lists a number of key cost drivers:

- Economies of scale and learning effects.
- Patterns of capacity utilisation.
- Linkages and interrelationships.
- Integration.
- Timing.
- Discretionary policies.
- Location.
- Institutional factors.

These are relatively broad factors, and should not, as is argued by Kaplan (1988), be mistaken for more operationally specific cost drivers. Kaplan recommends (wisely) that we should concentrate on analysing the costs of primary activities between direct and indirect costs, and then focus on more specific cost-driver categories, particularly in terms of indirect costs.

For instance, depreciation and interest need to be traced to specific products (as suggested by Tomkins, 1991).

The moral from this is that we should not get stuck trying to use a generic framework which will apply equally well to all businesses. It is more helpful to work out the key cost drivers which are industry specific and also those which are organisationally specific. In the latter case, some of the most important cost drivers are rooted in style and are inseparable from the organisational paradigm of 'how we do things around here'.

Another useful distinction is that between:

- Structural cost drivers – those cost drivers which reflect the fundamental design of the business – operationally, technologically and in terms of market focus and scope.
- Executional cost drivers – those cost drivers which hinge on the firm's ability to execute effectively.

This distinction (Riley, 1987) is useful because it helps to pin-point both the internal and external 'hard' drivers of cost which are concerned with design, and also the more interactional 'soft' elements which are concerned with delivery. Not only must SCM embrace tangible issues such as product complexity and product design, but also softer issues such as organisational structure, style and management processes. For instance, when SCM was applied in a division of Mercury Communications – Mercury Data – the soft elements were found to be more important, especially within the management processes involved in new business development.

Costs programmes as investment decisions

A second (financial) strand of thinking is that a large element of costs are actually, in effect, investment decisions (for instance, see Grundy, 1992b). Yet so rarely do we see these longer-term cost programmes appraised as such, even by using relatively crude measures like payback.

In reality, there are many areas of cost where the bulk of the benefit is felt after the immediate, one-year budgetary period. Examples of quasi-investment decisions include:

- Acquisition costs of new customers.
- Advertising and promotion.
- Business process re-engineering.
- Culture change.
- Entry costs into new markets or segments.
- Major consulting projects.
- Management and organisational development.
- Product development.

- Research and development.
- Restructuring programmes.
- Systems development.
- Total quality management.

In Chapter 7, we discussed the need to consider the 'do nothing' or *de minimis* case for investment decisions generally. For major cost programmes, parallel issues are raised – for instance, without undertaking a particular cost programme, the question should be asked, what will the adverse effects be through competitive decline? Also, what edge can be gained through cost programmes over and above competitors? For how long is that edge likely to be sustainable, and at what further cost?

If managers were prepared to appraise their internal cost programmes as if they were investment decisions, they might gain some interesting insights, for instance:

- Many cost programmes might provide a much faster payback and higher ratio of present value (of outlays) than many more tangible areas of investment. This can be appraised using a net present value/payback matrix to help managers to examine their project preferences (see Figure 8.3).
- Some cost programmes have dubious benefits, many of these benefits being largely claimed to be 'intangible'. When exposed to scrutiny, however, this intangible nature might be revealed as being due to their being not very well thought through and targeted.
- Note that on balance a project with shorter payback should be preferred to one with a similar NPV, but longer payback is to be preferred (especially if there are opportunities to do other similar projects) (see Figure 8.3). Here value can be 'turned-over' faster than with slower payback projects. A proviso, however, is that managers should avoid unbalancing the portfolio of cost programmes/projects, especially where valuable projects with harder-to-quantify benefits may be at an unfair disadvantage.

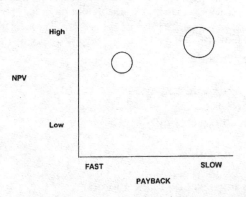

Figure 8.3 Trading off NPV and payback

A useful approach to dealing with the issue of appraisal process is to insist on major cost programmes being defined as projects and thus to require a formal business case. Cost programmes can then be grouped more readily as project sets and subsumed into the business plan. This can be done to show both the cross-functional effect of strategic cost programmes and also the impact within each function. This should help to break down at least some of the monolithic bureaucracy which surrounds many business planning processes.

For example, at Hewlett Packard a number of short-term operational projects were evaluated using a mini-business case method. This took only about half a day for each team using a workshop approach. The projects included achievement of the European quality standard ISO 9000, simplifying the order fulfilment process and centralising the provision of Hewlett Packard's customer demonstration equipment. These mini-business cases highlighted that direct cost savings were actually far less important than external benefits. The benefits involved protecting HP's quality image which could be evaluated in clear, if illustrative, financial terms, of what might or would happen if the changes were not implemented.

Cost structure analysis

Finally, before we leave what financial management's contribution to strategic cost management, it is worthwhile just to touch on parts of cost theory which may seem to be self-evident but which are often neglected or misunderstood by managers. Some key points are:

- Many costs are taken for granted, for instance 'fixed' costs may be fixed short-term but are variable or part-variable longer term.
- There are often trade-offs between cost structure (fixed, variable and semi-variable costs) and also against operational flexibility. This is another reminder of the need to consider and challenge assumptions about operational volume by using scenarios for market size and share, and how these are likely to evolve, given assumed competitive dynamics.

Not only does cost structure analysis invariably yield insights about the fundamental financial health of a business, it also yields options for shifting the balance of the cost base. These options are best explored via operational and competitive analysis.

Financial management thus provides some useful inputs into strategic cost management through ABC, through appraising longer-term cost programmes as quasi-investment decisions and also through achieving a deeper understanding of cost structures.

Operations management

The main operations management themes of most relevance to strategic cost management are those of:

- Quality.
- Simplification.
- Customers.
- Unit cost analysis.

Quality management

Quality interfaces with cost management in three main ways. First, quality may add superior value to the external customer. By improving quality one might actually add more value to the customer than previously. But how will that value actually be harvested by the company? There are a number of ways in which this might occur:

- Through higher prices (and thus margins).
- Through reducing the likelihood and frequency of switching to another supplier.
- Through reducing the costs of preventing the customer from switching (for example, through reduced advertising and promotion and costs of customer visits).

It is rare to harvest most of this value, unless, of course, the company has higher bargaining power than its customer. Some of the incremental value, and often most, is thus absorbed by the customer. This means that the benefits of quality management are so often felt in protecting the business rather than in generating incremental financial returns.

As an illustration, a major IT company began a project to review the effectiveness of its order-fulfilment process. Very quickly the project team identified a number of significant overlaps and ambiguities in roles and responsibilities which contributed to problems in managing the customer interface. Remedying this problem would not of itself yield dramatic cost savings. However, the business case for change was easily (and appropriately) justified by pointing out the downsides of muddling through. In the long run, the chances of *losing customers* or *losing specific sales contracts* through these problems was likely to increase, given rising levels of competitive rivalry. The business case for change was therefore founded on the *protective* value of the project.

A second way of generating value through quality is through adding more value to the internal customer at the same or less cost. This necessitates internal bench-marking of internal supply against internal market need. Internal bench-marking is not analytically difficult, but it is hard in terms of process, especially in challenging preconceptions about whether existing cost programmes do or do not add value in the organisation.

The third area where quality can be of financial benefit is in reducing the cost of failure and error, or the cost of (poor) quality (called 'COQ'). These costs can be considerable, particularly as the costs of undetected error compound as a product or service is processed by the organisation. It is often a salutary experience to work out the cost of an error – for example, in one manufacturing company a single rubber glove dropped undetected into the production process and contaminated an entire batch. The result was that of the loss of a large customer who had very tight quality requirements.

According to the quality literature, investment in error prevention often adds much more value than investment in the appraisal and measurement of quality.

Simplification

Most organisations evolve incrementally over time, often adding to cost in ways which are both ineffective or inefficient. This may be through adding 'nice to do' activities, or through activities which may add value but which could be configured more simply and cheaply. Ironically, automation of information processes appears to have added to, or at least protected, this trend towards increasing complexity. Many processes have been automated without being subject to redesign and simplification first. This has given rise to business process re-engineering (or BPR).

There appears to have been much, perhaps unnecessary, hype surrounding BPR. However, the amount of interest that has been generated in BPR, particularly in large, complex companies, seems to be disproportionate to a mere fad. But unfortunately BPR is often (but not always) sold as a stand-alone – developed from other major change programmes and not necessarily well targeted financially.

As with many other management initiatives like total quality management, BPR can be not well targeted either in terms of joint competitive/financial benefits. The costs of change involved in implementing BPR, and maintaining it, can also be unmeasured.

An exception to this pattern of uneven success is that of ICL Logistics. Here, management held a six-hour workshop to 'reinvent the business' with no frills, at a very low base cost. Several teams of middle managers were charged with coming up with a bid to run the business, as if they were doing a management buy-out. The result of this exercise was that they bid half of the cost level (for the full case, see Grundy, 1993).

In order to extract some sustainable benefit from business process re-engineering, we believe that it is best to focus on the idea of business simplification and redesign. This message is echoed by the project manager of a major organisational change within a very large and complex service business who tells us:

> BPR. . . well, I would hesitate to say the word 'fashion' but what is at the root of it is some basically simple ideas. The trouble is, people get carried away with it – it appeals particularly to the 'techies' in our business who can play with some new software tools. And I speak as one who headed up our BPR function until a year ago.

> We tend to talk more of 'dismantling' – taking apart and discarding superfluous activities and processes which aren't adding value. It can be great fun, yes, just as much fun as building all these things in the first place.

Customers

Another key issue is how customers are serviced and at what cost. One of the key cost drivers of any business is the choice of customers and the customer need which it serves. Not only does each new customer have an *acquisition* cost, it also has a *maintenance cost*, these costs varying considerably between customers and customer types.

Despite the wealth of prescription in the marketing and strategy literature about *targeting* customers and market segments, managers are frequently deflected from pursuing these targets in practice by thinking that they need to respond to whatever customer comes through the door. This is partly due to the uncertainty factor of 'you never know what orders will be available tomorrow', but also because of a confusion between *responsiveness* and *reactiveness*. Responsiveness means understanding and fulfilling targeted customer demand; reactiveness means mechanically servicing the demand which happens to materialise on a day-to-day basis.

This leads us to the 'value-destroying customer' syndrome. Companies service customer needs which destroy value in many ways, for instance through:

- Accepting order sizes which are uneconomic.
- Agreeing to tailor customer specification beyond what competitors might do and without reward through a premium price.
- Supplying customers who will be inherently uneconomic either through geographical distance, cost of distribution channels, complex after-sales servicing requirement.
- Entering into competitive bidding when, in the long-run, the balance of probabilities means that you destroy, rather than create, value.

Customer analysis is a critical area of the case on Cotswold Technology, as we shall see later.

Unit Cost Analysis

Many important insights on cost can be attained simply by analysing what it actually costs to define a particular product or service unit. For instance, in one service organisation the business managers frequently reran a financial model of global risk. Every time there was a significant change to some area of the world they initiated a new run of the mainframe computer model. In one particular month the computing costs seemed to go through the ceiling. Apparently no one had realised that running the model once not only took several hours of central processing time but also cost tens of thousands of pounds.

The same principle of working out unit service costs can be applied to many other areas. For instance, in a major professional firm it was discovered that to send out a single memo to all 500 partners and 2000 managers cost over £5000. This is a classic illustration of what is a non-obvious cost driver.

Organisational behaviour

In the UK version of SCM, softer issues involving organisational behaviour play a very central role, precisely because they are harder to tackle and, at the same time, often offer bigger and more sustainable competitive benefits longer term. The three main areas of impact of organisational behaviour on costs are through:

- Organisational structure.
- Style and culture.
- Organisational change.

Organisational structure, style and culture, and organisational change, are so inseparable (because of their many interdependencies) that it is not appropriate to untangle them. Instead, one should look at organisational change as involving a single, strategic cost programme which can only really be evaluated by:

- Generating a 'base case' for organisational costs – what will their costs look like without major change – given incremental changes in organisational structure and extrapolating the existing style and culture.
- Developing an organisational strategy – this involves looking at how the capability of the organisation can be developed to meet the external and competitive needs, and at what cost. Again, this can be supported by a higher-level 'organisational scenario' which we described in the section on Strategic Management (see pp 206–7).

- Devising change programmes (for instance, operational, people-related or culture change) which might support the overall organisational strategy.
- Appraising the cost outlay of organisational change relative to illustrative benefits as a strategic investment decision.

The idea of 'organisational strategy' (in the second point above) goes beyond that of merely 'human resources' strategy. It is impossible to disentangle what senior management is trying to do with the 'people' resource from both the internal, operational strategy and the external, competitive strategy. They are part of an overall strategic project set (Grundy, 1992b) where the benefits of the set are effectively delivered only if the individual projects are all there and are suitably and continually aligned. In this case, human resource (HR) development is too interdependent with operational development to be separately targeted and effectively evaluated.

A synthesis

Figure 8.4 now brings together our inputs to strategic cost management. This highlights how strategy, operations and organisation are inseparable with finance, in terms of targeting and (ultimately) measurement. Not everything can be measured precisely, but in these cases it is invariably possible to devise some financial and non-financial indicators which will give a handle on performance.

Figure 8.4 How strategic cost management fits in

This discussion now completes our review of perspectives on costs, leaving us well placed to take a look at the strategic cost management process.

THE STRATEGIC COST MANAGEMENT PROCESS

This framework for a strategic cost management is based on the following premises:

- Without a systematic process, costs are likely to be managed on a purely or predominantly tactical basis.
- Managing costs involves managers with lots of complex, cross functional issues which need to be tackled therefore with a flexible set of tools and also as a team process to provide more challenge to the *status quo* and to build ownership of the change.
- This suggests that the initial *diagnosis* phase is crucial. This involves identifying and prioritising issues *prior to* exploring and evaluating key options.

The process shown in Figure 8.5 illustrates therefore how costs can be managed strategically, showing the stages of issue definition diagnosis, challenging options, more detailed evaluation, planning and implementation.

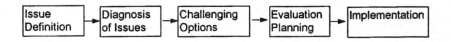

Figure 8.5 Strategic cost management – process

Following diagnosis, the next stage is to create challenging options – this tests the *status quo*. This stage is separated from detailed planning and evaluation so that managers do not just reinvent the existing pattern of cost allocation in a naïve way. This stage involves evaluating options against two dimensions:

- Their inherent attractiveness (in cost/benefit terms). Ideally, this boils down to quantitative and primarily financial indicators (these do not have to be exact).
- The implementation difficulty. This requires assessing how hostile or receptive the organisation is likely to be to changing its allocation of resources and the timely availability of appropriate resources to achieve project goals.

The two dimensions of inherent attractiveness and implementation difficulty can be pictured using the grid in Figure 8.6. Note that project A appears to be of medium attractiveness and relatively easy to implement, while project B looks equally attractive but much harder. Project C offers much higher net benefit still, but because of its apparent difficulty may be placed (erroneously) by management 'on the shelf'.

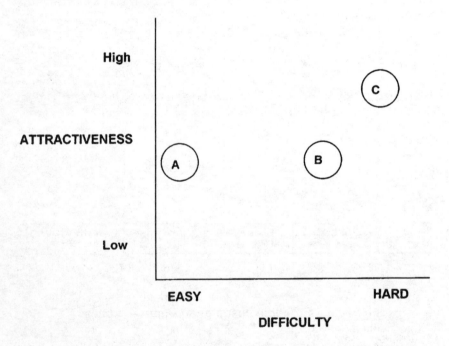

Figure 8.6 Attractiveness and implementation ('aid') analysis

The process can now be fleshed out using a series of checklists for each stage. These have been piloted successfully in a number of complex organisations – for instance, in the telecommunications, financial services and high technology sectors.

Let us now take each stage in turn before focusing on the Cotswold Technology case.

Defining issues

Before beginning the diagnosis of issues it is necessary first to brainstorm the universe of areas which might be addressed before prioritising these for analysis. Key questions to help identify the issues are:

1　Which discretionary costs exist within the organisation that might be managed more effectively?
2　Which overhead costs are incurred which generate limited value added?
3　Are marketing costs being well targeted and monitored in terms of their effectiveness?
4　What areas of operational cost might yield significant savings or might be refocused to add more value? Should these be selectively increased on account of their value leverage? (Consider for example, distribution, purchasing and information systems.)
5　What financing costs are being incurred in excess of what is really needed to run the business?
6　Are cost information systems genuinely effective or do these suffer from poor quality inputs, outputs and dissemination?
7　Is the prevailing culture a cost-aware one? Is this one of overly frugal management, or alternatively one of managing costs for both financial and competitive advantage?
8　What 'sacred cows' exist which incur cost without adding significant value to the business and also set an inappropriate example for how costs are managed elsewhere?
9　Are the costs of change evaluated, targeted and then monitored, and subject to a business case procedure?

Diagnosis of issues

1　How are costs made up and how can we creatively resegment costs, for example by activity, channels, customer types, etc?
2　To what extent are costs recurring or non-recurring, and does this suggest clues as to how both of these areas of cost can be more effectively managed?
3　What are the key cost drivers both at macro level and also at a much more micro level?
4　To what extent is poor quality or business complexity contributing to problems of controlling cost?
5　Which 20 per cent of areas of cost or cost drivers offers 80 per cent of the potential for improvement ('Pareto' analysis)?
6　What is the gap between current cost levels and where you need to be (target cost levels)?
7　How do these target costs stack up against the improvements which competitors are likely to be able to make over that period?

Creating challenging options

Once issues have been effectively diagnosed it is now timely to create genuinely challenging options, as follows:

1 Can costs be challenged either by using a zero-based approach (ie with no fixed assumptions of what is possible), or by building up from a very low base of cost?
2 Can target cost levels be established based on an assessment of how the business needs to compete effectively in, for instance, one, three and even five year's time?
3 Are these target cost levels linked to standards of output quality so that cost reduction is not pursued at the expense of a poorer quality?
4 Have these targets for cost and quality been bench-marked externally to help target them competitively?
5 Has this bench-marking process been used to generate a strategy for cost reduction which does not undermine the business strategy?
6 Has management unfrozen existing thinking about costs by encouraging a 'robbing Peter to pay Paul' climate, thus investing resources released in areas which can add more value.
7 Can costs be managed more effectively by substituting (in whole or in part) external for internal resource, thus refocusing the 'business activities that we are in'?
8 Is capacity there on a 'just-in-case' basis and is therefore considerably underutilised?
9 Are areas of 'fixed cost' really all that fixed, especially in the long run? What trade-offs exist within the cost structure between fixed and variable costs, financially, operationally and competitively?
10 What costs are based on internal allocations and transfer prices, and are these justifiable on any economic basis?
11 Are there many less tangible areas of benefit attributed to cost programmes which currently are unchallenged and loosely targeted?
12 Are there areas where new investment could generate a rapid pay back through cost reduction but have simply not been considered because of the perceived financial climate?
13 Are there areas of business which we should simply get out of because external shifts in the environment have increased the cost base substantially?
14 Can the industry's or company's value chain be restructured so as to give the company (sustainable) cost advantage?

Evaluation and planning

Evaluation and planning encompass not merely cost/benefit evaluation but also assessment of implementation difficulty and how this might be minimised. This phase thus combines 'hard' and 'soft' analysis as follows:

1 What are the key benefits of the cost programme, for instance:
   — strategically;
   — operationally;
   — organisationally?
2 How do these translate into financial benefits, whether these are relatively exact or inexact?
3 When will these be attained, ie what milestones have we set for ourselves and just how realistic are these?
4 What are the key costs and risks involved both:
   — in achieving the necessary changes;
   — in sustaining the improvement?
5 What are the direct and indirect benefits and how can these be targeted and effectively harvested?
6 What are the indirect costs and how can these be managed?
7 What might the impact be on customers', suppliers', distributors' value chains?
8 To what extent are gains in cost advantage relative to competitors likely to be sustainable, and if so, how?
9 What are the critical barriers to implementation, for example:
   — key stakeholders and their positioning and influence;
   — organisational style;
   — sufficiency of resource;
   — overload of staff;
   — complexity of the change involved;
     duration of the change;
   — leadership, and its active and visible support;
   — supporting measures and routines;
   — the impact generally on 'how we do things around here'?

Implementation

Implementation is a most critical phase and invites some obvious and less obvious questions:

1 Has the project manager for the programme got the necessary time, the technical and interpersonal skills, business awareness and clout to manage this project effectively?
2 Have the key constraining forces been dealt with in the implementation plan?
3 In particular, does the implementation plan recognise the softer areas of change which also need to be managed effectively – particularly communication, feedback and motivation?
4 Are the milestones and measures of change being actively monitored and has success (or failure) been highlighted at the right organisational level?

STRATEGIC COST MANAGEMENT AT COTSWOLD TECHNOLOGY

Introduction

Cotswold Technology is a niche technology company based in the UK with marketing operations worldwide. Over the past ten years it has been transformed from a product-led organisation to one which is marketed and with a strong commercial orientation.

In 1991 (the time of this case), Cotswold faced pressures to improve its financial performance following other board-level changes in 1990. A new Finance Director had just been appointed who was given a brief by the Chief Executive to review costs in a number of areas, including the logistics function. Since 1990 Cotswold's share price has almost quadrupled.

This case focuses on the logistics function which accounted for a considerable amount of Cotswold's costs (and its value added), particularly as Cotswold's sales were worldwide. Costs were also relatively high because of the sophisticated nature of the product which required special shipment requirements and high frequency of resupply.

The problem and opportunity

Initially the 'problem' of driving logistic costs down was framed as simply that – cost reduction. But rapidly it was realised that costs couldn't just be managed vertically downwards like that because there might be unpleasant side-effects, for instance loss of customer business and the rise in costs in other business processes. The last thing that management wanted was cost reduction becoming a 'dead cat' (Argyris, 1977), whereby problems in one department were solved by creating them elsewhere.

In 1991 the Head of Cotswold's Global Logistics function, whom we will call Ray Scot, decided to reframe the problem as one of opportunity. He decided to shift the question from: 'How can we make major reductions in Cotswold's logistics costs?' to 'How can we manage logistics costs for both financial and competitive advantage?'

Ray Scot reflects in 1994:

> The main thing now is that we are definitely commercially driven. We are in business teams now, a process which we started in 1991, meeting three or four times a year, led by senior management.

This change in emphasis had a number of key implications, as follows:

- Besides cost reduction, Cotswold would also be seeking opportunities for extra revenue generation.
- Any cost-cutting measures would be carefully probed to establish whether they might erode Cotswold's competitive position.

- Any changes in 'how we do things around here' in logistics needed to be managed in unison with changes in other business processes, particularly in manufacturing, marketing and information systems.

On the latter point, Ray Scot elaborates:

> We have worked with our manufacturing colleagues and got rid of taboos; like a product will only be available at 5 o'clock in the evening, now we can have it at 2 o'clock. It gives us so much more (flexibility of) options.

The subsequent review of costs was purely inward-facing and was supplemented by competitive bench-marking, both to establish whether Cotswold really did have 'a problem' and also to target continuous improvement.

Looking back, in 1994, Ray Scot expands on how this has taken root:

> It is a continuous process. . . Distribution effectiveness is going to be measured not only by cost but also by service and also, of course, in how we do against our competition. What we have done is to put in place measures, bench-marks, and as we speak we are undertaking a major study in France and in the UK which is trying to address all of those three issues.

We now turn to the process which proved to be a critical vehicle on the route to success.

The process

Ray Scot orchestrated a two-day workshop in logistics which was preceded by a one-day workshop on manufacturing. Participants in the logistics workshops were drawn from different parts of Cotswold's overseas operations worldwide. This proved invaluable not merely in obtaining data but also in building a commitment to effect change.

The two-day workshop was structured along the following lines:

Day 1
- Why we are trying to manage costs for both financial and competitive advantage.
- Presentation of data and distillation of issues.
- First-cut issues analysis.

Day 2
- Issues.
- Option generation.
- Option generation – relative financial benefits and implementation difficulty.
- Action planning and conclusion.

The workshop was attended by between 12 and 15 managers (different staff attending at different times). Ray Scot also used a facilitator who was knowledgeable both in terms of strategic and financial analysis – as it happens, the author of the case.

Initially I played the role of observer/commentator (in the first half day) but was drawn into more active facilitation during the afternoon and second day. This more active involvement followed relatively extensive presentations, lasting several hours with some discussion, which primed the participants for issue diagnosis and option generation.

This process of managing costs more strategically has since been embedded in Cotswold's culture:

> It is more of a process (than a system). I think that is more important than having rigid performance measures. You can almost fiddle them (performance measures), but at the end of the day what really matters is the truth – are the customers happy?

Managing the outputs

The sheer amount of ideas generated by syndicate groups on that first day came as a surprise to everyone – the participants, Ray Scot and, indeed, myself. The range of opportunities generated itself became a problem for the process. As one participant said in the bar later that night:

> We were coming out with so many different ideas – I couldn't see how we were ever going to pull it all together.

In fact, this proved easier than it looked. By continually sorting out the emerging ideas into a set of issue groups, it proved possible to generate a full issue framework. One of the benefits of using a facilitator is that there is always someone who has their 'hands and brain free' to collect and structure issues and options.

The issues (and opportunities) were then broken down into a number of natural areas. First, we distinguished between areas of costs which were variable, shorter term, offering relatively quick opportunities for saving. Secondly, there were areas of cost which might have been regarded as 'fixed' but in the longer term were variable. Thirdly, there was a big issue about service responsiveness and ensuring that customers were neither over- or under-serviced. Finally, there was a need for clear objectives and performance measures to be set. Subsequent to the workshop a lot of work was done on this, particularly using competitive bench-marking.

In terms of how the tools were used, Ray Scot reflects:

> I think it is good to use some tools. It is easy to get involved in too much detail too soon What is important is to rank things in terms of payback, importance to the business, relative importance, relative difficulty. If you

then get the right shape, the right focus, then you can concentrate on the detailed solution to implement. Implementation is about detail, strategy is more about 'Does it feel right, the shape of things?'. Most (business) deals are done on the basis of 'Does it feel right?'. They don't know exactly why they think it is right, it is intuitive. I think your intuition is more often right than wrong.

One of the particularly interesting outputs was service responsiveness. First, there were areas where Cotswold was making shipments to customers more frequently than they actually needed. This was due to a number of operational practices which had not previously been challenged. Secondly, there were instances where customers sought 'urgent deliveries'. Cotswold responded by delivering a separate shipment without any premium price for delivery. Not only did customers subsequently not mind the premium charge for urgent deliveries, they actually welcomed the formalisation of arrangements (this also helped to increase Cotswold's revenues).

Ray Scot reflects that:

We ended up with a premium (or 'tax') on certain orders. We looked at order size, timing, whether they wanted next day delivery or something special, and there was a tax put on it. In fact, the revenues generated out of it are not significant but the discipline that we put into the system is tremendous.

What we have always got to be careful of is putting ourselves in the position where it is difficult for (customers) to place an order. That is why it is important to bench-mark ourselves all of the time against our competitors, to make sure they aren't offering something better.

Thirdly, it was realised that attempts to take a 'blunt axe' to Cotswold's logistics service levels would be financially counter-productive. As an example, because some of Cotswold's products have a longevity measured in days (not weeks or months), the effect of doubling the intervals between delivery would be very significant indeed.

In tangible terms, net cost reductions (or revenue increases) per annum of over 15 per cent of logistics costs were targeted as a result of this exercise. Interestingly, it was not altogether self-evident as to what the total group's bill for logistics costs was. It needs to be remembered here that Cotswold operated in many countries and that the logistics costs would be spread over a large number of cost centres. This highlights the need for segmenting costs according to business process rather than purely along the lines of the financial accounting system. (The need to spend time pin-pointing current costs is a very common ingredient in applying strategic cost management for the first time.)

In all, over 70 options/areas of opportunity were identified which were then prioritised using the financial benefit/implementation difficulty grid (Figure 8.6, page 218). A sub-set of these were then translated into detailed action plans and then implemented over the next two to three years. This project was managed by Ray Scot.

Reflections on the process

Looking back in 1994, Ray Scot reflects on the impact of the strategic cost process. First, he describes how the cost environment has changed and how this has been managed via continuous improvement:

> Things are changing in the marketplace, with our competitors, changes in the customer base; in our case we are moving into new technologies where we have lower gross margins than our historical products which puts more pressure on costs.

> We are on a continuous improvement . . .kick. We have some specific business issues where the distribution channel in a marketing sense is questionable in some areas, and we are evaluating whether we are in the right channel. Depending on those decisions, that will have an impact on physical distribution. So it [our focus] is now more on effectiveness rather than efficiency. Given the way we operate, we are reasonably efficient, so our opportunities for improving profit are back to effectiveness, so it all leads us back to the marketplace. Should you be operating through a subsidiary, should you be going direct to the market? Should you be operating a wholesale service or a retail service? These are real business issues.

> The degree to which we have implemented an approach to manage costs more strategically varies. Some people are excellent at looking at the process, brainstorming the issues out, and then trying to develop the key strategies and tactics. They call it all kinds of things, but it is the same thing.

He now looks at how performance measures have been refocused in order to sustain the shift towards strategic cost management:

> . . . we were budget controlled (before we became market-driven). Now our key performance measure is in terms of costs as a percentage of sales, not in terms of absolute costs.

> We have to make a trade-off between costs and service and share of the market. What we try to do is we sit down with our (internal) customers once a year to agree performance measures, and those will be a combination of financial and non-financial.

> Quarterly, we get them to give us a satisfaction rating. We also ask them, 'Are you happy?' – it's just a feel. 'If you are not happy, what is it that we are not doing?' Then that might be quantified. We get a tremendous amount out of this, it can be pretty honest, quite brutal.

> We ask them to pull no punches. Equally, we ask them about things that they are adding cost to or inhibiting service.

One of the big issues which came out of the 1991 review was the extent to which distribution could or should become a strategic business unit in its own right.

> We looked at it, but at the end of the day we discarded it. We have decided that distribution is a core competence; we are not going to dilute it by offering services to other companies elsewhere. The amount of money that we might be able to make relative to the business is not worthwhile. We had divested a business which had left a great big hole in terms of unrecovered overheads, particularly in our overseas subsidiaries. For a while we focused on whether we could pull in other companies to fill this gap. What we found is that we would have to put a tremendous amount of effort into it. At the end of the day that was too big a distraction.

Distribution costs were also perceived to be a key strategic issue in post acquisition management:

> Acquisitions bring their own problems; there are synergy benefits. For example, by combining our buying power for one acquisition we could save almost half a million dollars. However, there was a cost to the acquired company (which was much less). So we had this debate, who was right and who was wrong, so that is just one small example.

The above highlights once again the considerable barrier of managing the organisational politics generated non-intentionally from traditional, perhaps inflexible, control processes.

As one measure of success, we see that strategic cost management has exceeded its original expectations in terms of benefits, even if it has taken longer to deliver these and was harder than was originally anticipated.

> When we started out at 1991, we were running at something in the order of (distribution costs) a percentage of sales just over 10 per cent. We are now at 8 per cent.

The impact of the savings in distribution costs represents about 15 per cent of Cotswold's annual profits in 1994, highlighting the significance of strategic cost management just in one key business function alone.

Some key lessons from the case

A number of key lessons for strategic cost management emerge from this case:

- How the original problem is framed is of vital importance – to manage costs for both financial and competitive advantage is non-trivial.
- The current situation needs to be defined very clearly – for instance, what exactly are our current costs?
- Sufficient time must be created for both workshop preparation and for issue generation, diagnosis and evaluation.

- The process frequently yields a very large number of opportunities which then have to be skilfully evaluated and prioritised.
- Some large opportunities may be longer term or may be perceived to be relatively difficult. However, these do not tend to go away but need to be brought back on to the agenda – for instance, the implications for 'what businesses are we in?'.
- It is crucial to get the right people involved, from a variety of functions, so that they own the need for change and for continuing improvement.
- It may be extremely advisable to have an internal or external facilitator – it is absolutely imperative to have a project manager.
- The strategic cost team needs proactively to influence upwards to shape the expectations (and sometimes the perceptions) of key stakeholders and to bring them on board rather than to adopt a 'leave alone' strategy.
- There is invariably a good deal of organisational politics associated with making SCM work. This needs to be tackled directly, otherwise much of the potential gains will not be harvested.
- To sustain the benefits, key performance measures need to be reshaped and also made more externally orientated, for instance by competitive bench-marking.
- There is invariably more work than the managers anticipate in the detailed planning and implementation process, there is a danger that some of the areas for greatest financial benefit do not get addressed because of perceived implementation difficulty.

On the final point above, implementation, Ray Scot reflects:

> I think that the honest truth is that we underestimated that [the amount of work required in implementation]. This was double at least what we expected. Then you have to rationalise the situation and you say 'What's important?', and you agree with your [internal] customers what is important and, in our case, the customer is the commercial people. They set the direction and then we figure out the optimum solution. It doesn't mean to say that all good ideas come from the marketplace – they don't.

After an initial focus on increasing efficiency, it may be a natural evolution to shift more into reviewing effectiveness – are we doing the right things (as opposed to doing things right)?

CONCLUSION

By now the argument for managing costs strategically through SCM is both overpowering and, we hope, complete. We have shown how costs can be managed as a coherent process, for both financial and competitive advantage. This process draws in a variety of analysis tools and recipes for diagnosing cost issues, for creating challenging options and for testing implementation plans.

Costs have often been relegated within finance as a 'systems' or budgetary issue. To a large extent they have been viewed as being merely operational and tactical. But the increasingly competitive pressure we have seen over the past few years has put the spotlight very much on costs. This increase in competitive pressures has been accompanied by stagnant economic conditions, deregulation in many sectors and also many former growth industries reaching maturity. Sometimes this spotlight has been focused purely internally and in the short term was without regard for the interdependencies within the business system. More rarely cost management has been sensitised to avoid the negative impact on the competitive position. A way forward here is to highlight and amplify the message that this generates weaker financial performance, not only longer term but also indirectly through impact in other functional areas.

Strategic cost management is therefore not merely a philosophy which integrates perspectives from strategic management, financial management, operations and organisational behaviour; it is also a practical approach which enables managers to rise above the narrow and political budget games which beset so many of our larger and more complex organisations.

References

Argyris, C (1977) 'Double Loop Learning in Organisations', *Harvard Business* Review, September–October, pp 115–125.

Cooper, R and Kaplan, R S (1991) 'Profit Priorities from Activity-Based Costing', *Harvard Business Review*, May–June.

Ghemawat, P (1985) 'Building Strategy on the Experience Curve', *Harvard Business Review*, March–April.

Grundy, A N (1992a) 'Strategic Cost Management – The Land that Strategy Forgot', *Strategic Planning Society Journal.*

Grundy, A N (1992b) *Corporate Strategy and Financial Decisions*, Kogan Page.

Grundy, A N (1993) *Implementing Strategic Change*, Kogan Page.

Grundy, A N (1994) *Strategic Learning in Action*, McGraw Hill.

Hammer, M and Champy, J (1993) *Re-engineering The Corporation*, Nicholas Brealey Publishing, London.

Kaplan, R S and Johnson, H T (1987) Relevance Lost – The Rise and Fall of Management Accounting, Harvard Business School Press.

Kaplan, R S (1988) 'One Cost System Isn't Enough', *Harvard Business Review*, February.

Porter, E M (1985) *Competitive Advantage*, The Free Press, Macmillan, New York.

Riley, D (1987) 'Competitive Cost Based Investment Strategies for Industrial Companies', *Manufacturing Issues,* Booz, Allen and Hamilton, New York.

Shank, J K and Govindarajan, V (1993) *Strategic Cost Management – The New Tool for Competitive Advantage*, The Free Press, Macmillan, New York.

Tomkins, C (1991) *Corporate Resource Allocation – Financial, Strategic and Organisational Perspectives*, Basil Blackwell.

9

USING THE STRATEGIC MANAGEMENT PROCESS TO ESTABLISH COST-EFFECTIVE SERVICES IN THE NHS

Keith Ward, Ruth Bender and Julie Quinlan

OVERVIEW

The change in emphasis in the NHS towards a more market-led culture has led to the introduction and widespread adoption of competitive tendering and contracting-out of non-core services such as cleaning and catering. Before decisions can be made on contracting-out, managers need to understand their organisations and their cost structures, to be able to determine what services they should offer for tender and the relative cost at which it becomes more satisfactory to use an outside firm.

Issues to be considered within this decision frame can be divided between those which focus on strategy, organisational issues and, of course, the financial ones.

If the organisation has not clearly defined its mission and strategy, it may be unclear as to which services are non-core and suitable for competitive tendering, and which are of such fundamental importance that it should develop them in ways which will improve their effectiveness and efficiency. Furthermore, it may find difficulties in specifying the desired outcomes of the services to be contracted-out, which in turn would reduce the advantages of that option.

Contracting-out will have a fundamental impact on the organisation of the hospital. Managers who were skilled at managing staff in their employ will have to adopt new styles in order to deal with contractors. Furthermore, the reorganisation which almost inevitably follows a competitive tendering exercise can be disruptive and needs to be carefully understood and managed.

In order to support the strategic decisions, a management accounting system must be more sophisticated than those previously adopted in the NHS. The ability is needed to identify committed costs and to differentiate those costs which are discretionary. The 'true' cost to the organisation of running a service must be established in terms of the cost saving to the hospital of contracting it out. Management accounting systems must be set up with enough flexibility to be able to supply information to meet these one-off decisions.

INTRODUCTION

The National Health Service

The National Health Service (NHS) in its current form dates from the implementation of the National Health Service and Community Care Act of 1990. Prior to that Act, the NHS was organised in a traditional hierarchy, with hospitals reporting to district health authorities which in turn were managed by regions. The new regime, a product of the market-orientation that marked the Thatcher years, separated out those who decided on the care to be provided from the patient-facing organisations that delivered the care. An 'internal market' was formed in which the *purchasers* acquired specified levels of health care from the *providers*, to satisfy the health needs of the populations under their remit.

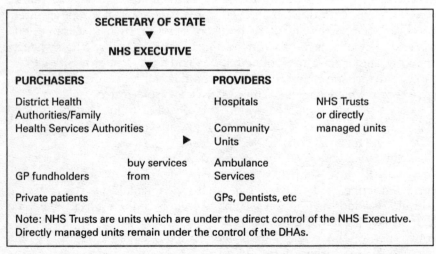

Figure 9.1 A simplified view of the new NHS structure

In this chapter, hospitals are used as a proxy for all provider units in discussing the implications of contracting-out.

Competitive Tendering

The testing of a hospital's in-house services against external service providers, a practice known as *market testing* or *competitive tendering,* is one route to competitive advantage and an efficient allocation of resources in the internal market. Comparing services to see which supplier can provide the required level of service and at what cost is a credible method of ensuring that resources are utilised efficiently. Where the external service provider proves to be the most suitable supplier, then the service should normally be contracted-out.

The contracted company then provides the goods or services specified in the contract between itself and the hospital. It is responsible for the operation, maintenance and provision of the specified service. Such companies can often provide services more efficiently than an in-house team because they can capture economies of scale in areas such as new technology, personnel, management, research and development and equipment purchase. Thus, by contracting-out activities which can be provided more efficiently by other service providers, hospital management can concentrate its scarce resources in those areas in which the maximum value can be added.

The concept of compulsory competitive tendering was introduced to the public sector in the late 1970s as part of the government's drive to improve efficiency and to promote a more businesslike culture. However, the idea that an organisation should focus on its core business and employ outsiders to undertake the non-core activities is common in the commercial world.

Contracting-out in the private sector

Contracting-out has been used extensively by much of industry for many years to provide the components it requires for its in-house manufacturing process. The result is that several previously highly vertically integrated industries now comprise a limited number of large assembly-focused companies whose needs are supplied by a large number of sub-contractors. Success in this area has meant, more recently, that the concept has been applied to other less tangible areas of their operations. Many companies now contract-out functions such as training, recruitment, ancillary services, personnel and information technology. For example, BHS contracts-out its business re-engineering, development of IT links into the supply chain and other similar functions to outside suppliers. Whitbread entered into a £12.5m contract for its systems development and maintenance. IBM contracts-out the handling of its customer requests for information to Manpower Services (Financial Times Survey, 1993).

Increasingly, companies are using the contracting-out concept to improve the running of their operations. In a 1991 survey of 500 Chief Information Officers (CIOs) and Information Systems (IS) directors (Schwartz, 1992), 53.6 per cent contracted-out in order to obtain knowledge and expertise and 39.8 per cent to relieve labour constraints. John Kerry, head of outsourcing at Ernst & Young, in a Financial Times report (20 February 1992) identified skills shortages, reducing costs and capital investment as some reasons for contracting-out. In a similar report in 1993, the FT identified the need for flexibility, reduced costs, quality of service and the ability to concentrate resources on the core business. Clearly, if these expectations were not being met, this strategy would not continue to be pursued.

Healthcare

The success of contracting-out has also been reported in the provision of healthcare in the US. A survey of 1,090 hospitals by *Hospital* in 1992 (Hard) showed that 90 per cent of respondents were satisfied with the performance of their hospital management firms. They usually met the hospitals' total quality management and cost goals and provided specialist expertise necessary for the provision of the service. Another study of four hospitals in 1991 (Gardner) looked at the contracting-out of information technology. They adopted this strategy for the effective use of capital, personnel issues, the ability to cope with technological change and cost stability. A survey of clinical service contracting also reported similar findings (Lumsdon, 1992). These examples show the benefits that can be obtained by a successful application of the market testing and contracting-out concept.

Contracting-out initiatives in the NHS

The government has realised the benefits that contracting-out can achieve. It has therefore advocated and sometimes enforced the use of market testing and contracting-out on a number of occasions. For example, in 1983 compulsory competitive tendering (CCT) for the provision of domestic, catering and laundry services was established. The aim was to ensure that hospitals test 'the cost effectiveness of their domestic, catering and laundry services by putting them out to tender in the market' (Milne, 1987).

Contracts with external service providers were advocated where this proved to be the most 'cost effective way of providing support services'. In the White Paper 'Working for Patients' (1989) the government's commitment to the benefits of contracting-out is also quite clearly stated:

> [One of] the most important aims behind these changes [is] to contract-out more functions which do not have to be undertaken by health authority staff and which could be provided more cost effectively by the private sector.

The government clearly supports the contracting-out concept as a means of securing the efficient and cost-effective provision of services. In fact, in a White Paper (1989) it has proposed an extension of the concept into the provision of clinical services:

> ...there is scope for much wider use of competitive tendering beyond the non-clinical support services which have formed the bulk of tendering so far. . . health authorities and their managers will be expected to consider such opportunities as an option in carrying out their new role.

Unfortunately, the strategic requirements of the contracting-out process have sometimes been misunderstood by those in charge of implementing it. Those in charge of policy appear to have assumed, as part of their 'market philosophy', that contracting-out will automatically lead to efficiencies; those charged with implementation have often merely accepted contracting-out as being necessary to satisfy their political masters, without much regard to whether it is meeting their needs. To quote an article in the *Health Service Journal* (1995), although contracting out is often seen as useful and successful, there is concern over the time and resources that it takes, such that 'scarce resources may well be diverted into unprofitable procedures for the sake of quasi-political dogma.' The outcomes of contracting-out have therefore been mixed, with both successes and failures being documented.

The Results of Contracting-out

Not surprisingly in view of the political sensitivities of the issues, the perceived success or otherwise of competitive tendering in the NHS varies dependent on whether the research results are being presented by representatives of the NHS management or by the trade unions and employee representatives. Although the government has repeatedly stressed the benefits of competitive tendering, and these are borne out in the private sector, there is a substantial amount of evidence which demonstrates the failure of the contracting-out mechanism. For example, a report entitled 'More Contractors' Failures' by the Trades Union Congress (TUC, 1986) detailed 42 cases of tendering that had 'gone wrong', leading to falling standards and high staff turnover. A report by the Institute of Personnel Management (IPM) in 1986 reported adverse effects on industrial relations and conditions for workers. Newbigging and Lister's research for the Association of London Authorities (1988) also concluded that:

> An ever-growing list of scandals and failures; a toll of suffering, inconvenience, hygiene risks. . . these are the fruits of the government's policy of putting hospital ancillary services out to tender.

A study by Griffith, Iliffe and Rayner (1987) found that any efficiency gains achieved were at the expense of the employee. In 1988 Sheffield City Council conducted an investigation, using questionnaires and interviews, into the effects of CCT on hospitals in the area. It found that costs had been reduced by £900,000 but that standards and morale had also fallen, sometimes to the detriment of the service. In 1987 Galbraith said that:

> ...public sector purchasers do not always obtain good value for money from competitive tendering, despite contracts often being awarded to the lowest-priced tender. In many cases the lowest priced tender is not the lowest price which could have been achieved, or, alternatively contracts end up taking much longer than they should or need to take, or else the quality of service is poorer than it should be.

Although the political beliefs and ideologies of these authors may well have tarnished some of the results, a number of independent studies have also been conducted to support their claim. A study conducted by Warwick Business School (Bach, 1989b) looked at one health authority's decision to contract-out its cleaning. The cleaning function was the first of many that were put out for tender in response to the government's claims of improved efficiency and quality service. Tenders were based on price (mainly of staff, materials and equipment), the result being that other issues, particularly those of quality, were ignored and subsequently found to be unacceptable. The study by Newbigging and Lister (1988) of contracting-out in the London region reported on the:

> disastrous effect which competitive tendering and privatisation has had on the London NHS.

In the PhD thesis by Kelliher (1993), case studies were conducted in four hospitals. Her findings led her to conclude that:

> in efficiency terms it could not seem to have been a wholly successful exercise since major savings were not brought about.

Other significant contributions in this area include works published by Kakabadse and Chandra (1985), The National Audit Office (1987), The Nuffield Provincial Hospital Trust (1987), Weale (1988) and HM Treasury (1992).

SUCCESSFUL CONTRACTING-OUT AND THE STRATEGIC MANAGEMENT PROCESS

Strategic management can be defined as:

> the process by which an organisation establishes its objectives, formulates actions designed to achieve these objectives in the desired timescale, implements the actions and assesses progress and results (Thompson, 1993).

Thus in order to achieve success it is necessary for the organisation to have a clear statement of its objectives and an understanding of the process by which these can be achieved.

As a first step, the mission/goals of the organisation need to be established. These are usually quite general statements which are not changed every year; they are statements of what the organisation is and what it wants to be. These goals are then translated into strategic objectives which the organisation will aim to achieve in the long term. The methods used to achieve the objectives are then selected and implemented at a functional level. The outcome is then monitored and a feedback process established so that the performance can be measured and any changes in the strategic plan and its implementation made as the environment changes.

Within this model, a successful contracting-out decision requires that a series of steps be undertaken (see Figure 9.2). The starting point is to

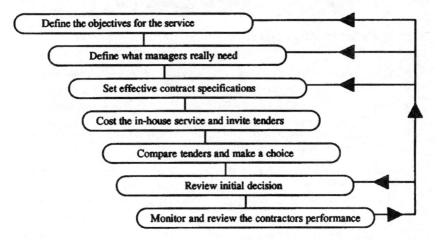

Figure 9.2 The steps leading to contracting-out

define the objectives of the service, which should flow from the strategic objectives of the organisation. The level of service that is required should then be established. This requires the manager to have a clear idea of what service is actually needed, or indeed if the service is needed at all. Thus, a thorough review of the service should take place at this point. From this review, clear and unambiguous contract specifications should be set. This is a crucial stage. A careful specification of the service, in terms of the required outcomes, is vital if a valid comparison is to be made between the competing potential internal and external sources. Such a specification should also include measurable performance criteria by which the service can be judged, now and in the future.

The in-house service should then be costed. It is crucial that such costings are based upon the costs that would be incurred if the service were outsourced and the savings that would be made if the internal department were closed (*avoidable costs*). Any apportioned costs, or long term committed costs which would still be incurred even if that particular department were closed, should be excluded from the comparisons. The tenders should then be compared and the least costly or most cost-efficient service provider should be chosen (always bearing in mind the quality of the service on offer). This provider should then be monitored by the performance criteria that were specified in the tender and the results fed back to the relevant decision makers. Throughout this process, employees should be consulted and kept informed of developments. This will help to prevent a decline in morale and should also ensure that the service specifications set are realistic and effective.

Critical success factors in contracting-out

In an article by Peisch (1995), a vice-president of Sun Microsystems, a US company which uses contracting-out extensively, states:

> Most companies choose to outsource [contract-out] carefully selected non-core activities that can be accomplished quicker, cheaper and better by outside resources. The intent of outsourcing is to focus management on core competencies and to expose certain activities to the competitive pressures of the marketplace, ensuring that they are performed by the highest quality and most efficient means possible.

The article goes on to discuss a fictional case study of outsourcing the anaesthetics service in a hospital, and problems encountered when the contractor fails to provide this core service to a satisfactory standard. Its conclusions are that outsourcing has to be fully understood, managed carefully, and should not be used to fulfil core needs unless proper safeguards are in place. It does, however, support the use of contracting-out when handled as part of an integrated strategy.

Contracting-out has the potential to be a powerful tool in the NHS battle to make the best use of its resources. Strategic management is one means by which the process can be controlled to lead to a positive outcome. The organisation needs to understand its own core competencies and its own strategy; if these are not clear, the contracting-out exercise may not only be ineffective, it could actually destroy value by diminishing those areas in which the hospital makes a positive contribution.

In order to be successful in contracting-out, all parties must have a clear vision of why they are entering into the process and how it will be done. To do this, they must appreciate which factors are key to the success of the process and manage those factors.

The critical success factors in NHS contracting-out will include the following:

Strategic issues

- Strategic direction.
- Specification of the service to be contracted-out.
- Flexibility.
- Satisfying the customer and the client.

Organisational issues

- Reliability and experience of contractors.
- Effects on the organisation.

Financial issues

- Price.
- Redundancies.
- Life-cycle costs.

In the following section these factors are examined in more depth.

STRATEGIC ISSUES

Strategic Direction

The contracting process has major strategic implications and cannot be entered into without considerable thought as to the future shape of the organisation. By contracting-out a service the hospital may be reducing its future ability to adapt to change. Two examples were quoted to us:

- A hospital which contracted-out its laundry services but neglected to take account of the cash-generating potential of using its sophisticated laundry facilities to provide such services to other surrounding organisations.
- A hospital which contracted-out its cleaning service and the following year contracted-out its catering. The finance director was now concerned as to how to manage the logistics of implementing a combined contract for hotel services, which he believed could be a more effective option.

A further strategic option for these hospitals, which would seem to be a logical next step, would be for a group of hospitals in the same geographical area to contract jointly for hotel services. This could provide the contractor with economies of scale, and the hospitals with a more streamlined and cost-effective service. However, having entered into their individual separate contracts, they have effectively prevented this from happening for several years, until existing arrangements are unwound.

Specification of the Service

Identifying the Service

The purpose behind contracting-out is that a hospital – or indeed any organisation – should devote its resources to its core business, concentrate on ensuring that this is operating at maximum efficiency and effectiveness, and delegate the non-core activities to other organisations that can carry them out better and at a lower cost. In order to be able to do this it is necessary for the hospital to be able to define its core business, from which everything else follows. Without a clear understanding of what is core, the hospital cannot know which activities should be entrusted to outsiders and which should be kept in-house.

For example, running an Accident and Emergency unit is obviously core to the functioning of most hospitals, and it could be argued that to contract-out this service would be to deny the function of the hospital. The most important aspect is the geographical location of the service, not testing whether it could be provided more efficiently elsewhere. However, other 'clinical' services may not be core themselves and could be contracted-out. One example, which is being adopted by some hospitals, is basic pathology services. Although carrying out the diagnoses and performing the operations may be core activities, there is no reason why the organisation should not look to a contractor for this particular ancillary service.

Research reported in *The Economist* (1995) shows that at least one hospital has considered contracting-out its cardiac services. This would at first sight appear to be a core activity for an acute hospital, and it would be interesting to know the thinking behind it. Taken to the extreme, hospitals could almost certainly contract-out their core services as easily as the non-core. There is a view that this is the path being taken through the government's private finance initiative (PFI). It is now NHS policy that hospitals seeking to undertake capital projects must attempt to seek private finance in a joint venture with a non-government contractor, before seeking NHS funding. This is leading to initiatives such as the private financing of an entire NHS hospital.

Ultimately, this leaves the question to be asked – why do we need hospitals – surely the purchaser could go direct to a separate unit and purchase the service without the 'middle-man' provider? Taken to extremes, the provider industry could ultimately contract itself out of a role. (Such a question provokes one to ask the question, which is not within the remit of this chapter, of whether, regardless of the inevitable public outcry, such a configuration would be of advantage to the NHS as a whole.)

One way in which the unit might identify the services to be contracted-out is by the techniques associated with activity based costing – setting down in detail what is done in the organisation and where each process adds value. In this way, activities which turn out to add no value can be eliminated totally, rather than just contracted-out to be done more efficiently! What is important is not to use more resources than are necessary to achieve an end. The aim is to find all those combinations of resources that meet the organisation's objectives. Having determined these objectives, the activity analysis can then be focused to identify clearly how the hospital adds value, which services are non-core, and which are perhaps being done for historical reasons but have lost their relevance and outlived their usefulness.

Efficiency is concerned with *doing things right* and focuses on the relationship between inputs and outputs. Cost efficiency is therefore concerned with the lowest cost combination of inputs to produce the required outputs. In contrast, effectiveness relates to how well the objectives of the organisation have been achieved and is concerned with *doing the right things*. It refers to how resources can best be combined to meet the goals of the organisation. A cost-effective service is, therefore, one which maximises its contribution to the hospital's goals in the most cost-efficient manner. Clearly, a failure to perform an effectiveness evaluation before a review of efficiency takes place could result in the provision of a service which is 100 per cent efficient but totally ineffective! Unfortunately, this seems to be exactly what some hospitals have been doing when they market test their services.

Specifying the service

For any organisation contracting-out, it is vital that the service is specified in detail so that the organisation knows what it is getting and the contractor knows what is expected. It is only when this is done that it can be seen if the contractor's tender really does represent better value for money than the unit itself can provide, on a like-for-like basis.

For example, Bach (1989a) cited one example of a region which specified that 'the inside windows' of the hospital must be cleaned. The chosen contractor did not interpret this to be the inside face of the external windows, as the hospital had intended. Instead, it was interpreted to be all windows inside the hospital which were not on an outside wall! Problems inevitably arose between the hospital and the service provider. The study by Domberger, Meadowcroft and Thompson (1987) also found that poorly thought out specification led to contractors making their own assessment of the service required. Paine (1984) and The Joint Privatisation Research Unit (1990) reported similar findings.

However, detailed specification of a service by means of the inputs to be used – for example, two cleaners to visit each ward for two hours every day – is not the most effective means of specifying a contract. Far better is to specify the outputs rather than the inputs. Stating that a ward always has to maintain at least a given level of cleanliness, with spillages cleared within a stated time-frame, is likely to result in a better service. The hospital should not really be interested in the inputs, in *how* the contractor does the job. Instead, having defined the outcomes that are required, it should be left to the contractor to devise the most efficient way of achieving this. The hospital thus benefits from the contractor's accumulated experience, and can adapt to changes in practice far more easily than if it had specified the nitty-gritty details of how things should be done.

Although being done for the purposes of a contracting-out exercise, it would appear that one of the chief benefits to the organisation is in the processes of identifying and specifying the services. Regardless of whether the service is later contracted-out or kept in-house, the fact that management now understands clearly how the function is operating and where it is adding value can only be of benefit to a well-run organisation.

Evaluation of Tenders

Having determined which services are suitable for contracting-out, and specified the level of service required, the organisation has to develop a clear set of procedures for the evaluation of the resultant tenders. Until recently, NHS organisations were obliged by law to accept the lowest tender received. This placed considerable emphasis on a detailed specification of the service, generally focused at the 'input' level, to ensure that they were following the rules and comparing like with like. Recent changes in the law mean that the hospitals must now accept the tender which presents the best 'value for money'. Before this can be achieved, the unit must have a clear view of what would comprise 'value for money' in the context of any particular contract. This should be defined in terms of the strategic objectives, the overall impact on the hospital, and various other factors discussed later in this chapter.

The evaluation of tenders can be a costly exercise for the hospital in terms of manpower, which should not be underestimated. Procedures need to be determined and the appropriate staff fully briefed so that they appreciate the factors to be taken into account in the decision. Having set up procedures and received the resultant tenders, the mere act of reading all of the tender documents received from prospective contractors, and comparing and evaluating them, will take a substantial amount of time and probably involve the use of (paid) external assessors. It is important that the hospital management appreciates in advance the requirements of this exercise, for if the evaluation is imperfect the resultant contract is unlikely to be a total success.

Monitoring

Having evaluated the tenders and accepted that which offers the best value for money, it is important that the hospital actively monitors the resultant work. Ideally there should be a team in the hospital which is involved in all aspects of the tender evaluation and monitoring to ensure continued adherence to standards, to enable subsequent negotiations of tender alterations and to facilitate an effective retendering process at the end of the allotted contract term. This needs to be done regardless of which bidder wins the tender. As one hospital finance director stated to us, 'Winning in-house cannot be seen as the easy option – we still monitor as if it were an external contractor.'

Flexibility

The climate within the NHS changes rapidly, and hospitals are often swept along with these changes without having any significant input into them.

In devising a successful contract, both parties need to be winners. The hospital needs to be able to change its contracts to meet the changing needs of, for example, GP fundholders, but the contractor needs to have the security of knowing that it will be able to meet the contract terms at a suitable profit level. Thus a level of flexibility should be built into the contract, while retaining a suitable balance. (Referring back to an earlier point, such flexibility is likely to be achieved more easily in a contract that specifies outcomes rather than inputs.)

Satisfying the Customer and the Client

NHS provider units are in the unusual position that their services are provided to the customers – the patients – but paid for by the clients – the purchasers. This inevitably leads to a tension, in that the patient's interest is in the 'best' service (however defined) but the providers must also be concerned with the cost effectiveness of the service.

Contracting-out can be used to satisfy both parties. By obtaining the best value for money the unit can ensure that the required service level is achieved at lower cost than would have been the case if it were kept in-house. Thus the purchaser can be assured of cost effectiveness and the patient of continued high service.

ORGANISATIONAL ISSUES

Reliability and Experience of Contractors

Perceptions

For any business it is important that the contractor who takes over the work has the ability to deliver. Within the NHS there is the added dimension of public service and public perception. Few organisations attract the public's interest and sympathy in the way that the NHS does, and that sympathy is almost inevitably with the medical and 'caring' staff rather than the management. Almost without exception, management innovations are seen as cost cutting exercises rather than a means of improving services, and hospital management have to convince purchasers, patients and staff (particularly the latter) that the actions being taken will be of benefit to the service as a whole.

Because of this, using contractors who have known reliability and proven experience is a vital part of the PR exercise of bringing along the staff and the community to support the contracting-out initiative. Indeed, one of the benefits of the change in rules from having to select the lowest cost tender to taking the one offering the best value for money is that this factor can legitimately be brought into the equation by management in evaluating alternatives.

Alternatives

In taking the decision to contract-out a service because it is not core to the hospital's business, care should also be taken not to be blinded to the feasibility of the alternatives. One example quoted to us was the case of an NHS trust hospital which determined that it would be of benefit to contract-out its sterile supply services. Having explored the market, including wide circulation of potential tender details, the hospital discovered that there were no contractors with sufficient knowledge or experience to undertake the work. Sensibly, it concluded that the service should remain in-house for the foreseeable future, rather than attempting to work with prospective contractors who might not be able to provide the required quality.

Effect on the Organisation

Impact on Morale

The impact on hospital morale of contracting-out a service which had previously been done by an in-house team is considerable. Even when the contract is won by the in-house team, there are often claims that cost-cutting has been put ahead of patient comfort and safety, and the new service will in some way be inferior to that previously provided. (In one NHS Trust hospital, this culminated in claims to the newspapers by a disgruntled staff member that the hospital's catering service, which had been won by the in-house team, was resulting in 'almost 90 per cent of food being wasted'. This was despite the fact that the new service provided more variety at a higher standard and lower cost – and was more highly rated by the patients!)

In order to combat these claims, and indeed in order to fulfil what is likely to be a key part of the hospital's mission statement, management and the contractors must be able to show that this is not the case, and they must be satisfied that contracting-out the service has indeed been of overall benefit. The use of experienced and reputable contractors can assist in this, as their 'brand name' can be taken as an indicator of quality. Furthermore, if possible some concrete measurement of savings and service improvements should be defined, to be offset against a measured impact on morale over a period of time. (In the catering example above, the use of patient questionnaires and surveys provided some of this useful management information.)

Patient morale should also be considered. One aspect of this is shown in the impact on ward patients of the contracting-out of a cleaning contract. Ward cleaners form an integral part of the hospital community and inevitably have patient contact. It is important that both hospital management and the contractor work to ensure that the impact of the contract on ward relationships is favourable. This extends to ensuring a high level of nurse commitment to the new contract in order to preserve positive staff attitudes on the ward.

Impact on other services

In any organisation, individual services cannot be looked at as discrete units, with no impact on each other. The NHS is no different to this, and in contracting-out a service it is important to identify and control the impact that this will have directly on other parts of the hospital.

One example of such impact is in the possibility, already mentioned, of hospitals contracting-out their basic pathology services. There are commercial organisations in existence with central facilities which can no doubt undertake this standard work, with the required 24 hour turnaround, at a lower cost than can the hospitals, due to the benefits of economies of scope and scale. However, in addition to standard pathology work, hospitals need the ability to do specialist work at very short notice and with the results available immediately. Such a service would almost certainly have to be done on site. Hospitals which are addressing the possibility of contracting out basic pathology face the problem that many in-house pathology units needed for this emergency work, become non-viable if they lose their 'bread and butter' work. This problem has been solved by at least one hospital by outsourcing all of its pathology work, transferring that risk to the contractor. The key success factor here will be in maintaining the essential relationship and trust between the consultant and the pathologists.

Management skills and systems

It has already been stated that the hospital will need an in-house team to monitor the contractors, regardless of whether the contract is won in-house or by an external firm. What is not always appreciated by hospitals is that in doing this they need to develop different management skills. Monitoring and liaising with a contractor differs from managing the hospital's own staff, and it is important that the hospital's team appreciate this and are trained in the relevant techniques. Having an experienced contractor monitored and evaluated by an 'amateur' hospital team is unlikely to lead to the operational efficiencies and improvements that were originally anticipated when the contracting process commenced.

The changes in reporting and management responsibilities will lead to structural changes in the organisation – it is unlikely that the structure set up to administer a traditional NHS hospital will still be the best organisational form in the new regime. However, in a traditional and heavily unionised environment such as the NHS such changes, although ultimately essential, will be difficult to implement, and the transition will need to be carefully managed.

FINANCIAL ISSUES

Price

As stated above, the legal obligation to accept the lowest priced tender has been removed, although the hospital is obliged to (and indeed, should wish to) accept the tender which represents the best value for money. 'Value for money' is somewhat intangible, but in addition to the expected criteria of price and quality, it should be taken to include the reputation and experience of the contractor – as mentioned above, these are particularly important in assessing the impact on the rest of the hospital.

One of the objectives of contracting-out is to reduce the costs of the service being provided, while retaining or improving the quality of the output. In order to achieve this objective the hospital needs to specify the service carefully, but also to know its existing costs. It would be impossible to determine the level of cost saving from contracting-out unless the management had a clear knowledge of current cost behaviour. Thus the hospital should have calculated the cost of the service and understand the effect on the organisation as a whole of changing this one aspect. Managers should appreciate which costs are incremental and will disappear when the contractor takes over the service, and which costs are merely allocated from one activity to another and will have no overall effect on financial performance.

A further aspect of the pricing of contracts is that the NHS as a whole operates under a regime of efficiency savings. Annual budgets are set to include an efficiency gain each year, effectively reducing the cash available. For example, in 1994–5 budget increases were based on the assumption that there would be an across-the-board efficiency saving of 3 per cent over the previous year's spending. This being so, it is important either that contracts build in price reductions for such efficiency savings, or that management are aware of the need to make additional savings in other areas. Without this, management could find that a large part of their costs were fixed and that they would have to cut back in some core business areas or fail to meet their budgets, with the consequent penalties imposed by the NHS Executive.

Redundancies

If a tender is won by an external contractor, or sometimes even if the in-house team wins the bid, the hospital will have to make part of its existing workforce redundant. This inevitably leads to the tensions and impact on morale mentioned above, but there is also a financial impact.

Government guidelines state that when comparing the financial cost of competing tenders, a hospital should amortise its anticipated redundancy costs over a five-year period – if it did not do that, then the in-house bid would almost inevitably be the lowest cost option, as the only one not entailing a redundancy package. However, it is important for the management to appreciate that it is only the 'profit' impact which is deferred; the cash impact of redundancies will obviously take place in the first year. As all NHS units are constrained by having to meet an annual cash budget (the 'external financing limit'), this could lead to an overspend unless the situation is previously identified and carefully planned and monitored. A contracting-out exercise which forces spending and service cuts in other parts of the hospital can hardly be considered to be a total success.

Life-cycle Costs

A further financial point for management's consideration is the cost of the contract over the entire life-cycle, including the retendering at the end of its life. In the initial contracting-out exercise the current cost of running an in-house operation is known and can be compared with the tenders.

Furthermore, the option always remains of retaining the service in-house. However, once an external contractor has been awarded the contract that in-house option is no longer available or would be costly to resurrect. At that stage, the hospital is totally dependent on commercial contractors who, knowing that there is no in-house competition, may increase their prices in the retendering. In the 1980s this was seen as a problem in the first rounds of compulsory competitive tendering for cleaning services etc. Although, in fact, the situation appears not to have arisen in these areas, hospital managers will certainly need to consider it when implementing the PFI.

THE IMPLICATIONS FOR MANAGEMENT ACCOUNTING

Most of the points made in this chapter relate to the thought processes and decisions surrounding the contracting-out process. As such, they have an impact on the organisation's management accounting systems, for management accounting is about producing information to assist in decision making rather than just about keeping score of what has been spent.

It is obvious to everyone that one of the key information requirements of hospitals seeking to contract-out services is the cost of the services as they currently exist, so that comparisons can be made to determine the most cost-effective route. However, this in itself was a challenge for many hospitals in the early days of the development of the internal market. Hospitals had developed their information systems to comply with the requirements of the district and regional health authorities that governed them and, prior to the NHS reforms, those bodies had had little use for information on profitability and comparative costs. Even now, some management information systems are rudimentary, collecting data with minimal analysis and forethought. Much information is being collected in one-off exercises, with the supporting analysis being done only to support the particular decision of the moment, and systems developed to collect information that is seen to be relevant at that time only.

The management information systems need to be configured so as to be flexible, to be able to collate and analyse data from various different sources. In order to support contracting-out decisions, it is vital that the hospital can differentiate committed costs from those which are discretionary, otherwise it will be impossible to determine the true saving from contracting-out a service. Similarly, records will need to be able to substantiate the relationship between 'engineered' costs (those which move strictly in relation to levels of activity), in order to prepare reasonably accurate forecasts and assessments. Thus the accounting systems must enable data to be analysed and collated in different ways, to provide the information to support each decision.

In addition to the historical analysis to support decisions, important as that is, the management accounting system should also be able to be used to identify further areas which may be appropriate for future contracting-out exercises. To do this, information will need to be collated on the cost of activities and also on the comparative costs in the external world, shadowing external organisations to see what is currently on the market. It is only with this input that the management accounting can become proactive, rather than merely reacting to each government initiative as it is announced.

It is also important that the management accounting system can collect and present information which delves beneath the situation as it is and considers the situation as it might be. One example of how this could be important is in situations where costs are temporarily high (or low) as a reaction to some short term market condition – for example, a shortage of qualified pathologists, which is leading to high costs, but which it is known will be corrected in the near future. Such market imperfections can distort both the internal cost and the cost of an external contract, and it is vital that they are acknowledged and included in the information package to be considered before deciding whether, or how, to contract out.

The strategic management accounting system requires commitment from the hospital's top team if it is to work. Management accounting information is not just the province of the accounts department, but should involve the whole organisation. In assessing what is done in the hospital and where value is added, it is important to include management from clinical and operational functions. Cross functional teams will be needed to review each area, and people will need to understand the advantages to the organisation of providing accurate information for the purposes of the analysis.

This is of particular relevance in collecting data in areas which may not at first sight seem to be the natural province of the management accountant – areas such as quality and performance. In a period of change (and it should be remembered that the NHS is *always* in a period of change!) employees fear for their jobs and may see any new initiative as being designed to reduce staffing. Biased data is no basis on which to make decisions, and ways need to be found to ensure accurate and responsive data capture.

Finally, the accountant should remember that the only purpose of a strategic management accounting system is to produce information to support decision making, and that generally those decisions are made by non-financial managers. The information must be in a format which is both relevant and understandable by the user. Its use must generate behaviour patterns which are congruent with the hospital's mission and goals. The comment made to us by a senior member of the NHS Executive was: '[there are still] a number of people who get confused between accounting and decision-making'. Without this distinction, the most sophisticated management accounting systems will not be doing their job.

CONCLUSION

The NHS is an unusual environment, heavily regulated and subject to great public scrutiny. However, the principles of strategic management accounting can be applied here as they can to any commercial organisation – and lessons learned in the NHS have general applicability.

Contracting-out has become a part of the commercial and public sector way of operation. Research shows that if done well it can have great benefits in streamlining an organisation and making it concentrate on the profitable core business. However, undertaking competitive tendering for the 'wrong' reasons – for example, in response to government (or head office) edict – can damage morale and lead to a waste of resources.

The management accounting system must generate information to enable management to anticipate and plan for future developments, and make one-off decisions about service provision. A good management information system is essential to plan, implement and monitor all services, and especially to ensure that maximum value is obtained from those which are contracted-out.

References

Bach, S (1989a) 'Trading For Health Services: Lessons from the Competitive Tendering Experience', *Journal of Management in Medicine*', Vol 4, No 3, pp 160–166.

Bach, S (1989b) 'Too High a Price to Pay: A Study of Competitive Tendering for Domestic Services in the NHS', Warwick Papers in Industrial Relations, No 25, Industrial Relations Research Unit, University of Warwick: School of Industrial and Business Studies.

Barker, L (1994) 'Managing the Contract – Building in Quality Controls', presented at the Financial Times Conference on Resource Management in the Public Sector, 7 February.

Bowman, C and Asch, D (1987) *Strategic Management*, Macmillan Education Limited, London.

Carnaghan, R and Bracewell-Milnes, B (1993) 'Testing the Market', Research Monograph No 49, Institute of Economic Affairs, London.

Clarke, K (1983) Hospital Caterers Association, *National Study Day Report Document*, 28 September, Health Caterers Association.

Cleaning and Support Services Association (undated – about 1991) 'Safe in their hands: the record of private contractors in public services', London.

Contract Cleaning and Maintenance Association (1990) 'The Facts on the NHS Privatisation Experience: a response to "The NHS Privatisation Experience" by the Joint NHS Privatisation Research Unit', London.

Culyer, A J (1990) "The Internal Market: An Acceptable Means to a Desirable End', Discussion Paper 67, Centre for Health Economics, University of York.

Decker, D (1995) 'Market Testing – Does It Bring Home the Bacon?', *The Health Service Journal*, 19 January, pp 26–28.

Department of Health and Social Security (1983), 'Competitive Tendering in the provision of Domestic, Catering and Laundry Services', HC(83)18, HMSO, London.

Domberger, S, Meadowcroft, S, Thompson, D (1987) 'The Impact of Competitive Tendering on the Cost of Hospital Domestic Services', *Fiscal Studies*, Vol 8, No 4, pp 39–54.

Economist, The (1995) 'The Making of NHS Ltd', 21 January, pp 27–28.

Enthoven, A C (1985) 'Reflections on the Management of the National Health Service', Occasional Papers 5, Nuffield Provincial Hospitals Trust, London.

Financial Times Survey (1992) 'Contracted Business Services', Financial Times, 20 February.

Financial Times Survey (1993) 'Resource Management: Buying-in Services', Financial Times, 28 July.

Galbraith, D (1987) 'Achieving VFM from competitive tendering', *Public Finance and Accountancy*, 11 December, pp 9–10.

Gardner, E (1991) 'Going on line with outsiders', *Modern Healthcare*, 15 July, pp 35–47.

Griffith, B, lliffe, S, Rayner, G (1987) *Banking on Sickness: Commercial Medicine in Britain and the USA*, Lawrence and Wishart, London.

Hard, R (1992) 'Hospitals look to Hospitality Service firms to meet TQM goals', *Hospitals*, 20 May, pp 56–58.

Harrisson, S (1986) 'A valuable part of the team', *The Health Service Journal*, 96 (5029), 11 December, pp 1608–1609.

Health Service Journal (1993a), Thursday 14 October.

Health Service Journal (1993b), Thursday 21 October.

Hayes, K (1994) 'Managing Market Testing of Pathology Services: A Case Study', presented at the SMI Conference on Market Testing in the NHS, 4–5 July.

HM Treasury (1992) 'Market Testing and Buying In', Public Competition and Purchasing Unit, London.

Institute of Personnel Management and Incomes Data Services (IDS) (1986), 'Competitive Tendering in the Public Sector', Public Sector Unit, London.

Joint NHS Privatisation Research Unit, The (1990) 'The Privatisation Experience: Competitive Tendering for NHS Support Services', London.

Kakabadse and Chandra (1985) *Privatisation and the National Health Service*, Gower Publishing, Hampshire.

Kelliher, C (1993) 'Competitive Tendering, Management Strategy and Industrial Relations in the Public Sector', PhD thesis, London University, p 383.

Levene, P (1994) 'The UK Government's Market-Testing Programme – Opportunities and Threats', presented at the Financial Times Conference on Resource Management in the Public Sector, 7 February.

Lumsdon, K (1992) 'Clinical Contracting: CEO's see demand for specialized skills, advanced services', *Hospitals*, 20 August, pp 44–46.

Mially, R (1986) 'Competitive Tendering Approaches Adopted in the NHS', *Health Care Management*, Vol 1, No 3, pp 24–29.

Milne, R G (1987) 'Competitive Tendering in the NHS: an economic analysis of the early implementation of HC(83)18', *Public Administration*, Vol 65, Summer, pp 145–160.

Moore, W (1993) 'HA calls in private sector to tender for clinical work', *The Health Service Journal*, 2 September, p 6.

National Audit Office (1987), 'Competitive Tendering for Support Services in the National Health Service', HMSO, London.

Newbigging, R, Lister, J (1988) 'The record of private companies in NHS support services', Association of London Authorities, London, pp 5–6.

Paine, L (1984) 'Contracting Out In The Bethlem Royal And Maudsley Hospital', in 'Contracting Out In The Public Sector', proceedings of a conference, Royal Institute of Public Administration, London.

Peisch, R (1995) 'When Outsourcing Goes Awry', *Harvard Business Review*, May–June, pp 24–37.

Reynolds, I (1994) 'Selecting Counterparties: Who Should You Be in Bed With?', presented at the SMI Conference on Market Testing in the NHS, 4–5 July.

Scofield, R (1994) 'Market Testing in the National Health Service' presented at the Financial Times Conference on Resource Management in the Public Sector, 7 February.

Schwartz, J (1992) 'Ordering Out for IS', *CIO*, February, p 18.

Sheffield City Council, Employment and Economic Development Dept (1988) 'Competitive Tendering for Support Services in the National Health Service: Who Pays the Price?', Sheffield City Council, Sheffield.

Thompson, J L (1993) '*Strategic Management: Awareness and Change*, 2nd edn, Chapman Hall, London, p xiv.

TUC (1986) *More Contractors' Failures*, TUC Publications, London.

Waldgrave, W (1994) 'Public Service and the Future', opening address at the Financial Times Conference on Resource Management in the Public Sector, 7 February.

Weale, A (1988) 'Cost and Choice in Health Care', King's Fund, London.

White Paper (1989) 'Working for Patients', CM 555, HMSO, London pp 8 and 70.

White Paper (1991) 'The Citizens Charter: Raising The Standard', HMSO, London.

White Paper (1991) 'Competing For Quality: Buying Better Public Services', HM Treasury, London.

Part Five

STRATEGIC FINANCIAL ACCOUNTING

10

USING PUBLISHED FINANCIAL STATEMENTS FOR STRATEGIC ADVANTAGE

Keith Ward

INTRODUCTION

Financial accounting is normally perceived as the historic, backward, looking part of the finance function. It is seen as involving the recording of the underlying financial transactions of the business and then by many observers, such as Allen (1994), summarising these actual transactions into a profit and loss account, a cash flow statement and a balance sheet for publication to the external world. This means that all the data included within a set of published financial statements must be regarded as being generally available to the 'public', where 'public' must be assumed to include all external parties which have an interest in the financial performance and position of the company. Competitors are clearly one external group which is very interested in the performance of the company as, in many industries, are the company's suppliers and customers.

Corporate and competitive strategy is by definition forward- and outward-looking and hence, at first sight, it may appear strange to include financial accounting in a book on strategic business finance. This perception may well be heightened when the problems involved with preparing generally available financial information is placed in the context of the competitor analysis discussed in Chapters 5 and 6; the temptation is to avoid giving away anything which may have value to competitors or present potential future negotiating opportunities to suppliers and customers.

However, published financial statements represent the major communication medium between the company and its shareholders at least; for many companies, they are also the major medium for communicating with a broader range of stakeholders. Hence the company should think carefully about how it handles this communication process and what information should be supplied to the shareholders. This is particularly true for a large public group where its future share price movements are heavily dependent upon the company's ability to attract new investors as well as to retain its existing shareholders.

Both existing and potential shareholders are primarily interested in the future returns which they can expect from an investment in the company. Therefore, as in any strategic analysis, information regarding the past is only relevant in as far as it provides an appropriate indicator as to the future performance which may be expected. Also, as discussed in detail in Chapter 2, the current share price of the company already incorporates the existing expectations by shareholders of this future performance. Hence a key element in the communication process should be to highlight any changes to these existing expectations; published financial statements and the associated press releases can, and should, therefore be used *to manage* shareholder expectations. If this is not done, then the share price of the company is often unnecessarily volatile as the financial markets respond to a series of unexpected financial results and shock announcements. Again, as already mentioned in Chapter 2, any required changes to the corporate financial strategy, such as an increase in the dividend payout ratio, must be carefully explained and justified to shareholders if adverse impacts on shareholder value are to be avoided.

Therefore this chapter attempts to draw together a number of factors which could lead to a more strategic approach to the preparation of published financial statements and the ways in which they are subsequently communicated to the interested stakeholders. This starts by reconsidering the risk/return relationship, which is so fundamental to all shareholder value considerations, and the way in which this is impacted by published financial statements. Ways in which this role could be improved are then considered and this leads into a discussion of the target audience for externally focused financial communication.

It can be strongly argued that major publicly quoted groups compete for investors against other similarly large publicity quoted companies rather than necessarily against their direct competitors. The implications of this are considered for the presentation of strategically focused published financial statements and for the types of investors which companies should be trying to attract.

The chapter goes on to consider how the company can indicate the types of investment opportunities and their associated levels of return so that future likely levels of returns are more clearly understood by investors. All of this has to be achieved, of course, through the use of generally available information to which competitors will be able to gain complete and immediate access; therefore the chapter concludes by considering some of the issues relating to the practical implementation of a more strategic approach to financial accounting.

THE RISK/RETURN RELATIONSHIP REVISITED

If published financial statements are the major tool of communication between the company and its shareholders, they should be focused on the key items of common interest to these two parties.

As has been repeated frequently throughout the book, the key financial objective for a commercially run company should be to create long-term shareholder value. In Chapter 1 this was distinguished from the commonly stated objective of enhancing corporate value, which is the real underlying focus of much of the earlier literature on shareholder and corporate wealth creation (see Rappaport, 1986 and Donaldson, 1984), in that any increase in corporate value (which is the increase in the net present value of the expected future cash flows of the business) needs to be translated into increased *perceived* value by the shareholder. An important role for strategic financial accounting must therefore be to aid this translation process, ie to minimise the gap between corporate value, as defined in Chapter 1, and shareholder value. As stated in Chapter 2, the rational shareholder has a *required* rate of return which is dictated by their perception of the risk associated with their investment in the company; clearly, in the case of existing shareholders, they are concerned

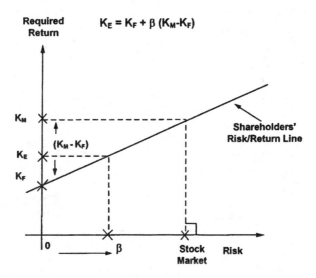

Figure 10.1 Capital asset pricing model

with the actual risk on their existing investment, while the equally important prospective investors are concerned with the perceived risk associated with their potential investment. There is a fundamental positive correlation between perceived risk and the required rate of return (normally referred to as the company's cost of capital). This means that it is not sufficient simply for a company to increase its actual rate of return in order for the share price to increase correspondingly. The resulting movement in share price will depend upon the shareholders' perception of any change in the risk associated with this increased rate of return.

In practical terms, the shareholders' perception of risk is driven by the volatility concerned with the returns generated by the company (thus a zero risk investment refers to one with a guaranteed level of return with no volatility). Diagrammatically this can be shown, as in Figure 10.1, as the Capital Asset Pricing Model (CAPM). The CAPM, which is the dominant model used in the major financial markets around the world, states that investors can calculate their required rate of return on any particular investment by reference to three variables. These are the risk-free rate of return which is available in this financial market (this controls the point of intercept with the vertical axis), the premium which is required over this risk-free rate for taking on the risk associated with this stock market (this effectively sets the slope of the shareholder's risk/return line), and the particular risk associated with the company under consideration. The company's specific risk is referred to as the β factor (the stock market as a whole has a β of 1, which is dictated by the linear equation of the CAPM: $K_E = K_F + \beta (K_M\text{-}K_F)$; hence the important characteristic of a company's β is its position relative to the stock market level of unity.

Many issues relating to the application of the CAPM and the resulting required rates of return around the world are considered in detail in Chapters 3 and 4 and their theoretical development is comprehensively

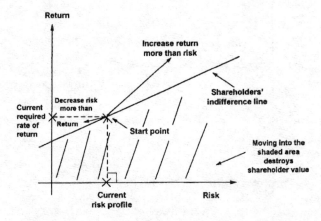

Figure 10.2 Added value possibilities

covered by the author in *Strategic Issues in Finance* (1994) and hence need not concern us here. From the company point of view, it is important to focus upon how this model affects the company's ability to create shareholder value.

As should be clear from the previous discussion and can be seen in Figure 10.2, the CAPM line of shareholders' required returns for different levels of perceived risk can be regarded as the shareholders' indifference line; moving up and down the line merely compensates investors for the comparative change in their risk perceptions. Equally clearly, any strategic initiative by the company which moves the company below this indifference line will result in a reduction in shareholder value. The consequences of such a reduction will be that the share price falls until the expected return once again equals the required rate of return; in other words, the share falls below the line temporarily and the price adjustment then moves the share back on to the CAPM line. (In a perfectly efficient capital market, as discussed in Chapter 3, these changes would be instantaneous.)

Conversely, any strategic initiative which *created perceived shareholder value* would lift the particular share above the indifference line, ie until the share price increased sufficiently to move it back down on to the line (the share price increase being the crystallisation of the enhanced shareholder value). In practical terms, as shown in Figure 10.2, this leads to two different types of value-enhancing strategies. The company can select a return-increasing strategy, where the expected resultant increase in financial return is greater than any proportionate perceived risk increase. These strategies should be built around the sustainable competitive advantages of the company as discussed in Chapter 5.

Alternatively, the company can seek to reduce the volatility associated with its returns and accordingly reduce its perceived risk level. This can be achieved through a variety of hedging strategies (taking out insurance cover, etc) or by giving key customers discounts in order to guarantee a continued level of business and hence future return, but all of these strategies will result in a reduced level of return (the payment of the insurance premium, the level of the long-term discount, etc). Shareholders' value therefore is only created if the reduction in the level of perceived risk is proportionately greater than the reduction in the rate of return.

PROBLEMS OF THE RISK/RETURN RELATIONSHIP

This shareholder value creation concept should lead to a clear decision for any company facing the opportunity depicted in Figure 10.3. This company has an opportunity to make a strategic investment in a project with a risk profile lower than that which the overall company has at present. Thus, although the proposed investment is expected to produce a return which is below the company's current required rate of return (ie its existing cost of capital), because of its much lower risk profile, the investment *should* enhance shareholder value.

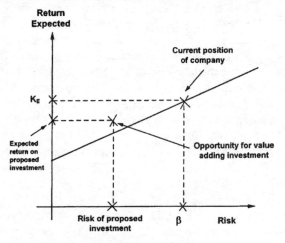

Figure 10.3 Risk reduction strategies

Unfortunately most research in this area indicates that very few companies would be willing to undertake such a low-risk/low-return project because they believe that, in the short term at least, the investment would in practice destroy shareholder value. Their logic is based on the way in which they believe risk perceptions are created and then changed in financial markets. For shareholder value to be created in the short term by such a strategic initiative, the financial market would have to reduce its required rate of return immediately to take account of the new, less volatile investment (the new cost of capital should simplistically reflect the weighted average cost of capital for the original business and the new investment). Most large, publicly quoted company finance directors seem to believe that this reduction in risk perception and consequent reduction in required rate of return will only take place *over time* as the company actually delivers these more stable, less volatile financial returns.

However, the first communication resulting from such an investment will be that investors will see a reduction in the overall rate of return actually being delivered by the enlarged group. If the *required* return has not been more than proportionately reduced, there is a significant risk that the decreased *actual* rate of return will result in a drop in value. In the longer term, when the risk perception has been changed, the combined rate of return should lead to an upward reassessment of the company's value (by more than it went down initially), but very few senior corporate managers seem prepared to risk seeing their company's share price fall now so that it can rise even further in the medium-term future.

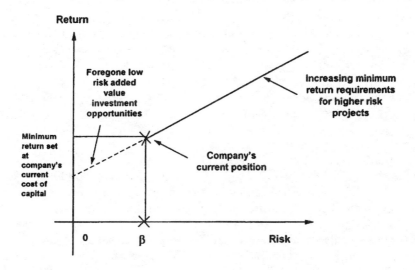

Figure 10.4 Foregone low-risk opportunities

As a consequence, many companies set their minimum required rate of return on new investments at the current cost of equity capital for the company. As shown in Figure 10.4, this results in the company potentially foregoing low-risk but value-enhancing opportunities. Equally significantly, such a strategy almost inevitably leads, over time, to an increasing risk profile for the company as it seeks to find investment opportunities which generate an expected rate of return which is greater than the risk adjusted required rate of return. This is considered again later in the chapter.

It would seem logical that a more strategically focused approach to communicating with shareholders would place a greater emphasis on the risk/return relationship so that these lower risk alternatives could be undertaken by the company. However, current incentive schemes given to senior managers of these companies do not encourage risk-reduction strategies as they reward return-increasing strategies, often irrespective of whether they create enhanced shareholder value or not. (This area is not considered in detail here as it is dealt with in Chapter 12.)

COMPETITION AT THE CORPORATE LEVEL

The argument for emphasising the risk/return relationship in communications with shareholders is considerably strengthened when one considers the real competition faced by large publicly quoted companies. Many very large, publicly quoted groups consist of a unique collection of only vaguely related businesses. Each of their operating businesses, subsidiaries, divisions, strategic business units, or whatever they are called, should be able to identify specific businesses which they compete against at the product/market interfaces where they actually do business, ie sell goods and services to external customers. (Indeed, a key issue for describing any subdivision of the group as a strategic business unit is the identification of specific external competitors.) However, at the corporate or group level where outside shareholders are primarily involved, there may be no readily identifiable direct competitors.

In Chapter 1 the Marlboro Friday case study was briefly introduced which showed the financial strategy of Philip Morris Inc in its very strong tobacco business. However, Philip Morris Group also contains the second largest food business in the world (following the acquisitions and integration of General Foods, Kraft and Jacob's Suchard) and Miller Brewing. Its largest worldwide competitor in the tobacco business is BAT Tobacco Group but this is part of BAT Industries and here the other major element of the group is in financial services (Eagle Star and Allied Dunbar in the UK and Farmers Insurance in the US). Further, one group is based in the US, while the other is located in the UK (despite the fact that BAT does not have a UK-based tobacco business for historical reasons).

As a consequence, while these companies are serious competitors and will spend much senior management time on competitor analysis and developing specific competitive strategies for individual markets and product segments, they are not necessarily seen as direct alternative investments by existing or potential shareholders. Indeed, at this very large end of the corporate world, these companies effectively compete for investment funds with all the other major companies in their financial markets or, at least, with *all* those with similar general characteristics. Thus Philip Morris might be classified as a branded, fast-moving consumer goods company which is using its US success to drive a global, product- and brand-based strategy. A US based investor might quite logically consider alternative investments therefore to be in Coca-Cola or Procter & Gamble.

Procter & Gamble's global competitor, Unilever, might not feature as a direct investment alternative to P&G due to its Anglo-Dutch corporate structure and the resulting complexity of its shareholdings. BAT Industries, however, might well include Unilever in its comparative analysis of financial performance as both of them are significant elements within the UK stock market and BAT's mix of businesses makes it a unique investment opportunity without direct comparisons. Increasingly, large groups are explicitly acknowledging exactly this by placing their financial objectives in the context of the overall capital market expectations or requirements (eg stating that they intend to pay a dividend yield equivalent at least to the average of their stock markets or the top 100 companies in that market, or expressing earnings per share growth in terms of outperforming the average for their stock markets as a whole). Indeed, when they make presentations to financial analysts and investment fund managers, many of these companies will compare their overall financial performance against these other alternative investments, rather than against their direct, but less relevant competitors.

The logic of this is based on a key difference between economic and managerial performance measures. A sound managerial performance measure must only include measures over which managers can exercise control, as it is clearly unfair to judge a manager's performance on anything over which no control is possible. These managerial performance measures therefore indicate how well the management team have performed, particularly with reference to their competitors. Although of importance to their investors, these comparisons on their own do not provide sound information as to whether the 'company' has been and, more importantly, will continue to be successful in an overall sense.

Thus the role of economic performance measures is to place the overall performance of the business into its appropriate context, which should be a comparison against the opportunity cost of the *alternative* investments which could have been made, ie the other large companies in the same financial market. In simple terms, this is saying that the external investor would rather have invested in an average management team which happened to be in the most attractive sector of their market than in the best managers in the world if they are stuck in a dramatically loss-making industry. It should be clear that modern published financial statements for diversified groups are fulfilling the role of economic performance measures (which, of course, do include assessments of relative managerial performance), but these measures are being used for setting the shareholders' required rate of return in the future far more than for assessing the actual performance in the period which has already finished.

Following on from the earlier discussion on the risk/return relationship, the management of shareholders' risk perception of one company relative to the alternative investments is clearly therefore of critical importance. Hence the presentation of consistent, continuing and *sustainable* levels of return can be fundamental to the strategic use of published financial statements, if the strategy is to reduce the perceived risk associated with the company. However, another objective could be to show how the corporate strategy adds shareholder value through the specific types of business which are combined together in the group (eg Philip Morris with its cigarettes, food and brewing, or BAT Industries with its tobacco and financial services). This area has been directly considered by Campbell et al (1995) and more indirectly by Hamel et al (1993) among others, but there has been little if any consideration as to how these *corporate* added value strategies (as opposed to the more specific competitive strategy issues) can be communicated, in advance, to the shareholders in a believable way. (If the corporate strategy *does* indeed add value, the excess financial performance will eventually be delivered and at this point the shareholders' value should become crystallised, but this could be a long way off.)

ATTRACTING THE RIGHT INVESTORS

The published financial statements should be seen therefore as an integral part of a financial strategy designed to demonstrate that the company is a good investment relative to a broad range of alternative investments, rather than by simple comparison to its direct competitors. A key role for the published financial statements within this strategy is to ensure that both existing and potential investors understand properly the relative risks associated with the company and the potential level of sustainable future returns which the company can produce. This communication process should also endeavour to attract those investors to whom the particular risk/return offering of the company will appear most attractive.

Due to the linear form of the CAPM, this point may not seem particularly relevant. If individual investors have a genuinely linear trade-off between risk and return across the entire range of potential investments, they should be both able and willing to adjust their portfolio to accommodate any attractive prospective investment, wherever it is in terms of its relative risk profile. However, in practical terms the shareholders' *line* (or the capital market line to give it its more formal title) should be regarded as the tangent to an infinite array of indifference *curves* for individual investors, as shown in Figure 10.5. In other words, for the CAPM theory to hold it is not necessary for individual investors to have a linear risk taking appetite across the whole range of potential investments; after all, no economist would ever discuss an indifference *line*.

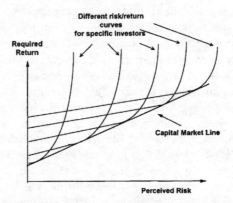

Figure 10.5 Different risk/return profiles

Any individual investment will be bought by the investor who requires the lowest return for taking on its specifically associated risk, ie they will pay the highest price for the particular share. As long as there are a broad enough range of investors with different risk-taking appetites, the overall market risk/return will be represented by the straight line which is drawn as the tangent to the lowest point of all the individual indifference curves. Thus, as discussed in Chapter 2, when a high risk-taking investor such as a venture capitalist takes on a very high risk investment in a new start-up company, a correspondingly high return is required. However, if the company is successful, its risk profile is likely to reduce quite rapidly and hence the required return should also reduce proportionately. Unfortunately for this company, the risk/return curve for the venture capital investor is likely to be much less steeply inclined than the capital market line, as the venture capitalist will normally require a relatively high return on any investment they make.

Consequently it would add value if the company was able to attract new investors whose risk-taking appetite more closely matched the company's new risk profile. These new investors should be able both to buy out the original venture capitalists and to inject the necessary growth financing at a much more acceptable required rate of return. Similarly at the other end of the spectrum, a low-risk company should have appropriately low-risk taking investors. These risk averse investors are likely to have a very steeply increasing return requirement for increasing risk perceptions, as indicated in Figure 10.5.

Thus, if the strategy of the company changes to increasing value through increasing return *more than risk,* any such successful increase in corporate value may not be translated into a comparable increase in shareholder value. However, this company could create enhanced shareholder value by attracting investors who are more willing to bear the increased risk which is now associated with the changed strategy, ie for bearing this level of risk they will require a lower return than the existing investors in the company.

Theoretically, it can be argued that this changing profile of investors would occur automatically, if it was needed. The process would be that the change in the risk perception would lead to an adjustment in the required return of the existing investor. Since, in both examples, their new risk-adjusted return position would be well above the capital market line, the value of the shares in the company would fall substantially. As the price of the shares fell, other investors would find that the shares had now become attractive and so would seek to buy them, thus bidding up the share price back to the capital market line. This degree of fluctuation in share price is unlikely to be attractive to the company's management (the very strict theoretician would, of course, again argue that the changes would be instantaneous) but, more importantly, the new investors are only likely to be attracted if they understand the new risk profile of the company.

The new risk-taking strategy should therefore be communicated to both existing and potential investors so that they can base their future investment decisions on the most relevant information. This must be in the long-term best interests of the company as, if it misleads its shareholders, the share price will be very adversely affected when the deception becomes apparent, particularly as shareholders with the wrong risk profile will still be invested in the company.

REINVESTMENTS WITHIN THE COMPANY

A clear example of the problems that can arise can be developed by building on the theoretical models discussed in Chapter 2. A key element in any approach to shareholder value creation is the relationship between the two methods of giving a financial return to shareholders, ie dividend yield and capital growth. Capital growth in the share price is generated because future profits and hence future dividends are expected to be greater than those produced today. This future growth in profits and dividends is created at the expense of the current dividends because growth normally occurs through the reinvestment of current profits, ie retained earnings. Current profits which are retained for reinvestment cannot, of course, be paid out as dividends.

Thus a good signal to shareholders as to the future rate of sustainable growth in both earnings and dividends is given by the dividend pay-out ratio or the related retention ratio. However, the other critical component of the very important sustainable growth prediction is the rate of return which will be achieved on these reinvested funds. Clearly the higher the rate of return is expected to be, the faster the company can grow for any given retention ratio.

Unfortunately this is the element which is not directly observable by the financially rational investor (the other components all are) and therefore an assumption is required. Not surprisingly, the most common assumption (and the one which is built into the theoretical and practical models) is that, in the absence of any information to the contrary, the rate of return on reinvestments will be the same as the rate of return currently being achieved by the company, ie its current return on equity.

For many companies, the application of this assumption may not create any significant problems, but for other companies it may dramatically over- or under-represent what the senior managers expect to happen. This can be particularly significant where the currently reported accounting return on equity is affected by large balance sheet adjustments (such as the writing off of goodwill, or the capitalisation of certain intangible assets, etc).

Senior managers of large companies should be well aware of the type of forward-looking analyses which investors are carrying out based on their historically focused published financial statements. Therefore they should, as far as possible, ensure that their investors are fully aware of any distortions in the current figures which could affect their perceptions of the future: putting a large *caveat emptor* sign on the front of the published financial statements is not a sound way to build a long-term relationship with your shareholders. As discussed in Christopher et al (1991), any long-term relationship marketing strategy must be built on a sense of mutual trust and this should be the fundamental basis for preparing published financial statements. If the company can assist their investors to make their forward-looking investment decisions more soundly based by highlighting where historic performance is not a good guide to the future, they should do so, as long as it does not require them to give away competitively sensitive information through these 'public' documents.

A key way of doing this in a large diversified group is to ensure that investors do not use the overall average rate of return for the company, if this is significantly different from the rate which is being achieved in the area where the major reinvestments are actually being made. Yet many such groups seem to go out of their way to make it difficult for even the serious analyst to compute a remotely accurate rate of return on a segmented basis.

An even clearer signal can be given through a publicly stated financial strategy which some groups now have. This could quite simply state, as some companies do, that the company will not reinvest funds unless the expected rate of return is greater than the shareholders' required rate of return. However they do not then go on to state anywhere what the company considers this required rate of return to be! The issue here, of course, is that senior managers do not wish to be too specific as it can be used against them in the future, however, a long-term trust relationship is a two-way process. Many of the issues related to reinvestment strategy and corporate resource allocation decisions are dealt with in the existing literature (see Tomkins, 1991).

CAN INVESTORS READ THE SIGNALS?

If companies produced more signals as to their future sustainable performance and the associated risks, these would not result in better long-term relationships unless investors were capable of recognising and understanding the signals. (It is clearly impossible for companies to start publishing specific profit and cash flow projections together with the detailed competitive strategies which it intends to implement in order to achieve them.)

In most developed capital markets there is no doubt that there are sufficient skilled investors and advisers (eg analysts, etc) who are quite capable of applying the models discussed in this book and elsewhere in the

financial literature. Indeed, as the UK capital market becomes more dominated by professional fund managers (the second stage in the two stage
agency theory discussed in Chapter 12), this capability should increase. It
could be argued that this is to the disadvantage of the less sophisticated,
small investor, but the developments in technology, information systems
and trading processes generally have already achieved this. In fact, if companies produced more strategically relevant information directly, it could
redress part of the current imbalance as the small investor probably cannot afford to carry out a lot of the fundamental industry analysis which
the big funds already do.

Of course, any discussion of the value of improved information is of no
relevance to anyone who believes that financial markets are already highly
efficient.

PUBLISHED FINANCIAL STATEMENTS AS A MARKETING TOOL

The whole concept of using published financial statements as a means of
communicating appropriate and relevant (ie forward-looking and strategically oriented) information to both existing and potential shareholders
places them properly into context. They should be seen as a principal element in marketing the company, rather than as the enforced reporting to
the minimum historic financial information which will comply with the
regulatory requirements.

Many companies are very clearly using their published financial statements as a positive marketing tool by including much more general information about the company, its strategy, its products and the markets in
which it operates. Technically this additional information does not form
part of the audited financial statements and, not surprisingly therefore,
auditors are very specific as to what elements are reported in their audit
report.

However, the latest trend is now to produce two documents which are
often put into one outer folder. In one section is all the marketing information and the other includes all the detailed financial accounts, ie the
profit and loss account, cash flow statement, balance sheet and detailed
notes to the accounts. Many companies are now including a simplified
version of the detailed financial accounts in the first glossy, marketing section; this financial presentation is often made much more user friendly
still by showing the key numbers in a graphical or pictorial way.

Many shareholders seem to have responded very favourably to this
type of presentation and often tell the company that they no longer want
to receive the detailed financial reports. Interestingly, some very large
companies report that they have even received these requests from some
of their significant, professionally managed fund investors. Perhaps the

earlier comment regarding the sophistication of these professional investors needs to be revisited.

CONCLUSION

Much more positively, perhaps the lack of interest in financial reports should be taken as an indication of the increasing sophistication of these investors. As a guide to their future investment strategy, the detailed financial accounts are of little use on their own. The continuing insistence of the accounting profession to publish *the* profit for the year and to show *the* state of affairs of the company at the end of the year is decidedly unhelpful for any strategic perspective. It is very well accepted that there are a vast range of judgements that need to be exercised in order to produce any set of financial statements, whether historical or projected. Consequently any profit figure and balance sheet position are the result of the ways in which those judgements have been exercised.

Rather than prescriptively legislating as to how these necessary and inevitable judgements are to be exercised, a much more strategic approach would be to disclose the impact of exercising them in different ways. After all, this is the role of sensitivity analysis, scenario planning, etc in strategic planning. The plan is based on a series of key assumptions and the impact of different outcomes for these key assumptions is evaluated and considered before implementing the plan.

If the impact of different accounting treatments was made clear, intelligent outsiders could form their own views as to the most appropriate treatment and put the reported financial performance into a much more appropriate context. More importantly, they could then use this actual performance as a much more relevant base from which to project their expectations for the future financial performance. On these projections they will then base their investment decisions.

The company can further improve the basis of these decisions by highlighting where the historic performance is inappropriate as the base from which to project and indicating where other changes need to be made if a sensible view of the future is to be developed. Clearly, as has been stated throughout this chapter, all of this information must be checked for commercial sensitivity but the decision *not* to publish useful and helpful information should be carefully justified, rather than the other way around.

Hopefully such a development trend will make published financial statements a much more helpful strategic investment aid in the future. If such amendments are not made, it is likely that the current trend of investors only wanting to receive the simplified, picture-book version will continue. This will eventually result in the underlying financial information becoming ever more discredited and irrelevant until it is finally ignored completely. Acquiring strategic relevance should not therefore be regarded as a nice optional extra for published financial statements; it is a matter of long-term survival!

References

Allen, D (1994) *Strategic Financial Decisions*, Kogan Page, London.

Christopher, M, Payne, A and Ballantyne, D (1991) *Relationship Marketing*, Butterworth Heinemann, Oxford.

Campbell, A, Goold, M and Alexander, M (1995) 'Corporate Strategy: The Quest for Parenting Advantage', *Harvard Business Review*, March/April.

Donaldson, G (1984) *Managing Corporate Wealth,* Praeger, New York.

Hamel, G and Prahalad, C K (1993) 'Strategy as Stretch and Leverage', *Harvard Business Review*, March/April.

Rappaport, A (1986) *Creating Shareholder Value*, Free Press, New York.

Tomkins, C (1991) *Corporate Resource Allocation*, Blackwell, Oxford.

Ward, K (1994) *Strategic Issues in France,* Butterworth Heinemann, Oxford.

11

25 YEARS OF CURRENCY DEBASEMENT AND THE ACCOUNTS OF LUCAS INDUSTRIES

D R Myddelton

INTRODUCTION

This chapter looks at the financial results of Lucas Industries over 25 years from August 1969 to July 1994. The focus is on differences between historical money cost and constant purchasing power accounts, as well as on absolute performance. We look first, briefly, at how to adjust HMC accounts into CPP terms; at some special features of Lucas accounts; and at how Lucas itself reported the impact of inflation on accounts. The main section then considers key aspects of the HMC and CPP results, and differences between them.*

Going concerns split their accounts into arbitrary one-year periods for legal and tax purposes. But the margin of error in year-end adjustments can affect the results of such short periods and make them hard to interpret. In this chapter, therefore, we examine the results of Lucas Industries over 25 years, looking at five periods of five years each. Thus we allow for the cumulative impact of inflation over a long period, and we present the results in a way that is easier to follow and less subject to distortion.

Few assets have a life of more than 25 years, and the period between 1969 and 1994 covers most of the UK's post-war currency debasement (so

---

*HMC refers to Historical Cost accounting in terms of Money (perhaps with some fixed assets revalued). CPP refers to Constant Purchasing Power accounting, which *dates* HMC amounts, and uses the Retail Prices Index to index them. Money amounts in **bold** are in July 1994 purchasing power; other amounts represent normal current money.

far). Between 1945 and 1995 the pound has lost no less than 95 per cent of its purchasing power. The average rate of currency debasement was 3½ per cent a year between 1945 and 1969, but 8 per cent a year between 1969 and 1994.

Lucas Industries is a well-established company with few large acquisitions or divestments during the period, and with little real growth. Thus the company is more recognisably the same over the whole period than most other UK groups of its size. Also currency debasement affects fairly capital-intensive companies such as Lucas more than many others, such as retailers or service industries. Lucas itself recognised this even before 1969, by publishing details of replacement cost depreciation in its annual report.

Finally, Lucas Industries now (1995) has new senior management. It will be interesting to see whether 'improved' results genuinely change losses into profits, or whether larger losses merely become smaller losses. To tell this, one needs to look at the real (CPP) results, not at fictional ones.

ADJUSTING HMC ACCOUNTS INTO CPP ACCOUNTS

Adjusting historical money cost (HMC) accounts into constant purchasing power (CPP) terms is like translating foreign currencies into domestic currency. ('The past is a foreign country. . .') Indeed, for this purpose the Retail Prices Index (RPI) is, in effect, an 'exchange rate over time'*.

The two main differences between HMC and CPP accounts relate to fixed assets and net monetary assets (NMA).

Fixed assets

Because fixed assets last for many years, the 'adjusted cost' in CPP accounts (and straight-line depreciation thereon) can be much higher than in HMC accounts. For example, if inflation averages 10 per cent a year, assets with a 15-year life produce a CPP expense nearly double HMC depreciation. In a capital-intensive business, this level of adjustment can easily translate an HMC profit into a CPP loss.

There are two special problems with fixed assets in CPP accounts: revaluations and disposals. Most so-called 'historical cost' accounts in the UK revalue some fixed assets from time to time – especially land and

---

*The current Retail Prices Index (January 1987 = 100) stood at 17.4 (equivalent) in August 1969, and at 144.0 in July 1994. Over the 25-year period, the annual rate of inflation (rising prices) was 8.8 per cent; while the annual rate of currency debasement (fall in purchasing power of money) was 8.1 per cent. If the rate of inflation is 25 per cent, the rate of currency debasement is 20 per cent (= 25/(100 + 25)). In preparing CPP accounts the working unit is the January 1987 pound; but the amounts published here are in July 1994 purchasing power.

buildings, where the extra depreciation is likely to be small. CPP accounts should normally ignore these: they partially match CPP's regular restatement of money cost in real terms. In fact, CPP represents a 'purer' form of historical cost accounting than the mongrel UK version (a mixture of cost and value) common today. (The acronym is thus HMC, not HC, because CPP, too, is a form of HC accounting.)

Since Lucas revalued fixed assets in August 1970, after only one of the 25 years, it seems sensible for CPP accounts to include the change. Land and buildings rose from £26m to £55m, and plant and equipment from £30m to £36m – a total increase of £35m (CPP: **£268m**).

It also seems right for CPP accounts to allow for any implied lengthening of asset lives. Thus in 1981 Lucas reduced cumulative depreciation on plant and equipment by 1/6, from £159m to £134m, and increased the implied average life from 12½ to 15 years. And in 1989 Lucas reduced cumulative depreciation on land and buildings by ½, from £46m to £24m, and increased the implied average life from 33 to 50 years (The CPP reductions were **£151m** and **£181m**.)

Lucas also revalued stocks in August 1976 (RPI = 40.2) from £183m to £208m, following Statement of Standard Accounting Principles (SSAP) 9 on treatment of overheads. (The CPP increase was **£91m**. Assuming a *mid-year* increase (RPI = 43.7) would cause a CPP rise of only **£84m**, which illustrates the kind and scale of error that can easily occur.)

The CPP accounts have ignored two other HMC fixed asset revaluations:

1. £24m in 1981, in respect of overseas assets (5 per cent of the total).
2. £113m in 1989, of which £94m was in respect of all UK properties (48 per cent of land and buildings).

The second special problem with fixed assets relates to disposals. CPP profits may be less than HMC profits because of larger *losses on disposals* of fixed assets (which represent adjustments to earlier depreciation charges). For example, over the 25 years Lucas reported total HMC *profits* on disposals of tangible fixed assets of £41m. (Total CPP *losses* on disposals amounted to **£360m**.)

Net monetary assets

In times of inflation there may be losses of purchasing power in respect of net monetary assets. Clearly there is no similar expense item in HMC accounts. It is simplest (and normally makes little difference) to treat stocks as part of NMA, even though strictly they are 'real'. Every item in working capital is then 'monetary', and deducting long-term liabilities gives the net position (which equals current assets less total liabilities).

To determine the purchasing power loss in respect of NMA requires a number of simple steps:

1. Calculate the money amount of NMA at the start and end of the year.
2. Translate these amounts into CPP terms, using different exchange rates for the start-of-year and end-of-year money amounts; and average the two.
3. To find the CPP loss on NMA, multiply the average CPP amount of NMA during the year by the rate of currency debasement. If the average balance of NMA is *negative*, then the CPP *gain* is income.

General

After making CPP adjustments to HMC accounts, it is useful to reconcile changes in CPP equity capital during each year. The main items will normally be as follows:

1. Retentions = CPP profit after tax, less dividends paid.
2. Proceeds from issues of shares.
3. Revaluations of assets (where appropriate in CPP accounts).
4. Goodwill written off against reserves.
5. Various small items.

Due to the nature of the adjustments and estimates, there will often be a remaining unexplained difference. 1 per cent (per year) of the average equity is well within the normal margin of error; but larger differences are not uncommon. The average annual errors in Lucas CPP accounts for four of the five-year periods were less than 1 per cent. In period D (1985–9), however, the errors (negative in each case) were larger, ranging from 2.7 to 5.8 per cent between 1985 and 1988. Without affecting CPP profits, these amounts (totalling £160m) have been used to reduce CPP accumulated depreciation.

It is, of course, extremely ambitious at the best of times to try to represent accurately in two summary financial statements the complex affairs of a large international business. Financial accounting is an art, not a science. There are two further reasons why CPP adjustments using the annual accounts can only be approximate. Certain assumptions have to be made, which will not be entirely accurate, and which, over a long period, may lead to significant error. And the Retail Prices Index is not a perfect reciprocal measure of the fall in the general purchasing power of money. There is no such measure. The implicit index used in historical money cost accounting is 1969 = 100, 1994 = 100. This compares with the Retail Prices Index (used in CPP accounting): 1969 = 17.4, 1994 = 144.0. While the RPI is certainly not perfect, it is a great deal less inaccurate than the implicit index in HMC suggesting that, over long periods of time, 'a pound is a pound is a pound'.

SPECIAL FEATURES OF THE LUCAS ACCOUNTS

It can be difficult to estimate the minority interests share of CPP profit after tax. The Lucas amounts are small, so minority interests have been included with equity, and total profit after tax, less dividends, has been treated as 'retained profit'.

Deferred tax (1970–8 and 1989–93) has been treated as a liability, and investment grants (1970–7) as part of equity, and both combined with tax in tax expense.

From 1986 to 1992 the HMC depreciation charge in the details of tangible fixed assets slightly exceeds the profit and loss account expense. The CPP expense has been reduced by a similar amount.

Two 'prior year' expenses (£3m interest in 1992 and £33m employee benefits in 1994) have each been treated as expenses in the previous year.

Between 1985 and 1990, 'extraordinary items' ranged up to 3 per cent of sales, mostly in respect of costs of withdrawing from businesses. Larger charges against profits are £88m provisions in 1992 for restructuring, and in 1994 £87m for 'restructuring and legal claims by US government' (not split), £17m for writing down Aerospace stocks, and £16m for other items. All these have been treated as 'ordinary' expenses, with suitable tax adjustments.

In two cases I have followed the company's approach. To repeat: we are here mainly dealing with the differences between HMC and CPP accounts, not with the 'real' performance of Lucas Industries.

There was a £94m goodwill expense in 1994 (following a disposal), which still leaves £172m net goodwill written off over the 25 years against reserves (CPP: **£309m**). (Treating this as an asset and expensing it against profit over time would reduce HMC RONA in period E from 7.1 to 5.5 per cent. It would also represent another difference between HMC and CPP accounts.)

In 1992 Lucas received £150m out of a pension fund surplus, and included the *net-of-tax* amount of £90m in profit *before* interest and tax.

LUCAS AND INFLATION ACCOUNTING

It would be wrong to imply that over the 25 years there was no reference to inflation accounting. On the contrary, Lucas accounts probably did more in that respect than most UK companies. For many years until 1977, the company transferred an estimate of replacement cost depreciation to fixed asset replacement reserve. Thereafter, like other UK companies, Lucas published supplementary current cost accounts, first under the Hyde Guidelines (1978–9) and then under SSAP 16 (1980–3). Between 1975 and 1983 replacement cost depreciation averaged exactly twice the HMC amount, very similar to the CPP charge.

The 1977 Report of the Directors discussed accounting for inflation:

> There have been a number of attempts to issue directions regarding the introduction of the effect of inflation into the published accounts of companies. On each occasion these proposals have proved to be either unworkable or unacceptable and have been dropped and the debate still continues. The Board has decided there should be a fully accepted standard established before formally adopting inflation adjusted accounts for the Company.

Between 1978 and 1982 the auditors reported on the Lucas current cost accounts, but not in 1983. Then in 1984 the directors expressed their opinion that the cost of producing the current cost accounts exceeded their value. So for the only time in the 25 years the auditors qualified their report, noting that: 'The accounts do not contain current cost accounts as required by SSAP 16.' (Throughout the whole period the auditors remained the same, though their name changed from Whinney Murray, to Ernst & Whinney, then to Ernst & Young.)

Lucas published estimates of replacement cost depreciation from the mid-1960s, long before the accountancy profession proposed any action on inflation accounting. Yet the tone of the 1977 paragraph is decidedly sharp; and it seems strange for Lucas, of all companies, to omit current cost accounts in 1984 and thus have the auditors qualify their report. In fact, the more the profession (or the government) tried to issue standards on the subject, the more disenchanted the company seems to have become.

HMC VERSUS CPP RESULTS

Introduction

For ease of discussion, the 25 years' results from Lucas Industries have been split into five equal periods of five years each, as follows:

Period A:	1970–4
Period B:	1975–9
Period C:	1980–4
Period D:	1985–9
Period E:	1990–4

Appendices and most of the figures show HMC and CPP results covering the five-year periods above, although a few of the figures show results for each of the 25 years.

Sales

Perhaps the most obvious difference between HMC and CPP accounts is in making comparisons over long periods of time. Figure 11.1 compares HMC and CPP sales. HMC accounts for Lucas show increases in sales every year except 1981, 1983 and 1992. HMC accounts show a 775 per cent increase in sales between 1970 and 1994, whereas CPP accounts show only an 11 per cent increase. But the RPI increased by 690 per cent over the period. Nearly all the apparent HMC increases in Lucas sales relate to inflation, not to real increases.

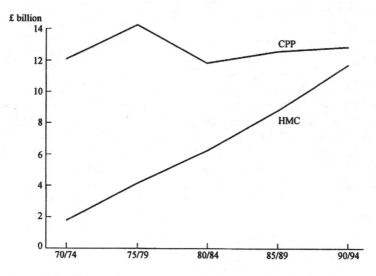

Figure 11.1 Lucas Industries PLC: sales

CPP sales have grown on average by only 0.4 per cent a year and have *fallen* in 11 of the years. Those who are content with reporting in terms of money seem to assume that people remember year-by-year rates of inflation. That is absurd. It is essential to look up the RPI numbers and make explicit CPP adjustments, even for an item as 'easy' as sales revenue.

Table 11.1 Annual rates of return for each five-year period, both on net assets and on equity, together with average annual inflation rates

	Average Inflation	Return on Net Assets			Return on Equity		
		HMC	CPP	Gap	HMC	CPP	Gap
	%	%	%	%	%	%	%
Period A	9.7	11.7	8.5	3.2	7.8	3.5	4.3
Period B	15.9	16.8	7.8	9.0	15.2	4.5	10.7
Period C	8.9	6.1	(1.3)	7.4	0.2	(6.9)	7.1
Period D	5.3	13.9	4.8	9.1	10.8	(0.4)	11.2
Period E	4.5	7.1	2.2	4.9	0.4	(5.5)	5.9
25 years	8.8	10.1	4.3	5.8	5.5	(1.0)	6.5

Profits

Figure 11.2 shows HMC and CPP rates of return on equity. Period A shows a fairly small difference between HMC and CPP rates of return, despite a high rate of inflation, whereas period D shows large differences, despite a fairly 'low' rate of inflation. This shows the importance of the *cumulative* impact of CPP adjustments. For example, even if there were no inflation at all in period F (from 1995 to 1999), CPP profits would still be less than HMC profits. In the same way, one can still get wet from walking under trees even after a rainstorm has ended.

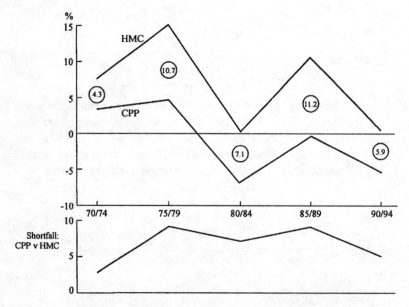

Figure 11.2 Lucas Industries PLC: return on equity

HMC accounts showed profits in all 5 periods (very small ones in periods C and E), but CPP accounts show losses in periods C, D and E (1980–94). In respect of that 15-year period, in 6 years there were already HMC losses, and in 6 years the adjustments translate HMC profits into CPP losses. In only 3 of the 15 years did Lucas make a CPP profit after tax.

In total, over the whole 25 years HMC profits totalled £628m, while CPP *losses* amounted to **£306m**. This is the crucial result which CPP adjustments often cause, transforming reported HMC profits into CPP losses. (The other main reason why companies report unreal profits is that profit and loss accounts make no charge for the (opportunity) cost of equity capital.) It should be emphasised that reported HMC profits are artificial while adjusted CPP losses are 'real'. Thus CPP losses mean that shareholder value is being destroyed.

In the 15-year period comprising periods B, C and D (from 1975 to 1989), annual HMC rates of return exceeded CPP rates by very large margins: over 8 per cent a year for return on net assets and nearly 10 per cent a year for return on equity.

Depreciation

Over the 25-year period, HMC depreciation totalled 2.8 per cent of sales revenue, while the CPP charge was 4.9 per cent of sales, including losses on disposals. Figure 11.3 shows the CPP depreciation charge as a percentage of HMC. In periods C and D the CPP charge is *more than twice* as

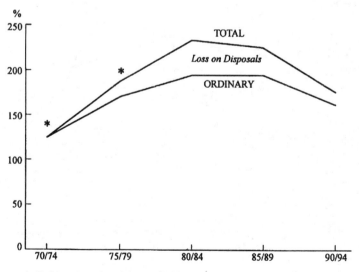

*= Replacement cost depreciation noted in Lucas accounts

Figure 11.3 Lucas Industries PLC: CPP depreciation as percentage of (adjusted) HMC

much as HMC. And over that 10-year period, HMC depreciation exceeded HMC profit after tax. Hence the CPP adjustments were enough to translate HMC profits into CPP losses in those years.

The CPP excess charge over HMC falls back only slowly from its peak in period C, even though inflation fell quite sharply after 1982. In period E inflation averaged 'only' 4.5 per cent a year, but CPP depreciation is still more than 75 per cent more than HMC. Even if there were no inflation after July 1994, CPP depreciation in period F (1995–9) would still be a good deal higher than HMC.

Net Monetary Assets (NMA)

Figure 11.4 shows average NMA for each of the 25 years and the loss of purchasing power thereon. HMC accounts, which calculate *in terms of money,* overlook this expense, but in the real world such loss of purchasing power is highly relevant. Over the 25 years, Lucas lost over **£500 million** purchasing power on NMA. This is a huge amount for HMC accounts to leave out. In times of rapid currency debasement, 'cash mountains' are very expensive in real terms, but you would never think so from HMC accounts.

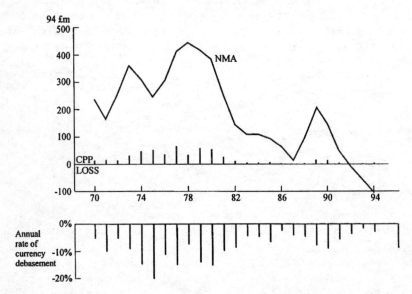

Figure 11.4 Lucas Industries PLC: annual loss (gain) on average net monetary assets (liabilities)

Of the **£500m** total NMA losses, Lucas lost **£400m** in the nine years from 1973 to 1981. During that period average NMA was **£350m** and the average rate of currency debasement was 12½ per cent a year. Over the remaining 16 years, average NMA was **£100m**, the average rate of currency debasement was 5 per cent a year and losses totalled **£100m**.

Tax

Whether Lucas makes a real profit or loss, the Inland Revenue still claims its tax take of around **£180m** per five-year period. Figure 11.5 shows CPP profit (or loss) and tax. In period D the tax bill exceeded profit before tax, and in periods C and E, when Lucas made real *losses,* the tax charge still continued remorselessly. (Over the 25 years, profit before tax had a mean of **£24m** and a standard deviation of **£92m**, while tax expense had a mean of **£36m** and a standard deviation of only **£11m**.)

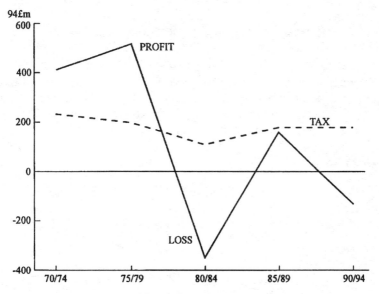

Figure 11.5 Lucas Industries PLC: real (CPP) profits and tax

Over the 25 years, CPP profits before tax amounted (net) to **£608m** and taxes amounted to **£914m**. Thus the average rate of tax on real Lucas profits works out at 150 per cent! Thank goodness the UK rate of tax on company profits is claimed to be one of the lowest in Europe, otherwise one dreads to think how much tax Lucas (and other companies like it) might have had to pay.

Debt ratio

As Figure 11.6 shows, the HMC debt ratio is slightly higher throughout than the CPP ratio. Both fluctuate between 15 and 30 per cent, until they increase to about 45 per cent in 1994. Another measure of gearing, however, tells a

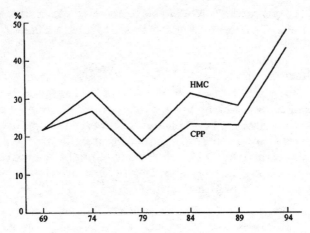

Figure 11.6 Lucas Industries PLC: debt ratio

different story. In the 15 years comprising periods C, D and E (1980–94), HMC profit covers interest more than twice, whereas interest is nearly twice as much as CPP profit before interest. Thus CPP adjusts gearing measures in *opposite* directions: 'improving' debt ratio (by increasing equity), while 'worsening' interest cover (by reducing profit).

Dividends

HMC accounts reported profits in each of the five-year periods, but HMC profits in periods C and E failed to cover dividends paid. Figure 11.7 shows CPP profits (or losses) and dividends. Lucas made CPP losses in

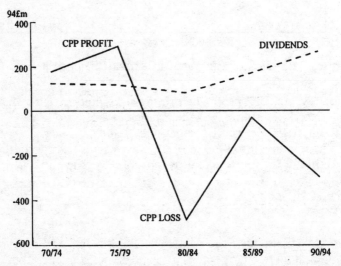

Figure 11.7 Lucas Industries PLC: real (CPP) profits and dividends

periods C, D and E, and paid large amounts of dividends out of CPP capital.

In total over the 25 years, HMC profits covered dividends 1.3 times, while CPP dividends were 2½ times as large as CPP *losses*. Thus, while HMC retained profits totalled £153m, CPP 'retained losses' amounted to no less than **£1,093m**! (But the proceeds of four separate rights issues over the 25 years totalled **£726m** – see Figure 11.9).

Figure 11.8 compares CPP profits (or losses) and dividends over each of the 25 years. CPP profits have covered dividends paid only in 2 of the 16 years since 1978. Even losses of around **£100m** a year (1981–4 and 1992–4) seem to lead to only modest reductions in real dividends.

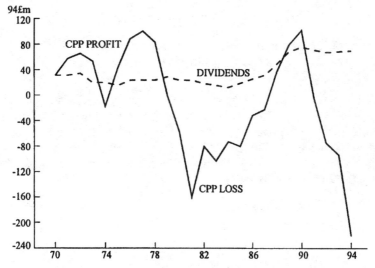

Figure 11.8 Lucas Industries PLC: annual profit after tax and dividends

Figure 11.9 compares in CPP terms total dividends paid over the 25 years with total proceeds from four separate rights issues of ordinary shares in that time. The two are nearly equal. So Lucas shareholders themselves have financed nearly all the purchasing power from which their dividends over 25 years have been paid out! In *money* terms, rights issues raised £325m, while total dividends amounted to £475m. Here again, CPP corrects the misleading picture given by HMC accounting.

Changes in Equity

HMC equity rose by £556m over the 25 years, but CPP equity rose by just £15m. Figure 11.10 shows changes in CPP equity each year. It portrays a significant decline since 1979. This is despite equity being increased by

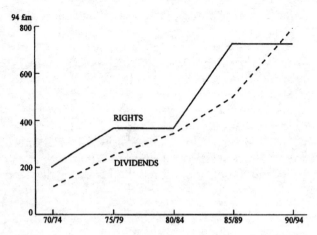

Figure 11.9 Lucas Industries PLC: cumulative dividends versus rights issues

two rights issues (total proceeds **£362m**) and two fixed asset revaluations (CPP total: **£332m**). The cause of the decline is the payment of dividends despite large CPP losses: in the 15 years from 1980 to 1994, dividends paid totalled **£532m**, while CPP *losses* amounted to £806m. That represents an average payment of dividends out of capital of about **£90m** a year – for a 15-year period!

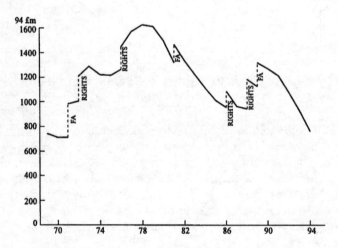

Figure 11.10 Lucas Industries PLC: CPP shareholders' funds (inc MI)

CONCLUSION

CPP adjustments evidently make a big difference to the Lucas results over the 25 years from 1970 to 1994. HMC sales growth over the period was almost entirely due to inflation, as CPP accounts show. CPP adjustments increase HMC depreciation on average by about 90 per cent (more than 100 per cent in the 20 years from 1975 to 1994). And CPP charges a loss of purchasing power on net monetary assets totalling **£500m**, which HMC accounts completely ignore. Hence the rate of tax on real CPP profits amounts on average to 150 per cent. CPP profits have covered dividends in only 2 of the 16 years since 1978; and in total HMC retained profits over the 25 years of £153m compared with CPP 'retained losses' of a staggering **£1,093m**. In times of rapid currency debasement, constant purchasing power results are far more relevant than money results. So it seems a pity that HMC accounts have continued to be so widely used. They pretend that companies are making profits which are really making losses. That seems worth knowing.

It might be argued that the contents of this chapter are, at best, only of historical interest – like inflation itself. After all, everyone now knows what damage inflation can do and governments are determined to see that it never recurs. But even seemingly 'low' rates of currency debasement can make a big difference to ordinary HMC accounts.

In the last ten years covered by this study (1984–94) the average rate of inflation was just under 5 per cent a year. Even so, the average CPP return on net assets (3½%) was only one third as much as the average HMC return on net assets (10½%). This is a very large difference. (Even larger was the difference in return on equity: 5½% a year on an HMC basis, but a negative 3% a year on a CPP basis.)

Thus while 5 per cent a year may sound quite a 'low' rate of inflation, its cumulative effect on conventional accounts can be striking. And the current yield gap between 15-year money gilts and index-linked gilts suggests future UK inflation of just under 5 per cent a year! So it would be premature to expect virtually no future UK inflation or to think that the relevance of CPP accounting lies solely in the past.

Table 11.2 Lucas: quinquennial profit and loss accounts

Money (c £millions)	A 1970–4	B 1975–9	C 1980–4	D 1985–9	E 1990–4		25 YEARS 1970–1994
Sales	1,795	4,218	6,216	8,708	11,769	=	32,706
Depreciation	44	92	147	227	401	=	911
Other expenses	1,635	3,766	5,870	7,891	10,907	=	30,069
Profit before interest & tax	116	360	199	590	461	=	1,726
Interest	26	52	130	145	288	=	641
Tax	36	62	64	136	159	=	457
Profit after tax	54	246	5	309	14	=	628
Dividends	19	37	46	124	249	=	475
Retained	35	209	(41)	185	(235)	=	153
CPP 94 £millions							
Sales	12,088	14,234	11,870	12,459	12,770	=	63,421
Depreciation	366	566	674	745	770	=	3,121
Other expenses	11,009	12,718	11,206	11,329	11,804	=	58,066
Loss on Net Monetary Assets	118	243	101	27	12	=	501
Profit (loss) before interest & tax	595	707	(111)	358	184	=	1,733
Interest	177	182	245	207	314	=	1,125
Tax	239	204	121	176	174	=	914
Profit (loss) after tax	179	321	(477)	(25)	(304)	=	(306)
Dividends	131	124	89	174	269	=	787
Retained	48	197	(566)	(199)	(573)	=	(1093)

Table 11.3 Lucas: quinquennial balance sheets

Money (c £millions) 31 July	1969	1974	1979	1984	1989	1994
Tangible Fixed Assets	45	114	247	370	647	755
Fixed Asset Investments	7	24	39	31	30	33
Net Monetary Assets	36	50	171	73	144	(144)
= Shareholders Funds	88	188	457	474	821	644
Debt ratio: (%)	22.0	31.1	18.7	31.4	28.1	48.2
CPP 94£million						
Tangible Fixed Assets	396	802	972	868	1,050	834
Fixed Asset Investments	59	171	219	140	91	72
Net Monetary Assets	292	262	423	118	180	(144)
= Shareholders Funds	747	1,235	1,614	1,126	1,321	762
Debt ratio: (%)	21.5	27.0	13.9	23.8	23.3	44.0

Table 11.4 Lucas: changes in shareholders' funds, 1970–94

Money (c £millions)	A	B	C	D	E	=	25 YEARS
Rights issues	29	43	-	253	-	=	325
Other issues of shares	-	–	3	75	73	=	151
Asset revaluations	38	21	36	37	(39)	=	93
Profits after tax	54	246	5	309	14	=	628
less: Dividends	–19	–37	–446	–124	–249	=	–475
= Retained	35	209	(–41)	185	(–235)	=	153
Goodwill written off	(–7)	(–4)	(–8)	(–146)	(–7)	=	(–172)
Miscellaneous	5	–	27	(–57)	31		6
	+100	+269	+17	+347	(–177)	=	+556
CPP ₉₄£m							
Rights issues	200	164	-	362	-	=	726
Other issues of shares	1	–	6	108	78	=	193
Asset revaluations	268	91	151	182	-	=	692
Profit after tax (loss)	179	321	(477)	(25)	(304)	=	(306)
less: Dividends	–131	–124	–89	–174	–269	=	–787
= Retained	48	197	(566)	(199)	(573)	=	(1093)
Goodwill written off	(55)	(16)	(14)	(202)	(22)	=	(309)
Miscellaneous	26	(57)	(65)	(56)	(42)		(194)
	488	379	(488)	195	(559)	=	15

12

CORPORATE ACCOUNTABILITY AND EXECUTIVE INCENTIVE SCHEMES

Keith Ward

INTRODUCTION

The issue of corporate governance has been and remains the subject of much debate and empirical research. Much of this attention has been focused on the area of senior executive compensation and its relationship with either, or both, of the relative performance of the business and the creation of shareholder wealth. However, most of the research in this area has concentrated on trying to establish a positive relationship between compensation and performance rather than in considering the causality of the relationship. In other words, under almost all common executive bonus systems an improvement in financial performance would lead to an increased level of bonus even if the improved financial performance was completely fortuitous and outside the control of the relevant senior executives.

The aim of this chapter is to re-examine some of the key underlying theoretical concepts on which the most popular executive incentive schemes are based, and to place these concepts in the context of current capital market conditions and modern large scale corporations. The logical starting point therefore is with the overriding financial objective of corporate and competitive strategies from the perspective of the shareholders in a company, ie the creation of shareholder wealth. The impact of this strategic objective on the managers within the company is then examined by considering the changes caused to agency theory by the increasing proportion of equity ownership held by professionally managed institutional investors. It is argued that this trend has effectively created a two-stage agency theory which significantly increases the complexity of incentivising managers to act in the best interests of their ultimate principals, ie the pension fund members and life assurance policy-holders. The major forms of managerial incentive schemes are then discussed in the context of this updated view of agency theory and some potential conceptual flaws are highlighted which may explain the current levels of concern being expressed regarding the motivational impact of such schemes. The final issue discussed in this chapter is the relative lack of research on appropriate executive incentive schemes at levels below the overall publicly quoted corporation, ie at the strategic business unit (SBU) or divisional level. This is surprising as it is now widely accepted in the area of strategic management that the success of most large modern corporations depends on the development and implementation of appropriate competitive strategies at this lower level, which is where real shareholder value can be created (Porter, 1980).

BACKGROUND

There has been a rising level of concern expressed in both the US and UK at the manner and degree of control being exercised over remuneration of senior company executives. In the UK this has been evidenced by a key recommendation of the recent Cadbury Committee (1992) that publicly quoted companies should establish a remuneration committee composed entirely of non-executive directors, following similar earlier recommendations of the Institutional Shareholders Committee (1991) and the Association of British Insurers (1990). In the US, the Securities and Exchange Commission have recently changed their policy to allow shareholders to challenge and debate executive remuneration schemes at company general meetings. In particular, in the US there have been growing complaints by shareholders at the increasing reliance on the use of share options to reward such senior executives. In the UK, this concern has led to one of the two major bodies representing institutional shareholders, the National Association of Pension Funds (1992), to recommend that quite severe conditions should be placed on the exercise of executive share options.

The extensive empirical research into this area has highlighted the major determinant of the total level of senior managers' remuneration as being the size of the company (Simon, 1957; Becker, 1964; Child, 1973; O'Reilly, et al. 1988). It is only when this total remuneration is broken down into its components of base salary, performance related payments and other monetary value elements that a meaningful correlation with performance has been found. For example, Finkelstein and Hambrick (1989) describe a positive relationship between the financial performance of the company (as measured by its return on equity) and the bonus element of the remuneration of Chief Executive Officers; however, they found no such relationship between base salary and their measure of financial performance. The importance of this area of executive incentive schemes is indicated in Forker (1992) where over 90 per cent of an extensive sample of top UK companies were found to be operating a share option scheme in one particular year.

The importance of competitive strategy

The logic of shareholders providing senior managers with financial incentives is not in contention but, before considering the required linkages by re-examining agency theory, the most relevant measure for such performance enhancing remuneration schemes should be reviewed. As shown in Figure 12.1, investment in a modern company is a two stage process with initial shareholders providing funding to the company, which then invests its available resources in a portfolio of projects. The key issue for the shareholders is whether the return achieved by the company on its investments more than adequately compensates them for the risk associated with their investment in the company. In a perfectly competitive market, there is by definition no possibility of achieving an above-normal level of return at either stage of the investment process (Modigliani and Miller, 1958).

SHAREHOLDERS
(AND OTHERS)
INVEST IN
COMPANY

COMPANY
INVESTS IN
PORTFOLIO
OF PROJECTS

IN A PERFECTLY COMPETITIVE MARKET THE

PORTFOLIO OF PROJECTS ACHIEVE

EXACTLY THE RETURN DEMANDED BY

SHAREHOLDERS AND OTHER SOURCES

OF FINANCE

Ie NO VALUE IS CREATED

Figure 12.1 Adding value: the two-stage investment process

It is therefore well accepted that shareholder value is only created through identifying or creating imperfections in the market and exploiting them successfully – what is now normally referred to in the strategic management literature as developing a sustainable competitive advantage (Porter, 1985). Without becoming embroiled in the academic debate as to the level of technical efficiency and perfection which exists in modern financial markets (and which is comprehensively reviewed by Fama, 1991), it should be uncontentious to assert that the major areas of potential market imperfection lie in the second stage of the investment process. Thus the opportunities to develop and maintain a sustainable competitive advantage (SCA) are far greater in the product/market interfaces than in the way in which the company raises its capital. This has always been supported by the strategic management literature which specifically addresses the linkages between competitive strategies and creating shareholder value (Rappaport, 1981; Branch and Gale, 1982; Donaldson, 1984). Therefore the objective of any sensibly structured managerial incentive scheme should be to encourage the selection and implementation of appropriate competitive strategies.

However, the development of most forms of sustainable competitive advantage, which generally consist of creating some form of entry barrier in order to reduce the effective operation of the forces of perfect competition, requires a considerable initial financial investment by the company. Indeed, it can be argued that the apparent excess return, which is subsequently achieved by such a successful competitive strategy, actually represents the financial return on the investment in the intangible asset created through the development of an SCA. Such an intangible investment will be expensed in the year in which it is incurred due to the normal prudent financial accounting policies, with a consequent short-term reduction in published earnings of the company. If the financial markets are operating effectively, this reported decline in profitability should not lead, of course, to a fall in the share price as this share price should adjust to reflect the net present value of the future cash flows to be generated from the newly created SCA.

Hence it is important that the managerial incentive scheme is properly related to the way in which the selection and implementation of competitive strategy actually affects shareholder value. At first glance, setting up a stock option scheme may appear far more attractive to shareholders than instituting a short-term profit based bonus, but this depends on the stage of development of the company and the type of competitive strategy being implemented, as discussed in Chapter 2.

IMPLICATIONS OF A TWO-STAGE AGENCY THEORY

The application of agency theory to the area of corporate governance has been well developed over many years (Pratt and Zeckhauser, 1985).

Indeed, arguments have been put forward (Fama, 1980; Fama and Jensen, 1983) that the operation of agency theory makes other forms of regulations or sanctions over managerial behaviour largely irrelevant. The current debate in the UK and the convoluted attempts at regulation in the USA over the last ten years indicate that this confidence in the efficient operation of an unfettered market is not universally shared (Tosi and Gomez-Mejia, 1989). This concern may be caused partially by a significant change in corporate ownership in these markets which, at least, is making the application of agency theory more complex and, at worst, is leading to its effective breakdown. In both the US and UK equity markets, the power of institutionally based investors has increased significantly so that pension funds and insurance companies now control the majority of the shares in most large publicly quoted companies.

This development should not lead, at first sight, to the breakdown of agency theory as the basic tenets of the theory can still be applied. The managers of a company are the agents (although a more appropriate term would be 'stewards') of the shareholders in the company because, in almost all such large modern corporations, the shareholders have delegated the day-to-day control of the business to these full-time, paid managers. In many cases, these professional managers have no significant personal financial investment in terms of ownership of the company. Therefore their remuneration (ie salary, bonuses, pension benefits, other benefits in kind, etc) is not automatically linked to the financial return received by their principals, ie the shareholders in the company.

The financial return to these shareholders obviously comes in the form of dividends paid out by the company and through an increase in the value of the shares. Equally obviously, there is a trade-off between these two forms of financial return for shareholders because if all the current profits are paid out as dividends, it is impossible for the company to fund future growth by the reinvestment of these same profits (Lintner, 1956). From the shareholders' perspective, it can be demonstrated easily mathematically that shareholder value is enhanced only if the minimum required return on such reinvestments by any particular company is set against the risk-adjusted cost of capital for that company (Clarke et al, 1990). It should be remembered that under the restrictive assumptions of a perfectly competitive market, the return on reinvestment will be exactly equal to the shareholders' required return, with the result that shareholders should be indifferent between receiving dividends now or at some unspecified time in the future (Modigliani and Miller, 1961).

The more realistically based need for the selection of the most appropriate dividend policy indicates a potential conflict between the interests of shareholders and managers (Fama and Babiak, 1968; Baker et al., 1985). In the absence of financially attractive reinvestment opportunities, shareholder value is maximised by the implementation of a high dividend pay-out ratio, but this reduces both the retained earnings and the cash balances held by the company. This reduction in the liquidity position of the company may also increase the risk of the future financial collapse of the company and hence lead to a decline in the share price. However, the higher short-term dividend payments received by existing shareholders may still have enhanced total shareholder value as expressed in the net present value of total future expected cash flows. If the senior management team are not shareholders in the company, they will not receive any of this increased dividend value, but they will potentially suffer considerably financially if the subsequent increased risk of corporate collapse actually takes place. Such an increased risk perception, without the normally required compensating increase in return, may make such a high dividend paying strategy unattractive to the senior management team. They may prefer to retain, within the company, a substantial net cash/liquid assets balance in order to provide a buffer against unforeseen fluctuations. An alternative managerially focused strategy is often to invest these surplus funds in diversifying the company so as to reduce any future risk of forced liquidation, in spite of the research which demonstrates that diversification strategies tend to destroy shareholder value (Porter, 1987).

If agency theory is working effectively, it should be impossible for managers to act other than in the best interests of their principals, ie the shareholders. These shareholders should utilise their ownership power to force managers to behave in accordance with their wishes. Their ultimate sanctions are either to sack the management team directly or to sell control in the company to new owners, who then change the top management. There was some expressed concern that developments in the 1970s and early 1980s might indicate a breakdown in the effective working of the agency concept. A number of very large, highly diversified, low dividend paying conglomerates started to build up huge piles of net cash from the operations of their mainly mature business units. These large cash deposits were almost all invested in financial markets and consequently earned a low-risk deposit, ie debt-based, level of return. It is very difficult to argue that this creates any shareholder value for professional investors who could, presumably, invest such funds at least as effectively if they were given the chance. The gross debt-based return is reduced still further before it reaches the shareholder by the management cost incurred by such a conglomerate.

However, some degree of faith in agency theory was restored in the second half of the 1980s with the targeting of several of these managerially focused groups by corporate raiders. Such raids highlight the potential for a badly designed financial strategy to destroy shareholder value because most successful corporate raiders do not change the detailed competitive strategies of the SBUs within groups which they take over. The added value to the corporate raider is that the whole group can be purchased for less than the sum of its component parts; this has proved particularly true when the target company was holding significant net cash balances at the time of the take-over.

Not surprisingly, this 'efficiency enhancing role' of the corporate raider has created a considerable response from senior management teams of possible or prospective targets, and many overall corporate strategies have been rapidly and dramatically altered. However, the interesting development academically has been in the increased debate about the role of major shareholders. In the UK and the US, these major shareholders are now professionally managed institutional investors (ie pension funds, life assurance funds, investment companies and unit trusts) as they control, by value, over two-thirds of their domestically held equity markets As their dominance has grown over the last 30 years, so has the debate over their ownership role. Historically, most such institutional shareholders took a relatively passive role as long-term investors in a company accepting the delegation of running the business to the incumbent management team. This seemed relatively logical as most of these professional fund managers (particularly pension funds and life assurance companies) are investing funds on a long-term basis and could look for companies which were likely to develop and maintain long term SCAs.

More recently, this position has started to change as both effective sets of principals in this two stage agency set-up have become more demanding of their agents. Effectively, as is shown in Figure 12.2, these professional fund managers are both principals and agents, since they are located in the middle of the expanded investment process model. They

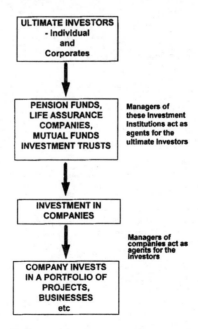

Figure 12.2 The two stage agency model

are clearly the agents of the ultimate investors in their fund (whether a pension fund, life assurance policy or mutual fund) but normally have delegated to them substantial levels of discretionary powers regarding the specific investments which they make. This means that, from the perspective of the senior managers of companies seeking to attract and retain such important shareholders, these fund managers assume the role of direct principals to their managerial agents. As long as there is total goal congruence between the fund managers and their real principals, this added complexity need not damage the effective operation of agency theory. However, the world of professional fund management has become increasingly competitive, with the regular publication of performance 'league' tables in certain areas. Elsewhere, performance is now regularly assessed by reference to the markets in general or to specific competitors. The result is that most fund managers now seek to outperform the 'market' within the assessment periods, which are becoming shorter and shorter. If professional fund managers in total dominate the market it is, of course, impossible for all of them to outperform the market, which itself increases the competitive pressure.

This inevitably focuses the attention of some fund managers on investments where they perceive an opportunity for a relatively short-term return well in excess of the total market. Such opportunities are most commonly found through acquisitions, mergers and corporate raids, so that many fund managers now have a much more open-minded attitude to the attractions of a potential bid for almost any company than would have been the case in the past. The effect of this pressure on professional fund managers for short-term performance can easily be converted, through their role as 'perceived principals', to increased demands for short-term performance in terms of total returns from 'their' agents, ie senior company managers.

The response of many such senior managers is to criticise their investor as now having a very short-term focus. It is argued that this restricts the company from making the optimum long-term investment decisions, which are needed to develop and maintain worthwhile sustainable competitive advantages (particularly in international markets against competitors which do not face such short-term pressure for instant returns). This plaintive argument is seemingly based on the age old economic rule that maximising the long-term return is not necessarily achieved by maximising the return in each of the short-term periods making up the long term; however, its application in this area is in direct conflict with the theory and empirical research of the way in which capital markets function.

As already stated, if the long-term competitive strategy requires expenditure in the short term which will result in lower reported profits, there is no reason to assume that this will inevitably lead to a collapse in the share price. The critical issue is in the perception by the financial market of the reason for the short-term downturn; if the longer term opportunities for the company can be seen to have been significantly improved, the share price should correspondingly be increased. Yet it appears that many senior managers do not trust the capital markets to respond totally rationally to signals where the short-term accounting indications are in conflict with the longer term strategic positioning of the company. This is in spite of the very large body of research which demonstrates how well capital markets can incorporate into share prices changes in accounting results due to amendments to accounting policies, etc (Beaver et al., 1980; Chow, 1983; Morris, 1975; Standish and Ung, 1982; Vigeland, 1981). Perhaps a useful new area for research would be into the relative success of those companies which invest more effort in communicating changes in their competitive strategy to their investors, particularly when it coincides with apparently adverse short-term accounting results. The obvious problem for the managers is that such a communication process is required to be completely open and the necessary information is of great strategic value to their competitors.

(As an aside, it is interesting to note that this argument by senior managers regarding short termism on the part of their institution shareholders is somewhat circular, particularly in the case of pension funds. The trustees of large pension funds have been placing greater emphasis on the performance of their professional fund managers, but many of these trustees are senior managers of the company. If the investment performance of the pension fund is particularly good, the required level of contributions from the company is reduced. For many companies, total payroll costs are a significant and critical expense item and pension costs can be a material element within this total. Indeed, the improved returns achieved by many UK pension funds in the 1980s enabled their companies to have several years of not needing to make any contributions to the fund, with a consequent substantial positive impact on the reported financial performance of the company.)

THE IMPACT OF STOCK OPTIONS

The demand by institutional shareholders for improved financial performance from the company has been assisted by the implementation of a much higher proportion of financial incentive schemes for senior managers in an attempt to restore the essential degree of goal congruence if the two-stage agency theory is to continue to function effectively. The most popular and most financially significant form of incentive scheme in publicly quoted companies is some type of executive stock option (Egginton et al., 1989). As illustrated in Figure 12.3, the attractions to the senior managers of such a scheme are that it permits them to achieve a significant capital gain if the share price rises sufficiently during the period of the option. This is done without them having either to invest the funds initially to buy the shares or to run the risk of suffering a significant capital loss if the shares go down in value; in such circumstances the senior managers simply are unable to realise a gain. They could be regarded as having suffered a financial loss if the present value of the option was treated as part of their total remuneration on the date on which it is granted. There is, of course, no theoretical problem in calculating the value of such an option using Black and Scholes (1973) or some alternative valuation model. Indeed, due to their generous exercise prices (which are often fixed either at, or by reference to, today's share price) and long terms to maturity, these present values of most executive stock options would be quite significant.

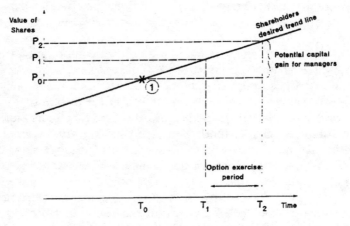

$\boxed{1}$ Managers receive option at time (T_0) to buy shares at today's price (P_0); but option can be exercised at any time during period $T_1 - T_2$
If price rises during this period to P_1 or P_2 (as per trend line), the managers can make an immediate capital gain by buying the shares at P_0 and selling them at P_1 or P_2

Figure 12.3 Executive stock options

However, even with such a dramatic innovation, the use of executive stock options would still fail to create an acceptable level of goal congruence between shareholders and option-holding managers. First, shareholders can receive financial returns from their investment either through capital growth or by receiving dividends from the company. As has already been discussed, the timing of these dividends can significantly affect total shareholder value, but dividends are not payable on stock options. Hence any increased dividends paid within the stock option period will not be received by the managers but, if the cash outflow from the company reduces the share price, the ultimate value generated by the exercise of the outstanding stock options will be reduced. (This type of price adjustment is easy to see in the changes occurring as a shares moves 'ex-div'.) This aspect could be taken into account by adjusting the exercise price of the share options to reflect any changes in the dividend pay-out ratio during the life of the option.

Secondly, shareholders have made a material financial investment in buying their shares in the company, and hence they have an opportunity cost of holding the shares. In other words, an increased value for the shares over the three to five years of the option scheme does not necessarily represent a real gain for the shareholder, whereas it would normally translate into a real capital gain for the manager. One potentially important factor is clearly inflation because, although the nominal value of the shares may have increased, the real value may have declined. As managers do not have to pay for their shares unless and until they buy them, they have no opportunity or carrying cost with the consequent potential for such inflation-generated losses. They will still be able to realise an immediate and real gain upon the exercise of their stock options, whatever the rate of inflation; indeed, the higher the rate of inflation, the more likely it is that the stock option will be worth exercising. The inflationary part of this problem can be solved by index-linking the stock option exercise price, so that managers only receive financial reward for a real increase in the price of the shares. The opportunity cost of carrying the shares could be taken into account by annually increasing the stock option exercise price by a net carrying charge, representing the gross financing cost to the investor, less the dividend yield paid by the company. A potential difficulty would be in arriving at the rate of the financing charge, should a debt-financing cost be used or the much higher shareholders' required rate of return on their equity investment. If the latter higher rate was included, managers would only receive a gain from their stock options if shareholders also received a more than acceptable total return. This would seem equitable if stock options are granted as a financial incentive in addition to the market-based normal remuneration package.

However, if the earlier suggestion was to be adopted under which the present value of the options was treated as an effective investment when they were created, a lower effective carrying cost would be more logical, as the manager has also now made a financial investment in the equity of the company. This analysis indicates that it is quite possible to remove some of the existing major drawbacks to executive stock option schemes, but the remaining problem is inherent in the other fundamental value driver of options.

Options have value because of the volatility in the actual price during the option period; it is clearly of no value to have an option to buy something if the price does not move at all. The value of the option is in being able to defer the purchase decision until the actual direction and scale of the movement has been revealed. Thus the greater the volatility, the greater is the option value. This is not necessarily in line with the desired objectives of the long term shareholders in the company, but it can certainly increase the returns from a management stock option scheme, as shown in Figure 12.4.

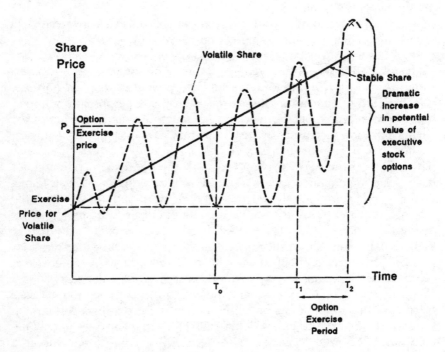

Figure 12.4 Stock options and volatility

It is not being suggested that senior managers would take any positive actions to increase the volatility of their company's share price during a stock option period, but it seems very strange to set up a financial incentive scheme where the returns are significantly increased if action is taken which is potentially directly contrary to the interests of the shareholders. A different perspective may be placed on this if the potentially increased volatility was seen by more aggressive professional fund managers as a way of increasing the total potential return from an investment in the company in the relatively short term.

One of the popular methods of trying to control stock option schemes is equally conceptually flawed and has recently been rejected by a leading group of institutional investors (National Association of Pension Funds, 1992). Many companies have incorporated financial performance triggers which have to be achieved before the full benefits of the stock option scheme can be realised by senior managers, with the most common triggers being based on the earnings per share achieved by the company. Some companies have gone even further by introducing significant annual bonus schemes driven by the growth in earnings per share (EPS) on a year-on-year basis.

These schemes suffer because of some apparent misconceptions regarding the relationship of EPS and share prices. The current share price of the company clearly results from the view taken by the financial market of the current financial performance of the company in terms of its sustainability and expected future improvement. This future expectation is reflected in the price/earnings (P/E) multiple which is applied to the current level of EPS to arrive at the market price of the shares; hence, a high P/E multiple indicates that shareholders not only expect but also have already paid for a substantial level of future growth in EPS. The subsequent delivery of this expected growth in EPS will not therefore lead automatically to a rise in the share price, and it is quite common to observe significant falls in the share prices of companies which, although they have reported improved levels of EPS, have underachieved against the expectations of the market. This is discussed in more depth in Chapter 2.

It is therefore important that the target levels set for any EPS bonus schemes or stock option triggering devices are established by reference to the expected performance which is already reflected in the existing P/E multiple of the company. These caveats are not observed in the vast majority of such schemes which exist in major UK companies today. Even if they were, there are still major problems with using such a basis for an incentive scheme if a key objective is to achieve goal congruence between senior managers and shareholders. By definition, an EPS growth bonus scheme is based on an accounting measure; in fact, in this case it is based on a ratio of two accounting ratios. The potential creativity which can be employed by managers in manipulating, massaging, or whatever it is called, profits from one accounting period into another is now well appreciated, as is the fundamental point that the total cash flow which can be generated by a business over time cannot be similarly manipulated. If the remuneration of senior managers is based on an annual accounting ratio, the question of the timing of profits can become significant, but this is not the major problem as good financial analysts should at least enable the capital markets to unravel the complexities of modern published financial statements so that shareholders are not misled by such reporting practices.

Figure 12.5 shows how the normal EPS growth calculation can influence managers to want to maintain a different financial structure to that which would normally be regarded as the optimum for the company. It can be seen that the EPS growth bonus will be triggered if profits grow from year to year by proportionately more than the increase in issued shares, or if the profits are stable but the number of outstanding shares is reduced sufficiently.

NORMAL SCHEME IS ➜ $\dfrac{EPS_1}{EPS_0}$ = $\dfrac{\dfrac{PAT \text{ in Year } 1}{No \text{ of Issued Shares in Year } 1}}{\dfrac{PAT \text{ in Year } 0}{No \text{ of Issued Shares in Year } 0}}$

DRIVEN BY

$$= \frac{PAT_1}{PAT_0} \times \frac{No \text{ of Shares in Year } 0}{No \text{ of Shares in Year } 1}$$

Where EPS$_1$ = Earnings per share this year

and EPS$_0$ = Earnings per share last year

Figure 12.5 Earnings per share growth bonus schemes

Share repurchase schemes by companies, particularly when offered as an alternative to extra dividend payments, should be reviewed carefully against the incentive schemes in operation for senior executives. It is far more common, however, to find rapidly growing companies which rely on higher risk debt financing to fund this growth rather than the more appropriate equity finance. Issuing new shares during a period of rapid growth, which is usually accompanied by relatively low accounting profits, would very often result in a decreased level of EPS in the short term. The consequent reduction in financial risk of the company at a time of high business risk would normally be a more sensible financial strategy from the perspective of the shareholders, but this may be in conflict with the short-term managerial incentive scheme.

All these incentive schemes require approval of the shareholders, although it is normally delegated to the remuneration committee of the Board of Directors. Therefore, shareholders really only have themselves to blame if they provide the wrong incentives to their corporate 'agents'.

APPLICATIONS OF INCENTIVE SCHEMES WITHIN THE COMPANY

This chapter has concentrated, so far, on executive incentive schemes at the corporate level, but it is often argued that in most large modern corporations the majority of any added value is produced at the SBU or divisional level. It is at this lower level of the organisation that detailed competitive strategies are developed and implemented; hence, it is here that SCAs can really be achieved. As stated at the beginning of the chapter, a primary objective of any managerial incentive scheme should be to encourage the development and maintenance of SCAs. It is therefore surprising that there has been little research into executive incentive schemes at the divisional or organisational sub-unit level within large companies. Fisher and Govindarajan (1992) investigated factors affecting profit centre manager compensation and found positive correlations with the size of the total company and the relative size of the profit centre. The only financial performance measure investigated was profitability at the total company level, and no assessment of profitability at the divisional level was made.

GROWTH	LAUNCH
CSF: Growth in market share	CSF: Successful development and launch of new products
Control measure: Discounted Cash Flow	Control measure: R & D milestones
MATURITY	DECLINE
CSF: Maintain market share at minimum cost	CSF: Minimise cost base
Control measure: Return on Investment	Control measure: Free Cash Flow

Figure 12.6 Tailored financial control measures

It is particularly important that companies develop suitably tailored management incentive schemes to fit the specific competitive strategy which is being implemented at the SBU level, but there is little empirical evidence to indicate that this is being done. These incentive schemes should be linked to the specifically tailored financial control systems which can be designed for the different stages of development (as illustrated in Figure 12.6) of the SBU and for the different types of competitive strategy being implemented by the subdivisions of the business (Ward, 1992). This area is discussed in more detail in Chapter 5.

If the management incentive schemes operate effectively at this lower level of the business, the long term success of these separate competitive strategies should ensure that the shareholders in the overall company receive a more than adequate return. Unfortunately at the lower levels of most businesses, the incentive schemes are normally based on very short-term financial performance measures which are exclusively internally focused eg profit or sales revenue compared to either budget or last year's actual. A competitive strategy is, by definition, outward-looking and therefore an appropriate managerial incentive scheme at this level must include some relevant external measure.

CONCLUSION

Most existing senior management stock option schemes and earnings per share bonus schemes contain various conceptual flaws which either reduce or completely destroy the critical goal congruence between the incentivised manager and the shareholders. This link through agency theory has been made more complex because of the development of a two-stage agency process with the potential for dysfunctional behaviour at both stages.

Many of the existing conceptual flaws could be removed by redesigning the schemes. However, a more fundamental linkage should be developed between the ways in which the company can create increased shareholder value and increased incentive payments for the senior managers who achieve this. This is particularly important at the divisional or SBU level of the business, which is where the major opportunities exist to create increased value through the development and maintenance of clearly defined sustainable competitive advantages.

References

Association of British Insurers mimeograph (1990). 'The Role and Duties of Directors – A Discussion Paper', 12 June, London.

Baker, H K, Farrelly, G E and Edelman, R B (1985), 'A Survey of Management Views on Dividend Policy', *Financial Management*, Autumn, pp 78–84.

Beaver, W H, Christie, A A and Griffin, P A (1980) 'The Information Content of SEC Accounting Series Release No 190', *Journal of Accounting and Economics*, No 2, pp 127–157.

Becker, G S (1964) 'Human Capital', *National Bureau of Economic Research*, New York.

Black, F and Scholes, M (1973) 'The Pricing of Options and Corporate Liabilities', *Journal of Political Economy*, May–June, pp 637–654.

Branch, B and Gale, B (1982) 'Linking Corporate Stock Price Performance to Strategy Formulation', *The Journal of Business Strategy*, Winter, pp 40–50.

Cadbury Committee (1992) 'Report on Financial Aspects of Corporate Governance', draft report published 27 May, London.

Child, J (1973) 'Predicting and understanding organizational structure', *Administrative Science Quarterly*, No 18, pp 169–185.

Chow, C W (1983) 'Empirical Studies of the Economic Impacts of Accounting Regulations: Findings, Problems and Prospects', *Journal of Accounting Literature*, Vol 2, pp 73–109.

Clarke, R G, Wilson, B D, Daines, R H and Nadauld S. D (1990) 'Strategic Financial Management', Richard D Irwin, Homewood, Illinois.

Donaldson, G (1984) 'Managing Corporate Wealth: The Operation of a Comprehensive Financial Goals System', Praeger, New York.

Egginton, D A, Forker, J J and Tippett, M J (1989) 'Share Option Rewards and Managerial Performance: An Abnormal Performance Index Model', *Accounting and Business Research*, Summer, pp 255–266.

Fama, E F (1980, 'Agency Problems and the Theory of the Firm', *Journal of Political Economy*, Vol 88, No 2.

Fama, E F (1991) 'Efficient Capital Markets: II', *The Journal of Finance*, Vol XLVI, No 5, December, pp 1575–1617.

Fama, E F and Babiak, H (1968) 'Dividend Policy: An Empirical Analysis', *Journal of the American Statistical Association*, December.

Fama, E F and Jensen, M C (1983) 'Separation of Ownership and Control', *Journal of Law and Economics*, Vol XXVI, pp 301–325.

Finkelstein, S and Hambrick, D C (1989) 'Chief Executive Compensation: A study of the intersection of markets and political processes', *Strategic Management Journal*, pp 121–134.

Fisher, J and Govindarajan, V (1992) 'Profit Center Manager Compensation: An Examination of Market, Political and Human Capital Factors', *Strategic Management Journal*, Vol 13, pp 205–217.

Forker, J J (1992) 'Corporate Governance and Disclosure Quality', *Accounting and Business Research*, Vol 22, No 86, pp 111–124.

Institutional Shareholders Committee (1991) 'The Role and Duties of Directors – A Statement of Best Practice', London.

Lintner, J (1956) 'Distribution of Incomes of Corporations among Dividends, Retained Earnings and Taxes', *American Economic Review*, May, pp 99–113.

Modigliani, F and Miller, M H (1958) 'The Cost of Capital, Corporation Finance and the Theory of Investment', *American Economic Review*, June, pp 261–297.

Modigliani, F and Miller, M H (1961) 'Dividend Policy, Growth and the Valuation of Shares', *The Journal of Business*, October, pp 411–433.

Morris, R C (1975) 'Evidence of the Impact of Inflation Accounting on Share Prices', *Accounting and Business Research*, Spring, pp 82–90.

National Association of Pension Funds (1992) 'Consultative Document on Implementation of Executive Stock Option Schemes', published 15 September, London.

O'Reilly, C A, Main, B G and Crystal, G S (1988) 'CEO compensation as tournament and social comparison: A tale of two theories', *Administrative Science Quarterly*, No 33, pp 257–274.

Pratt, J W and Zeckhauser, R J (1985) 'Principles and Agents: An Overview', in J W Pratt and R J Zeckhauser (eds), *Principles and Agents: The Structure of Business*, Harvard Business School Press.

Porter, M E (1980) *Competitive Strategy*, Free Press, New York.

Porter, M E (1985) *Competitive Advantage*, Free Press, New York.

Porter, M E (1987) 'From Competitive Advantage to Corporate Strategy', *Harvard Business Review*, May–June.

Rappaport, A (1981) 'Selecting strategies that create shareholder value', *Harvard Business Review*, May–June, pp 139–149.

Simon, H A (1957) *Administrative Behaviour*, Macmillan, New York.

Standish, P E M and Ung, S (1982) 'Corporate Signaling, Asset Revaluations and the Stock Prices of British Companies', *The Accounting Review*, Vol LVII, No 4, October, pp 701–715.

Tosi, H L and Gomez-Mejia, L R (1989) 'The decoupling of CEO pay and performance: An agency theory perspective', *Administrative Science Quarterly*, No 34, pp 169–189.

Vigeland, R L (1981) 'The Market Reaction to Statement of Financial Accounting Standards No. 2', *The Accounting Review*, Vol LV1, No 2, April, pp 309–325.

Ward, K R (1992) *Strategic Management Accounting*, Butterworth Heinemann, Oxford.

INDEX